# The WI book of Main Courses

# THE WI BOOK OF
# MAIN COURSES

**EBURY PRESS**
LONDON

Published by Ebury Press
Division of The National Magazine Company Ltd
Colquhoun House
27–37 Broadwick Street
London W1V 1FR

First impression 1989

ISBN 0 85223 727 8

The recipes in this book were originally published in *The WI
Book of Fish and Seafood* by Mary Norwak, *The WI Book of
Meat Cookery* by Angela Mottram and *The WI Book of Poultry
and Game* by Pat Hesketh.

Edited by Beverly Le Blanc
Illustrations by Cooper-West Graphic Design, James Farrant
and Vanessa Luff

Printed and bound in Great Britain at The Bath Press, Avon

# CONTENTS

# WHAT IS THE WI ?

If you have enjoyed this book, the chances are that you would enjoy belonging to the largest women's organisation in the country — the Women's Institutes.

We are friendly, go-ahead, like-minded women, who derive enormous satisfaction from all the movement has to offer. This list is long — you can make new friends, have fun and companionship, visit new places, develop new skills, take part in community services, fight local campaigns, become a WI market producer, and play an active role in an organisation which has a national voice.

The WI is the only women's organisation in the country which owns an adult education establishment. At Denman College, you can take a course in anything from car maintenance to paper sculpture, from book binding to yoga, or cordon bleu cookery to fly-fishing.

All you need to do to join is write to us here at the **National Federation of Women's Institutes, 39 Eccleston Street, London SW1W 9NT**, or telephone 01-730 7212, and we will put you in touch with WIs in your immediate locality. We hope to hear from you.

## Measurements

All spoon measures in this book are level unless stated otherwise.

3 tsp = 1 tbsp
8 tbsp = 5 fl oz = 150 ml = ¼ pint

Eggs are size 2 or 3 unless stated otherwise.

When following these recipes please use either the metric measurements or the imperial; do not mix them and then all will be well.

When a recipe states '450 g (1 lb) dough' it means dough made using 450 g (1 lb) flour. It does not mean 450 g (1 lb) prepared dough.

Measurements for can sizes are approximate.

### American equivalents

|  | Metric | Imperial | American |
|---|---|---|---|
| Butter, margarine | 225 g | 8 oz | 1 cup |
| Flour | 100 g | 4 oz | 1 cup |
| Currants | 150 g | 5 oz | 1 cup |
| Sugar | 200 g | 7 oz | 1 cup |
| Syrup | 335 g | 11½ oz | 1 cup |

An American pint is 16 fl oz compared with the imperial pint of 20 fl oz. A standard American cup measure is considered to hold 8 fl oz.

# POULTRY AND GAME

Poultry and game have been of great interest to the breeder, sportsman, hunter and cook for many hundreds of years.

Country people have always kept domestic poultry, particularly chickens and often geese and ducks. Rabbits and hares were regularly made into tasty dishes, though they would be considered luxury food by some poor families. Quite often they may have been poached from the local landowner's fields. The more exotic game such as pheasant, partridge and venison regularly graced the tables of the gentry.

Nowadays, poultry is readily available and specialist shops display a good range of game birds and animals which can provide something different for a dinner party or that special celebration meal.

This book deals with the choice and preparation of poultry and game – both feather and fur. It gives many interesting and exciting, as well as traditional, ways of cooking and serving.

**Choosing poultry and game**
*Chicken.* There are various types available.

Poussin: 6–10 weeks old; 700 g (1½ lb). Usually split down the backbone and best roasted, spit-roasted or grilled. One bird will serve 2 people.

Broiler: Spring chicken; 3 months old; 900 g–1.2 kg (2–2½ lb). May be roasted, pot-roasted or sautéed. One bird will serve 3–4 people.

Roaster: 6 months old; 1.5–1.8 kg (3–4 lb); the most popular size. Usually roasted or pot-roasted. One bird will serve 4–6.

Large roaster: 9 months old; up to 3.6 kg (8 lb). Cockerel which has been specially fattened for the table. Can be roasted; is a good size for boning out. One bird will serve up to 10 people.

Boiler: 12–18 months old; 1.8–2.5 kg (4–6 lb). Good for making broths, especially cock-a-leekie (see page 26) and for cold dishes served with sauces. There is a tendency for them to become fatty, so gentle boiling is required, then cooling, thus enabling the fat to be skimmed off.

*Turkey.* A hen turkey has a small frame and more meat in ratio to bone than a stag (male turkey), though the latter is often preferred for flavour. Whole turkeys are available as follows:

Clean-plucked: Head, legs and intestines intact. Should be dressed as for chicken.

Oven-ready: Giblets packed separately; ready for the oven.

Frozen: Giblets not usually included. Frozen turkey should be defrosted slowly in a cool place (not in the fridge) for 36–48 hours.

Turkey is also available (fresh and frozen) as turkey leg joints, turkey leg roasts and turkey breast roasts.

A 4.5–6.0-kg (10–13-lb) bird will serve 10–12 people, or 8 people with enough left over for a cold dish. A 4-kg (9-lb) frozen turkey is equivalent to a 5.4-kg (12-lb) clean-plucked turkey.

A 7.2–9.0-kg (16–20-lb) turkey should provide several meals for a family party of 6–8 people.

A 9.0–11.5-kg (20–25-lb) bird or larger will be required for a large household, and when lots of cold turkey is needed. When purchasing an extra-large turkey, your oven measurements should be checked beforehand.

*Duck.* Young ducks up to 8 months old may be roasted or spit-roasted. Birds over 12 months should be casseroled. They are at their best in early summer. They have a shallow breast and feed fewer people than a chicken of corresponding weight. A 1.8-kg (4-lb) bird will serve 3–4 people.

*Goose.* Available throughout the year but at its best at Christmas-time. A mature goose will weigh 4.5–6.3 kg (10–14 lb) and, like duck, is wasteful. Allow 450–550 g (1–1¼ lb) per person – a 4.5-kg (10-lb) bird will serve 8 people.

*Guinea-fowl.* A tasty bird with a flavour between chicken and pheasant. A young guinea-fowl is tender and good roasted. Older birds should be casseroled. Any recipe for chicken and pheasant may be used. One bird will serve 4–5 people.

*Pheasants.* They are sold by the brace – a cock and a hen. A young cock will have short, rounded spurs which become longer and pointed with age. A young hen has soft pliable feet which harden with age. Young birds have pointed feathers – rounded feathers indicate age. Young birds are excellent roasted, but older birds should be pot-roasted or casseroled. One pheasant will serve 2–4, depending on its size.

*Partridge.* There are two varieties – the English, or grey, partridge, which is considered to be better-flavoured than the larger French, or red-legged, partridge. The latter, although of continental origin, tends to be more common. A young bird will have a soft beak and pointed feathers. Young birds are excellent plain-roasted. One bird serves 1–2 people.

*Grouse.* Young birds have bright eyes, soft pliable feet and smooth legs and a soft pliable tip to the breastbone. In older birds the bones become hard and the feet scaly with sharp claws. Young birds are good oven- or spit-roasted; older birds require moist cooking by casseroling or can be used in pies and terrines. One plump bird serves 2 people.

*Black game or black grouse.* A member of the grouse family and about twice the size of a grouse. With the exception of very young birds, the meat is rather dry and a moist cooking method is recommended. Any recipes suitable for grouse may be used, but longer cooking time must be allowed. One bird serves 3–4.

*Ptarmigan or white grouse.* The smallest grouse, ptarmigan has not such a good flavour as grouse but young birds have a delicate taste when roasted. Older birds may be bitter and should be casseroled, with well-flavoured ingredients. Any recipe for grouse may be used. One bird serves 1–2 people.

*Capercaillie.* The largest member of the grouse family. Young birds have supple feet and smooth pliable legs, they may be roasted. Older birds have rough scaly legs and should be casseroled. The gizzard has an unpleasant taste and should not be used for giblet stock. A cock bird will serve 6–8 people; a hen bird will serve 3–4 people.

*Wild duck.* A collective name for a wide variety of duck species; the most usual ones being mallard, wigeon and teal. Although the mallard is the largest and the best known, it is the little teal which has most flavour. Unlike the domestic duck, the flesh is dry and needs plenty of fat for roasting. A mallard should serve 2–3 people, but teal will serve only one person. A duck shot on the fore-shore may have a 'fishy' flavour. This can be overcome by placing an onion or potato inside the cavity, and poaching the bird in salted water for 20 minutes. Rinse and dry thoroughly before roasting in the usual way.

*Woodcock.* Difficult to obtain in the shops and considered by many to be the best-flavoured of all game birds. Once a breakfast delicacy, it is now served for dinner either as a starter or main course. A minimum of one bird per person should be allowed

*Snipe.* A small bird and a great delicacy. One bird per person will do for a starter, but two for a main course.

*Quail.* Rare in the wild but now reared on game farms, this little bird is now widely available from poulterers and delicatessens and can also be bought frozen. One bird per person is needed for a starter and two for a main course.

*Pigeon.* All pigeons can be eaten but it is the wood-pigeon which can have a gamey flavour. It is readily available, cheap and nutritious. Young birds can be roasted, but for best results, long, slow cooking is advisable. For a pie, they are best pre-cooked.

*Rabbit.* Rabbits are at their best between 3 and 4 months old. They should be plump with bright eyes, flexible feet and smooth claws. The ears of young rabbits will tear easily. Native wild rabbits have much more flavour than those bred for the table or frozen imported rabbit from China. One large rabbit will serve 3–4 people.

*Hare.* There are two types of hare: English (brown)

and Scotch (blue) hare. The brown is larger and has more flavour. A young hare (leveret) has a smooth coat, small white teeth, soft ears and well-hidden claws. Older hares have a wavy coat, large yellow teeth, an evident cleft in the jaw and protruding blunt claws. Only leverets can be roasted without being marinated to tenderize the meat.

*Venison*. There are several species of deer in Great Britain, but generally it is only the meat of the red, roe and fallow deer that is eaten. Deer farms are now being developed all over the country and venison is becoming easier to obtain through country butchers and game shops. The quality of 'farmed' deer is normally good, as the age of the animal is known and facilities ensure good preparation of the carcase. Venison joints are available and also sausages and pâté. Being lean, venison freezes well. The best joints for roasting are the haunch and saddle; cutlets and steaks make good frying and the shoulder can be stewed. Game venison generally requires marinating before roasting, but with a good quality of 'farmed' venison, marinating is a matter of personal taste and not necessity.

**Plucking, trussing and drawing poultry and game birds**
Methods vary little from one type to another, so here is how to go about it:

*Plucking*. Either hold the bird by its legs, or suspend it by its legs. Start plucking the feathers from the breast. Work with the legs towards you, and pull the feathers away from you. From the breast work down the neck and then towards the tail, and down the legs. Turn the bird over and remove the feathers from the back and the wings. It may be necessary to use pliers on the strong wing-pinion feathers. Remember to keep some of the tail feathers of a pheasant for garnish if the bird is to be roasted.

*Drawing*. Remove the legs – cut through the skin approximately 2.5 cm (1 inch) below the knee joint, place the cut over the sharp edge of the table or a board, and with a sharp downward movement of the hand, break the leg. It should now be possible to remove the leg sinews by pulling the feet.

Remove the head – place the bird, breast-side down, and cut through the neck skin lengthwise from between the shoulders up to the head. Pull the skin away from the neck and sever the neck and skin just below the head. Cut through the neck by the shoulders, and retain the neck for stock.

Place the bird on its back, loosen the windpipe and food pipe from the neck skin, and remove the crop. If poultry has been starved before killing, the crop should be empty; in game it will usually be full of grain. Place the forefinger inside the neck cavity and loosen the lungs away from the ribs, by working the forefinger backwards and forwards around the rib cage.

Turn to the tail end, and with a sharp knife make a cut between the anus and the parson's nose. Insert the little finger and hook it around the back passage; insert the knife under the loop of the intestine and cut away from the parson's nose – this should cut out the anus completely.

Insert the forefinger into the cavity and loosen the intestines from the walls of the body cavity. Take hold of the gizzard (feels large and firm) and gently pull; the whole of the intestines should be removed, and also the lungs.

Carefully cut the heart away, and the liver. Cut the gall-bladder from the liver, taking care not to break it, otherwise it will impart a bitter flavour. Cut the gizzard away, cut through the muscular casing and remove the sack containing the partially digested food. Retain the heart, liver and gizzard casing with the neck for stock. Wrap the rest in newspaper and dispose of it.

Singe the bird over a clean flame to remove the fine down, then wipe with a clean damp cloth.

*Trussing.* Place the bird on its back, fold the wings to tuck behind the shoulders, and push the legs forward. With a trussing needle threaded with fine string, pass the needle from one hip joint through the body cavity to the other hip joint. Pass it up the length of one wing, across the back, just below the neck, and down the length of the other wing. Pull the string up tightly and tie the two ends together.

Take another length of string in the needle and pass the needle through the tail-end of the breast bone. Remove the needle, take the two ends of the string over the legs, cross them over the cavity and tie them behind the parson's nose.

Take the flap of neck skin and tuck it under the wings and string across the back.

*Trussing variations for game birds.* It is usual with game birds to leave the legs and feet on, although the toes should be cut off. Often with pheasant and other larger birds the feet and part of the leg may be removed. The scaly part of the legs should be dipped in boiling water and the scales scraped off.

Traditionally, small game birds such as quail, woodcock and snipe are not drawn. The head should be skinned and the eyes removed. (A woodcock should also have the gizzard removed.) The beak should be twisted around and used like a skewer to truss the bird. During cooking the trail (alimentary canal) turns to liquid and soaks into the toast on which the bird is cooked.

Today, many people prefer to draw and truss these birds as for other game birds.

## Jointing poultry and game birds

Place the bird, breast uppermost, tail towards you, and, with a sharp knife, cut through the skin between the leg and the breast; press the leg outwards and downwards, insert the knife in the hip joint, cut around and remove the leg. With a small chicken, the leg may be left as one portion; with a larger bird, it may be divided into two.

Cut down through the breast approximately 2.5 cm (1 inch) in from the wing, and cut the wing off – this ensures a reasonable amount of breast meat on the wing joint. Fillet the breast meat off the carcase. Repeat on the second side. The carcase may be used for making stock.

*Pigeons.* If acquired in large numbers, it is advisable to use only the breasts. With a sharp knife, cut along the breastbone, skin the breast area and fillet each breast 'steak' away from the carcase or, from the tail end lift the breast bone and, using scissors, cut through the skin and shoulder joints and lift the breast off completely.

**Boning out poultry and game birds**
Place the bird breast down, and with a sharp knife, cut the skin down the backbone; keeping the knife close to the carcase, carefully fillet the meat away until you reach the leg joint. Ease the knife through the hip joint, and break the leg away from the carcase. Fillet the meat from the leg. Pull the leg completely inside out to remove the bone (for some recipes you can leave the bones in the legs to give a better shape to the finished item).

Continue cutting away the flesh and skin towards the breastbone. Allow the knife to follow the carcase, removing the meat. Take care down the centre of the breastbone that the skin is not cut. Cut the wing off at the joint furthest from the body. Remove the meat from one side of the bird first, then work on the other side.

Read the recipe on page 22 for finishing. The carcase may be used for making stock.

Turkey, goose and pheasant are also ideal for boning out and can be finished in a variety of ways.

**Carving poultry and game birds**
Carving instructions are given with the recipes for the different types of bird. In each chapter, the basic recipe for each bird (usually a roasting recipe) contains the information you will need.

**Paunching and skinning rabbits and hares**
*Paunching.* Rabbits should be paunched (gutted) as soon as they are killed, by making a slit along the length of the belly and removing the intestine and stomach. They may then be hung.

Hares should be hung head down before gutting. A bowl or polythene bag should be placed or hung under the head to catch any blood. This can be used as a liaison to thicken the sauce of, for example, jugged hare (see page 75). A teaspoonful of vinegar added to the blood will prevent it from clotting.

*Skinning.* Start by removing the lower part of the legs. From the slit along the belly, loosen the skin around the back and peel it off towards the hind legs. Turn the skin of the legs and peel it off rather like removing a stocking.

Pull the skin down over the body and forelegs in a similar way. The head of the rabbit is removed, but the head of a hare is usually left on. The skin should be cut away from the head, and the eyes removed with a sharp knife.

From the liver, remove the gall bladder, taking care not to break it. Reserve the liver, heart and kidney, also the blood which has collected under the membrane of the ribs of the hare. From the hare remove the blue membrane which covers the meat. Rinse the meat well in cold water and dry well.

**Jointing rabbits and hares**
Remove the hind legs by cutting through the hip joint with a sharp knife. Remove the forelegs by cutting through the shoulder joint. Trim away the flaps of skin attached to the rib cage, and discard. The carcase may be divided in two lengthwise by cutting down the backbone, each half again being cut into 2 or 3 pieces depending on the size of the rabbit or hare. In a hare, the saddle (backbone) is often left whole for roasting. Joint as above, but leave the backbone complete.

**Hanging**
Hanging times will depend on personal taste and the weather. In warm humid weather, hanging time will be shorter than in cold dry weather. Game birds are hung by the neck, mammals by the hind legs.

## Game – availability and hanging times

| | Season | Best | Hanging times (in days) |
|---|---|---|---|
| Pheasant | 1 Oct to 1 Feb | Nov & Dec | 7–10 |
| Partridge | 1 Sept to 1 Feb | Oct & Nov | 3–5 (young birds) 8 (older birds) |
| Grouse | 12 Aug to 10 Dec | Aug to Oct | 7–10 |
| Black game | 20 Aug to 10 Dec | Aug to Oct | 3–10 |
| Ptarmigan | 12 Aug to 10 Dec | Aug to Oct | 2–4 |
| Capercaillie | 1 Oct to 31 Jan | Nov & Dec | 10–14 |
| Wild duck | 1 Sept to 31 Jan | Nov & Dec | up to 3 |
| Woodcock | 1 Oct to 31 Jan | Nov & Dec | 3–5 |
| Snipe | 12 Aug to 31 Jan | Nov | 3–4 |
| Quail | (Farmed) all year | | Little or none |
| Pigeon | All year | | Little or none |
| Rabbit | All year | | 3–5 |
| Hare | 1 Aug to 28 Feb | Oct onwards | 7–10 |
| Venison | 1 Aug to 30 Apr | Depends on species & sex | 8–10 (red deer) 7 (fallow & roe) |
| | (Farmed) all year | | 2–5 |

# POULTRY

# ROAST CHICKEN (1)

Serves 4–6

*1 chicken, 1.6–1.8 kg (3½–4 lb)*
*stuffing of own choice – traditionally*
*parsley and thyme (see page 88)*
*100 g (4 oz) dripping*
*streaky bacon rashers (optional)*
*1 tbsp plain flour*
*275 ml (½ pint) chicken stock (see*
*page 91)*

Heat the oven to 220°C (425°F) mark 7. Place the stuffing in the cavity of the bird and, if desired, place the bacon rashers over the breast – this will prevent drying out. Heat the dripping in a roasting tin, and place the bird in it, baste well and place in the oven. Reduce the temperature after 15 minutes to 190°C (375°F) mark 5, and roast for a further 1 hour, or until tender, basting regularly. 15 minutes before the end of cooking, remove the bacon rashers (if used) and sprinkle the breast with a little flour, baste well, and continue cooking.

To test to see if cooked, take a fine skewer, or a cooking knife with a fine point and insert it into the flesh of the thigh. If the juice that comes out is clear, the bird is cooked; if there is any pinkness, continue cooking.

Transfer the bird to a serving dish and keep warm. Remove most of the fat from the roasting tin, place the tin over the heat and stir in the flour; cook for 2–3 minutes, then gradually stir in the stock, bring to the boil and simmer for 3–5 minutes. Strain into a sauceboat.

Serve the chicken with bacon rolls (see page 94) and bread sauce (see page 89).

If time allows, the bird will be much easier to carve if, when cooked, it is placed on the serving dish, covered with foil and several layers of cloth, and allowed to stand for at least 30 minutes. This resting period allows the meat to set.

To carve, hold the bird firmly with a carving fork, insert the carving knife between the leg and the breast, and cut through the skin. Gently press the leg outwards and cut through the joint. Divide the leg into 2 portions. Slice down the breast about 2.5 cm (1 inch) in from the wing joint, and cut through the wing joint – this ensures that a reasonable amount of breast is served with the wing. Carve the rest of the breast into slices. Repeat the process for the second side of the bird.

# ROAST CHICKEN (2)

Serves 4–6

*1 chicken, 1.6–1.8 kg (3½–4 lb)*
*2–3 sprigs fresh thyme or rosemary*
*50 g (2 oz) butter*
*salt and pepper*
*275 ml (½ pint) chicken stock (see page 91)*
*1 tsp arrowroot or cornflour*

Heat the oven to 200°C (400°F) mark 6. Place the herb with a good nut of butter and seasoning inside the bird, and rub the outside of the bird with the rest of the butter. Place the bird breast side up in a roasting tin with half the stock, cover with buttered paper or foil and place in the oven. Roast for about 1 hour. After the first 15–20 minutes, baste the bird and turn it on to one side. Baste and turn again after another 15–20 minutes; finish off the cooking with the breast side up, removing the paper for the last few minutes to allow the breast to brown. Test to see if the chicken is cooked .

Place the bird on a serving dish and keep warm. Add the remaining stock to the roasting tin, and stir well to ensure that all the pan juices are incorporated. Thicken with 1 teaspoonful arrowroot on cornflour mixed with 1 tablespoonful water. Strain into a sauceboat.

*Variation*
Roasting in a chicken brick: soak the brick in cold water as directed in the instructions. Season the chicken well, inside and out, and place in the cavity either butter and herbs

(as in the recipe above), or for a delicate flavour, place 2 small onions and 1 lemon in the cavity. Place the bird in the brick and cook according to the manufacturer's instructions.

# ROAST BONED CHICKEN

Serves about 10 as a buffet dish

*1 large chicken, 2.7–3.6 kg*
  *(6–8 lb), boned out*
*700 g (1½ lb) pork sausagemeat*
*double recipe quantity parsley and*
  *thyme stuffing (see page 88)*
*4–6 lambs' tongues, boiled, skinned*
  *and boned*

Heat the oven to 200°C (400°F) mark 6. Place the boned out chicken, skin side down, and cover with the sausagemeat. Lay half the stuffing down the centre and place the lambs' tongues on the stuffing; cover with the remaining stuffing.

Bring the sides to the centre and over-sew with fine string. Turn the bird over and re-shape. Weigh the bird. Roast as for method 2.

This is ideal for a buffet; it may be eaten hot or cold, but will slice more easily when cold.

# FRIED CHICKEN PROVENÇALE

Serves 4–6

1 chicken, 1.6 kg (3½ lb)
8 sprigs fresh thyme
8 rashers bacon
50 g (2 oz) butter
2 tbsp oil
175 g (6 oz) onion, finely chopped
450 g (1 lb) fresh tomatoes, skinned
  and chopped, or canned tomatoes,
  chopped
1 tbsp tomato purée
1 tbsp plain flour
1 clove garlic, crushed with salt
275 ml (½ pint) white wine
salt and pepper
slices of French bread, fried, and
  chopped fresh parsley to garnish

Joint the chicken into 8 portions (see page 10). Lay a sprig of thyme on each, and wrap in bacon. Tie with string.

Heat the butter and oil in a large deep frying pan, and fry the chicken parcels to a golden brown. Remove from the pan to a plate. Add the onion to the fats in the pan and fry gently until soft. Stir in the tomatoes and purée, and cook for a few minutes. Stir in the flour and garlic and cook for a further 2–3 minutes. Add the wine and some seasoning. Bring to the boil, and replace the chicken joints. Cover and cook gently for 30–40 minutes, or until the chicken is tender. Remove the string.

Arrange the joints on a dish, skim the sauce, adjust the seasoning, and spoon over the joints. Garnish with slices of fried French bread and chopped parsley.

# CELEBRATION CHICKEN

Serves about 8 as a buffet dish

1 chicken, 1.6 kg (3½ lb), cooked
  and cut into pieces when cold
25 g (1 oz) butter
175 g (6 oz) onion, chopped
1 tbsp curry powder
150 ml (¼ pint) well-flavoured
  chicken stock (see page 91)
2 tsp tomato purée
2 tbsp lemon juice
2 tbsp sieved apricot jam
1 recipe quantity mayonnaise (see
  page 92)
3–4 tbsp single cream
lettuce leaves to garnish

Melt the butter in a saucepan, and gently fry the onion until soft. Stir in the curry powder and cook for 2–3 minutes. Add the chicken stock, tomato purée, lemon juice and apricot jam. Bring to the boil and ensure they are well mixed. Allow to go cold. Mix with the mayonnaise and cream, and combine with the chicken.

Line a large serving bowl with lettuce leaves and pile the chicken in the bowl.

# CHICKEN IN A CREAM SAUCE

Serves 4–6

*1 boiling fowl*
*1 litre (1¾ pints) water*
*1 onion*
*1 bayleaf*
*salt and pepper*
*100 g (4 oz) mushrooms, sliced, and*
*    sautéed in 25 g (1 oz) butter*
*25 g (1 oz) butter*
*25 g (1 oz) plain flour*
*275 ml (½ pint) chicken stock (see*
*    page 91)*
*150 ml (¼ pint) single cream*
*2 egg yolks*
*½ tsp ground nutmeg*
*1 tsp lemon juice*

Place the boiling fowl in a pan with the water, onion, bay leaf and seasoning. Cover and cook until tender (2–3 hours). Allow to cool slightly. Remove the bones and skin, and cut the meat into medium-sized pieces. Place in a serving dish and sprinkle the sautéed mushrooms over.

For the sauce – melt the butter in a pan, add the flour and cook for 1 minute. Gradually add the chicken stock, and bring to the boil, stirring constantly. Season to taste. Boil for 3–4 minutes, and allow to cool slightly. Mix the cream and egg yolks together in a basin and add to the sauce with the nutmeg and juice. Reheat without boiling and pour over the chicken pieces. Serve hot or cold.

The liquid that the bird was cooked in may be boiled to reduce in volume, and concentrate the flavour. It must be well skimmed. This may be used for the stock required in the dish, and the remainder used as the basis of a soup.

# SUFFOLK CHICKEN CASSEROLE

Serves 4–6

1 boiling fowl
1 onion
1 carrot
1 bay leaf
salt and pepper
1 litre (1¾ pints) water
25 g (1 oz) butter
1 tbsp oil
2 medium onions, thinly sliced
175 g (6 oz) mushrooms, sliced
425 ml (¾ pint) dry cider
2 tbsp Worcestershire sauce
1 tbsp cornflour
150 g (5 oz) natural yoghurt
2 medium apples to garnish

Place the boiling fowl in a pan with the onion, carrot, bay leaf, seasoning and water. Cover and simmer gently until the meat is cooked (2–3 hours). Allow to cool slightly. Skin the bird, and remove the meat from the bones. Cut the meat into pieces and place them in a flameproof casserole.

Heat the oil and butter in a pan and gently fry the onions until soft; add the mushrooms and cook for 4–5 minutes. Place the onions and mushrooms on top of the chicken pieces. Add the cider, Worcestershire sauce and salt and pepper. Cover tightly and simmer gently for ¾–1 hour.

Blend the cornflour with a little water in a basin, add 2–3 tablespoonfuls of the cooking liquid, mix, pour into the casserole and bring to the boil. Remove from the heat and stir in the yoghurt. Check the seasoning.

Meanwhile, core the apples and cut into 5-mm (¼-inch) thick rings. Fry these gently in a little butter and use to garnish the casserole.

# COLD CHICKEN SALAD

Serves about 8 as a buffet dish

*1 chicken, 1.6 kg (3½ lb), cooked,
    and cut into small pieces when
    cold*
*100 g (4 oz) mushrooms, sliced and
    sautéed in 25 g (1 oz) butter*
*4 eggs, hard-boiled and chopped*
*4 rashers bacon, crisply fried and
    chopped*
*425 g (15 oz) canned sweetcorn,
    drained*
*1 small packet frozen peas, cooked*
*1 red pepper, chopped*
*50 g (2 oz) walnuts, chopped*
*salt and pepper*
*150–275 ml (¼–½ pint)
    mayonnaise (see page 92), or
    vinaigrette dressing (see page 92)*
*1 tbsp lemon juice*
*asparagus spears, sliced cucumber
    and paprika pepper to garnish*

Prepare all the ingredients and when they
are cold, combine them together in a large
bowl, with the lemon juice and mayonnaise
(or vinaigrette). Pile on a large serving dish
and garnish with the asparagus spears and
cucumber slices; a light sprinkling of
paprika pepper will give extra colour.

Serve with a rice salad and a green salad.

# COCK-A-LEEKIE SOUP

Serves 4

*1 boiling fowl*
*4 medium leeks*
*bunch of fresh mixed herbs or
    1 bouquet garni*
*6 peppercorns*
*1 tsp salt*
*50 g (2 oz) long grain rice*

Place the boiling fowl in a large saucepan.
Prepare the leeks and cut into 5-cm (2-inch)
lengths. Add to the pan with the herbs,
peppercorns and salt; add sufficient water to
almost cover the bird. Cover, bring to the
boil, remove any scum and simmer for
approximately 2 hours or until the bird is
tender.

Remove the bird from the pan and cut the
flesh from the carcase. Cut the flesh into
bite-size pieces and return to the pan with
the rice. Bring to the boil, and simmer a
further 20 minutes or until the rice is soft.
Check the seasoning before serving.

# SIMPLE CHICKEN SOUP

Serves 3–4

1 chicken carcase, plus giblets, if
    available
1 medium onion, chopped
2 medium carrots, chopped
1 stick celery, sliced
1 matchbox-sized piece swede,
    chopped
bunch of fresh mixed herbs, or
    1 bouquet garni
6 peppercorns
salt
beurre manié (see page 92)
double cream and chopped chives to
    garnish

Place the chicken carcase, giblets, prepared vegetables, herbs and seasoning in a large saucepan. Cover with water. Bring to the boil, remove any scum, cover and simmer gently for approximately 1½ hours. Remove the carcase and the herbs. Sieve or liquidize the contents of the pan and thicken with beurre manié. Check the seasoning. Add any meat from the carcase, finely shredded, bring to the boil and simmer for 3–4 minutes.

Serve in individual bowls with a swirl of cream and a few chopped chives.

# CHICKEN LIVER PÂTÉ

225 g (8 oz) chicken livers
100 g (4 oz) butter
1 shallot, finely chopped
1 clove garlic, finely chopped
seasoning
1 tbsp brandy
good pinch of mixed dried herbs
clarified butter

Remove any sinews from the livers. Melt 25 g (1 oz) butter in a frying pan, and cook the onion and garlic until soft. Add the livers and sauté briskly (about 10–12 minutes) until the liver is firm to the touch.

Cool the liver, then rub through a fine sieve, mince, or liquidize. Cream the remaining butter and beat into the liver mixture. Season well, and add the brandy and herbs. Place in a china pot, or in small cocottes. Smooth over the top and cover with clarified butter. Store in the refrigerator, and use as required.

Clarified butter is butter which has been 'cleared' by heating until it foams, and then by skimming and straining off the clear yellow oil, leaving the milk solids behind.

# ROAST TURKEY (Slow Method)

See page 5 for servings

*1 turkey*
*stuffing(s) of own choice (see*
*pages 85–88)*
*50 g (2 oz) butter or dripping, or*
*225 g (8 oz) streaky bacon*
*plain flour*
*giblet gravy (see page 91)*
*bread sauce (see page 89)*
*cranberry sauce (see page 89)*
*sausages*
*bacon rolls (see page 94)*

Heat the oven to 170°C (325°F) mark 3.
Prepare the stuffings. A double quantity of
the recipe will be required for the cavity.
The neck and cavity may both be stuffed.
Weigh the bird after stuffing to calculate the
cooking time.

Either smear the breast with fat, and
completely wrap in foil, or cover the breast
with streaky bacon. Place the bird in a
roasting tin and cook.

Under 6.3 kg (14 lb), allow 45 minutes
per kg (20 minutes per lb) and 30 minutes
over (3 hours 50 minutes for a 4.5-kg/10-lb
bird).

Over 6.3 kg (14 lb), allow 35–40 minutes
per kg (15–18 minutes per lb) and
15 minutes over (approximately 5½ hours
for a 9-kg/20-lb bird).

45 minutes before the end of cooking,
open up the foil or remove the bacon
rashers. Sprinkle lightly with flour,
continue the cooking and allow the breast
to brown.

To test if cooking is finished, place a
skewer into the thickest part of the
drumstick: if it goes in easily and no liquid
runs out, cooking is complete.

Allow 20–30 minutes for dishing up.
During this time the bird may be placed on
a serving dish, covered with foil, and then
covered with several clean tea-towels or a
heavy cloth. This keeps the bird hot, and
allows the meat to 'relax' thus making
carving much easier. The bird can stand
like this for up to 1 hour, meaning therefore
that the oven is at liberty for roasting
potatoes, and preparing other
accompaniments for dinner. Use the pan
juices for the giblet gravy.

The traditional accompaniments to turkey are giblet gravy (see page 91), bread sauce (see page 89), cranberry sauce (see page 89), and sometimes sausages or bacon rolls (see page 94). Chestnuts are often used either in a stuffing, or served with Brussels sprouts; they may also be puréed and added to the gravy to make it richer.

To carve, cut through the skin between the body and a leg, then gently ease the leg away from the body, pressing the leg down towards the plate. This enables the knife to be put through the joint at the top of the thigh, thereby removing the leg completely. Carve the breast by slicing from the breast bone towards the wing. In the case of a small bird, it is usual to serve either a drumstick or a thigh from the leg together with slices of breast meat for one portion. With a larger bird, the leg meat is sliced off and served without the bone.

# ROAST TURKEY (Quick Method)

See page 5 for servings

*1 turkey*
*stuffing(s) of own choice (see pages*
  *85–88)*
*350 g (12 oz) streaky bacon rashers*
*100 g (4 oz) butter or dripping*
*plain flour*
*giblet gravy (see page 91)*
*bread sauce (see page 89)*
*cranberry sauce (see page 89)*
*sausages*
*bacon rolls (see page 94)*

Heat the oven to 220°C (425°F) mark 7.
Prepare the stuffings (see note on page 28).
Cover the breast with the streaky bacon.
Heat the fat in a roasting tin, place the bird
in the tin, baste well, and place in the oven.
After 20 minutes reduce the heat to 190°C
(375°F) mark 5. The bird should be
regularly basted throughout cooking.

Under 6.3 kg (14 lb), allow 35 minutes
per kg (15 minutes per lb) and 15 minutes
over (approximately 2¾ hours for a
4.5-kg/10-lb bird).

Over 6.4 kg (14 lb), allow 23 minutes per
kg (10 minutes per lb) and 10 minutes over
(approximately 3½ hours for a 9-kg/20-lb
bird). Finish the bird as on page 28.

# MOIST ROAST TURKEY

See page 5 for servings

*1 turkey (not exceeding*
  *6.3 kg/14 lb)*
*575 ml (1 pint) turkey or chicken*
  *stock (see page 91)*
*75–100 g (3–4 oz) butter*
*stuffing(s) of own choice (see pages*
  *85–88)*

Heat the oven to 220°C (425°F) mark 7.
After 15–20 minutes cooking time, reduce
the heat to 190°C (375°F) mark 5. Allow
35 minutes per kg (15 minutes per lb) and
15 minutes over (approximately 2¾ hours
for a 4.5-kg/10-lb bird).

Melt the butter in the hot stock. Place the
turkey in a roasting tin with one side of the
breast down. Pour the hot liquid over it and
place the tin in the oven. Baste regularly
with the liquid during cooking. After about
one-third of the cooking time, remove the
tin from the oven, turn the bird onto its
other side and continue cooking. After
two-thirds of the cooking time, turn the
bird onto its back, so that the breast can
brown. Test to see if cooking is complete
(see page 28). The basting liquid can be
used for gravy.

# WESSEX TURKEY

Serves 4

*1 turkey leg (thigh and drumstick)*
*2 medium onions*
*salt*
*275 ml (½ pint) water*
*100 g (4 oz) cooked ham or bacon*
*50 g (2 oz) butter*
*1 tbsp plain flour*
*150 ml (¼ pint) dry cider*
*pepper*
*croûtes (see page 93)*
*chopped parsley to garnish*

Place the turkey joints in a pan with one of the onions, quartered, ½ teaspoon salt, and 275 ml (½ pint) water. Bring to the boil, cover and simmer for ¾–1 hour, or until tender. Lift out the meat onto a plate, remove the skin and bone, and cut the meat into large pieces.

Strain the stock, and reserve it. Chop the cooked onion. Cut the ham or bacon into 1-cm (½-inch) strips. Slice the second onion, and fry until softened in the butter. Add the flour and cook for 2 minutes. Gradually stir in the cider and reserved stock. Bring to the boil, add the meats and the other onion, season to taste, and simmer for 7 minutes. Pour into a serving dish and garnish with croûtes and chopped parsley.

# TURKEY SAUTÉ ANNETTE

Serves 4

*1 tbsp cooking oil*
*25 g (1 oz) butter*
*2 small turkey legs (thigh and*
  *drumstick)*
*1 medium onion, chopped*
*1 tbsp plain flour*
*575 ml (1 pint) chicken stock (see*
  *page 91) or stock cube and water*
*275 ml (½ pint) white wine*
*salt and pepper*
*2 tsp chopped fresh chervil*
*2 tsp chopped fresh tarragon*
*1 tbsp chopped fresh parsley*
*1 tbsp lemon juice*
*chopped fresh parsley and strips of*
  *pimento to garnish*

Melt the oil and butter in a sauté pan, add the turkey joints and fry until golden brown. Remove the joints. Lightly fry the chopped onion, add the flour and cook for 2 minutes. Gradually stir in the stock and wine, bring to the boil, add seasoning, replace the turkey joints in the pan and add the chervil, tarragon, parsley and lemon juice. Bring to the boil, cover and simmer gently for approximately 1 hour or until the meat is tender.

Place the turkey joints in an oval dish, check the seasoning of the sauce, then pour it over the joints. Garnish with strips of pimento and chopped parsley.

# MARINATED TURKEY

Serves 6–8

Marinade
3 bay leaves
3 cloves garlic
4 peppercorns
1 medium onion, sliced
¼ tsp salt
575 ml (1 pint) white wine or white wine and water, or white wine and white wine vinegar

1 turkey approx 4 kg (9 lb), jointed
3 tbsp cooking oil
2 large onions, sliced
2–6 cloves of garlic, according to taste
2 tomatoes, skinned and chopped
4 peppercorns
2 cloves
½ tsp ground cinnamon
salt

Mix together the ingredients for the marinade. Place the turkey in a deep dish, and pour the marinade over; leave at least 4 hours, or overnight if possible. Turn the joints occasionally.

Remove the joints from the marinade and dry well. Heat the oil in a heavy saucepan or casserole, fry the turkey pieces until lightly browned, and remove from the pan. Add the sliced onion and fry gently until soft. Crush the garlic cloves and add to the onion. Add the remaining ingredients. Replace the turkey pieces in the pan, and pour over the strained marinade. Cover the pan tightly and cook over a low heat for approximately 2½ hours. Alternatively, if in a casserole, it may be cooked in the oven at 150°C (300°F) mark 2.

When cooked, test the seasoning. If desired, the sauce may be thickened with a little slaked cornflour.

# CARIBBEAN TURKEY

Serves 4

450 g (1 lb) white turkey meat
2 tbsp plain flour
salt and pepper
1 tbsp cooking oil
25 g (1 oz) butter
450 g (1 lb) canned apricot halves
2 tbsp Worcestershire sauce
2 tbsp vinegar
2 tbsp demerara sugar
2 tbsp lemon juice
150 ml (¼ pint) water
225 g (8 oz) long grain rice

Cut the turkey meat into 2.5-cm (1-inch) cubes. Place the flour, salt and pepper in a large polythene bag, add the turkey pieces and toss well.

Place the oil and butter in a flameproof casserole and heat. Add the coated turkey pieces and fry until brown.

Drain the apricot halves, reserve a few for the garnish and coarsely chop the remainder. Reserve the juice, and mix 150 ml (¼ pint) of it with the Worcestershire sauce, vinegar, demerara sugar, lemon juice and water.

Add any remaining flour to the turkey pieces and add the liquids to the pan. Stir gently and bring to the boil, add the chopped apricots, cover and simmer gently for 45 minutes, or until the meat is tender.

Meanwhile cook the long grain rice. Dry the rice, and place in a ring around a large serving dish. Keep warm. When the turkey is tender, check the seasoning and pour the mixture into the centre of the rice. Garnish with the remaining apricots.

# TURKEY DIVAN

Serves 4

450 g (1 lb) frozen broccoli
700 g (1½ lb) potatoes, cooked and mashed
25 g (1 oz) butter
350 g (12 oz) cooked turkey, sliced
1 can condensed chicken soup
2 tbsp dry sherry, or dry white wine
50 g (2 oz) Cheddar cheese, finely grated

Cook the broccoli in boiling salted water. Meanwhile pipe a bed of mashed potato into the centre of a warmed, flat, fireproof dish. Keep warm. Drain the broccoli and arrange around the potato; dot with butter. Place the turkey slices on top of the potato.

Heat the soup undiluted in a saucepan, add the sherry or wine, and pour over the turkey, leaving most of the broccoli uncovered. Sprinkle the sauce with grated cheese, reheat and brown under a hot grill.

# SHERRIED TURKEY

Serves 4

25 g (1 oz) butter
1 tbsp cooking oil
450 g (1 lb) turkey joints (leg or
  wing)
1 small onion, chopped
50 g (2 oz) lean bacon, chopped
50 g (2 oz) mushrooms, chopped
1 tbsp plain flour
salt and pepper
275 ml (½ pint) stock (see page 91)
3 tbsp dry sherry
chopped fresh parsley to garnish

Heat the butter and oil in a heavy pan, add the turkey pieces and gently fry until golden brown. Remove the turkey from the pan.

Add the onion and bacon and fry until the onion is soft, add the mushrooms and cook for 3 minutes. Stir in the flour and seasoning. Gradually add the stock, stirring continuously; bring to the boil, add the sherry, replace the turkey pieces, cover and cook for approximately 45 minutes or until the meat is cooked. Check the seasoning; bring the sauce back to the boil. Pour into a shallow oval dish and garnish with chopped parsley.

# TURKEY WITH BABY DUMPLINGS

Serves 4

575 ml (1 pint) béchamel sauce (see
  page 89)
450 g (1 lb) cold turkey
1 hard-boiled egg, chopped
1-2 tsp chopped capers
chopped fresh parsley to garnish

Dumplings
75 g (3 oz) self-raising flour
pinch of salt
35 g (1½ oz) shredded suet
1 tsp chopped fresh parsley and
  ½ tsp chopped fresh thyme or
  1 tsp mixed dried herbs
3 tbsp water

Make the béchamel sauce, cut the turkey into bite-sized pieces and place in the saucepan with the sauce; heat gently. Stir in the egg and capers.

Make the dumplings by sieving together the flour and salt into a bowl; add the suet and herbs. Mix with water to make a soft, but mouldable, consistency. Divide into 8, and shape each into a dumpling. Drop carefully into fast boiling water and cook for 7-10 minutes. Lift out carefully; place in the sauce, and cook for 2-3 minutes. Serve sprinkled with parsley.

# TURKEY TETRAZZINI

Serves 4

225 g (8 oz) spaghetti
1 tbsp cooking oil
3 tbsp strips of streaky bacon
1 large onion, sliced
25 g (1 oz) plain flour
275 ml (½ pint) stock (see page 91)
1 tsp concentrated tomato purée
1 green pepper and 1 red pepper,
  seeded, cut into strips and
  blanched
100 g (4 oz) small mushrooms,
  quartered
350 g (12 oz) cooked turkey, cut into
  strips
Parmesan cheese to sprinkle

Cook the spaghetti in a large pan in fast boiling salted water, until tender (approximately 15 minutes). Drain, and arrange around the edge of a warmed flat serving dish.

Meanwhile heat the oil, and gently fry the onion and bacon, until the onion is soft. Add the flour and cook for 2 minutes. Stir in the stock and tomato purée. Continue stirring and bring to the boil. Add the peppers, mushrooms, and turkey. Season to taste. Bring slowly to the boil, cover and simmer for 10 minutes.

Spoon into the centre of the spaghetti and sprinkle with Parmesan cheese.

# DEVILLED TURKEY JOINTS

Serves 4

4 turkey leg or wing joints
1 tsp curry powder
2 tbsp mustard powder
2 tsp Worcestershire sauce
salt and pepper
a few drops of tabasco sauce
  (optional)

Remove the skin from turkey joints, and score the flesh. Mix a sauce with the rest of the ingredients, and cover each joint thoroughly. Either grill the joints slowly until cooked, or bake in the oven at 180°C (350°F) mark 4, until brown and the meat is tender.

Serve with creamed potatoes and Brussels sprouts.

# TURKEY LOAF

Serves 4

350 g (12 oz) cooked turkey, minced
100 g (4 oz) fresh breadcrumbs
½ tsp dry mustard
1 medium onion, minced
75 g (3 oz) mushrooms, chopped
½ tsp celery salt
2 tbsp chopped fresh parsley
2 eggs, beaten
150 ml (¼ pint) milk
1 tsp Worcestershire sauce
salt and pepper

Heat the oven to 180°C (350°F) mark 4. Into a large bowl place the turkey, breadcrumbs, mustard, onion, mushrooms, celery salt and parsley. Mix well together. Add the beaten eggs, milk and Worcestershire sauce. Mix again, ensuring all the ingredients are well blended. Season to taste. Place the mixture in a well-greased 900-g (2-lb) loaf tin. Bake in the oven, until firm, for about 1 hour. Leave in the tin for 5 minutes before turning out onto a serving dish. Serve hot or cold.

# TURKEY WITH AVOCADO SALAD

Serves 4

2 avocados
fresh orange juice
½ small red pepper and ½ green
    pepper, de-seeded
225 g (8 oz) cooked turkey, diced
1–2 tsp Worcestershire sauce
2–3 tbsp mayonnaise (see page 92)
salt and pepper

Peel and core the avocados, slice, and arrange in overlapping slices in a circle on a serving plate. Brush with orange juice.

From each of the peppers, reserve a few fine slices for garnish, and finely chop the remainder.

Mix the turkey with the chopped peppers, Worcestershire sauce and mayonnaise. Season to taste. Pile the mixture in the centre of the avocado slices. Garnish with the reserved slices of peppers.

Chill well. Serve with a watercress salad.

# TURKEY SALAD

Serves 4

225 g (8 oz) cooked turkey, diced
225 g (8 oz) cooked long grain rice
½ red pepper and ½ green pepper,
  de-seeded and finely sliced
2 tbsp cooked sweetcorn kernels
25 g (1 oz) walnuts, chopped
25 g (1 oz) sultanas
vinaigrette dressing (see page 92)
sliced cucumber to garnish

Mix together the turkey, rice, peppers, sweetcorn, walnuts and sultanas. Add sufficient vinaigrette dressing to moisten.

Pile onto a plate, and garnish with a ring of finely sliced cucumber.

# TURKEY AND HAM SALAD

Serves 3–4

100 g (4 oz) cooked turkey, diced
100 g (4 oz) cooked ham, diced
150 g (6 oz) cooked long grain rice
3–4 tbsp fresh or canned pineapple,
  diced
3–4 tbsp melon, diced
2 eating apples, cored and sliced
4–6 tbsp mayonnaise (see page 92)
lettuce, tomato and cucumber to
  garnish

Mix together the turkey, ham, rice, pineapple, melon and apple. Fold in the mayonnaise.

Arrange the lettuce on a serving dish, and pile the salad on top. Garnish with sliced or quartered tomatoes and sliced cucumber.

# ROAST DUCK WITH ORANGE SAUCE

Serves 4

1 oven-ready duckling, about 2 kg
  (4½ lb)
salt and pepper
1 medium carrot, sliced
1 medium onion, sliced
4 navel oranges
150 ml (¼ pint) port or Madeira
2–3 tbsp Cointreau or Grand
  Marnier
a few drops of lemon juice (if
  necessary)
25 g (1 oz) butter, softened

Sauce
3 tbsp granulated sugar
3 tbsp red wine vinegar
275 ml (¾ pint) duck stock, using
  the giblets (see page 91)
1 tbsp arrowroot
2 tbsp port or Madeira
orange peel

Heat the oven to 220°C (425°F) mark 7.
Season the cavity of the duck. Remove the
zest from the oranges with a zester (or with
a potato peeler then cut into julienne strips);
simmer in 575 ml (1 pint) water for
15 minutes. Drain. Place one-third of the
zest in the bird's cavity.

Prick the skin around the thighs, back
and lower breast. Place in a roasting tin with
the vegetables. Roast in the oven for
15 minutes, reduce the heat to 180°C
(350°F) mark 4, and turn the duck on its
side. After 30 minutes, turn the duck onto
its other side. Remove any accumulated fat
occasionally. 15 minutes before the end of
roasting time, turn the duck on its back,
and sprinkle with salt. (Total cooking time
– 1¼ to 1½ hours).

Whilst the bird is roasting, prepare the
sauce. Place the vinegar and sugar in a pan
and heat to form a caramel. Remove from
the heat and stir in 150 ml (¼ pint) of the
stock. Simmer gently to dissolve the
caramel; add the remaining stock. Blend the
arrowroot with the port or Madeira, and
add to the stock, with the remaining orange
zest. Stir, bring to the boil, and simmer for
3–4 minutes until the sauce clears. Adjust
the seasoning.

Remove the remaining skin from the
oranges, and divide into segments.

When the duck is cooked, remove it from
the roasting tin, place on a serving dish and
keep warm. Remove surplus fat from the
roasting tin, add the port or Madeira and
boil, incorporating the pan juices; reduce
the liquid to 2–3 tablespoonfuls. Strain into
the prepared sauce; bring to the simmer.
Add Cointreau or Grand Marnier to taste
(correcting oversweetness with lemon

juice). Just before serving, and away from the heat, stir in the butter.

Garnish the duck with the orange segments and spoon a little sauce over; serve the rest separately.

Ducks are awkward to carve, so carving is best carried out in the kitchen. Cut straight through the breastbone and back, using scissors or game shears to cut through the bone. Lay each half cut side down, and make a slanting cut through the breast, separating the wing and the leg, ensuring that each piece has some breast.

# ROAST DUCK WITH BAKED APPLES

Serves 6

*1 duck, 2.25–2.7 kg (5–6 lb)*
*salt*
*6 medium-sized cooking apples*

Stuffing
*4 large onions*
*10 fresh sage leaves, chopped*
*100 g (4 oz) fresh breadcrumbs*
*25 g (1 oz) butter or margarine*
*salt and pepper*
*1 egg, beaten*

Heat the oven to 200°C (400°F) mark 6. Prepare the stuffing – boil the onions for 10 minutes, then chop finely. Add the sage, breadcrumbs, butter and seasoning. Bind together with the beaten egg.

Stuff the duck and truss it (see page 14). Sprinkle the duck with salt and prick the skin around the legs and the back. Place in a roasting tin in the oven, and when the fat starts running, baste well every 20 minutes until the bird is cooked. Roast for 35 minutes per kg (15 minutes per lb) and 15 minutes over.

Peel and core the apples and place in the roasting tin with the duck, 45 minutes before the end of cooking. Serve the duck on a shallow plate, surrounded by the apples.

*Variation*
Stuff each apple with well-seasoned sausagemeat, and cook as before.

# DUCKLING PROVENÇAL STYLE

Serves 4

*1.8-kg (4-lb) duckling, cut into
   4 joints*
*2 tbsp plain flour*
*salt and pepper*
*1 tbsp oil*
*25 g (1 oz) butter*
*225 g (8 oz) onion, chopped*
*2 cloves garlic, crushed*
*1 green pepper, de-seeded and
   chopped*
*2 tomatoes, skinned, pipped and
   chopped*
*1 tbsp tomato purée*
*2 tsp sugar*
*200 ml (7 fl oz) stock (see page 91)*
*200 ml (7 fl oz) white wine*
*2–3 stuffed olives, sliced*
*225 g (8 oz) long grain rice*
*lemon slices to garnish*

Heat the oven to 150°C (300°F) mark 2.
Mix the flour and salt and pepper in a
polythene bag, add the duckling joints and
shake well to ensure the joints are well
coated. Heat the oil and butter in a
flameproof casserole, and fry the joints until
evenly browned, then transfer them to a
plate.

Add the onion to the pan and fry gently to
soften. Add the crushed garlic, the pepper
and the tomatoes, and fry for 5–6 minutes.
Add the tomato purée and sugar. Stir in the
stock and wine, bring to the boil, replace
the duckling joints and add the sliced olives.
Cover tightly and place in the oven. Cook
for 1½–1¾ hours or until the meat is
tender.

Cook the rice. Remove the duckling from
the oven and check the seasoning. Skim off
excess fat. Serve with the rice garnished
with lemon slices.

# DUCK WITH SPICY ORANGE SALAD

Serves 4

*1.8-kg (4-lb) duck*
*salt*

Stuffing
*450 g (1 lb) onions, chopped*
*150 ml (¼ pint) water*
*salt and pepper*
*75 g (3 oz) fresh breadcrumbs*
*2 tsp chopped fresh sage*
*50 g (2 oz) margarine*

Spicy orange salad
*2 tbsp oil*
*1 large onion, sliced and separated*
  *into rings*
*4 oranges*
*¼ tsp cayenne pepper*
*2 tbsp stuffed green olives, sliced*
*1 tbsp finely chopped fresh parsley*

Heat the oven to 230°C (450°F) mark 8. To make the stuffing, place the onions in a saucepan with the water and cook for 10 minutes. Season well. Strain, reserving the liquid, and mix with the breadcrumbs, sage and margarine, adding sufficient of the onion stock to moisten. Cool, then stuff the cavity of the duck, sprinkle the bird with salt, and prick around the legs and back.

Place in a roasting tin, and roast for 30 minutes. Reduce the oven temperature to 190°C (375°F) mark 5, and cook for another hour, or until tender. Transfer to a serving dish.

While the duck is cooking, make the salad. Heat the oil in a frying pan and fry the onion rings for approximately 10 minutes, but do not brown. Lift out of the pan and drain on absorbent paper.

Cut the peel from the oranges, ensuring that all the pith is removed, and slice them into rings. Place the orange slices in a shallow dish, arrange the onion rings on top, and sprinkle with the cayenne pepper and the sliced olives. Chill for at least 30 minutes before serving. Serve sprinkled with the parsley.

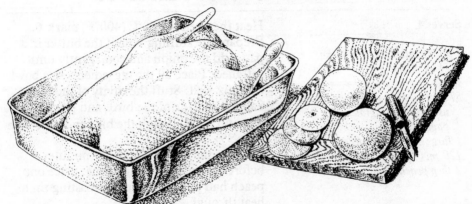

# BRAISED DUCK

Serves 4

*1 duck, cut into 4 joints*
*seasoning*
*1 tbsp oil*
*25 g (1 oz) butter*
*1 large onion, chopped*
*2 medium carrots, chopped*
*1 rasher bacon, chopped*
*1 tbsp plain flour*
*150 ml (¼ pint) red wine*
*275 ml (½ pint) stock (see page 91)*
*1 orange*
*bunch of fresh herbs – bayleaf,*
  *savoury, sage, parsley*
*50 g (2 oz) mushrooms, sliced*
*orange slices and watercress to*
  *garnish*

Heat the oven to 170°C (325°F) mark 3.
Season the duck joints well. Heat the oil and
butter in a flameproof casserole, and lightly
brown the duck joints. Transfer them to a
plate. Add the onion, carrot and bacon to
the casserole and fry gently until the
vegetables begin to soften. Add the flour
and cook for 1–2 minutes. Stir in the wine
and stock and bring to boil. Grate the
orange rind and add it to the stock with the
herbs.

Replace the duck joints in the casserole.
Cover tightly and cook in the oven for about
1¼ hours. Add the juice of the orange and
the mushrooms. Continue cooking for a
further 30 minutes or until the meat is
tender. Remove the joints to a serving dish
and keep warm. Strain the sauce, skimming
off any excess fat. Adjust the seasoning, and
pour the sauce over the joints. Garnish with
orange slices and watercress.

This recipe is suitable for an older duck.

# ROAST DUCKLING WITH PEACHES

Serves 4

*1 plump duckling, 1.8–2 kg*
  *(4–4½ lb)*
*salt*
*575 ml (1 pint) espagnole sauce,*
  *using the duck giblets (see*
  *page 90)*
*1 large can peach halves*
*120 ml (4 fl oz) dry sherry*
*2 tbsp peach brandy*

Heat the oven to 200°C (400°F) mark 6.
Prepare the stuffing – melt the butter in a
pan, add the onion and cook gently until
softened. Place all the ingredients in a bowl
and mix well. Stuff the cavity of the bird.
Salt the outside of the bird, and prick the
legs and back. Weigh the bird and cook (see
page 39).

Drain the peach halves. 10 minutes
before the end of cooking time, place one
peach half per person in the roasting tin to
heat through.

Stuffing
*100 g (4 oz) onion, finely chopped*
*50 g (2 oz) butter*
*25 g (1 oz) walnuts, chopped*
*50 g (2 oz) seeded raisins, chopped*
*rind and juice of ½ lemon*
*225 g (8 oz) pork sausagemeat*

Chop the remaining peach halves. When the duck is ready, place it on a serving dish with the peach halves and keep warm. Remove the surplus fat from the roasting tin, and add a little hot water to the tin to de-glaze it. Strain the liquid into the previously prepared sauce, add the sherry, peach brandy, chopped peaches and 3 tablespoonfuls peach juice. Heat gently, adjust the seasoning and pour into a sauce-boat.

# DUCKLING WITH BLACK CHERRIES

Serves 4

*1.8–2-kg (4–4½-lb) duckling*
*salt*

Stuffing
*25 g (1 oz) butter*
*1 medium onion, chopped*
*100 g (4 oz) walnuts or cashews,*
  *chopped*
*100 g (4 oz) fresh breadcrumbs*
*1 tbsp chopped fresh parsley*
*1 tsp chopped fresh sage*
*1 tsp chopped fresh thyme*
*pinch of ground cinnamon*
*seasoning*
*grated rind of 1 lemon, juice of*
  *½ lemon*
*beaten egg*

Sauce
*450 g (1-lb) canned black cherries*
  *(stoned)*
*3 tbsp red wine vinegar*
*2 tsp arrowroot or cornflour*

Heat the oven to 200°C (400°F) mark 6. To make the stuffing, heat the butter and gently fry the onion until it is soft; lightly fry the nuts to a golden brown. Place all the ingredients in a bowl and mix well, adding sufficient egg to bind. Place the stuffing in the cavity of the duck, and truss the duck.

Sprinkle the duck well with salt and prick around the legs and back. Weigh the duck and cook (see page 39).

When the duck is cooked, place it on a serving dish and keep warm. Remove the excess fat from the roasting tin, add a little hot water to the tin to de-glaze. Place this in a measure, add the red wine vinegar and strained cherry juice, and make up to 275 ml (½ pint) with water. Blend the arrowroot or cornflour with a little cold water, add the juice mixture, place in a pan, and bring to the boil stirring constantly. Add the cherries, and cook gently for 2–3 minutes. Pour into a sauce-boat.

Garnish the duck with watercress and serve with duchesse potatoes.

# SALMIS OF DUCK

Serves 4

1 duckling
salt

Sauce
25 g (1 oz) butter
duck giblets
1 small onion, diced
1 small carrot, diced
50 g (2 oz) bacon, cut in strips
1 tbsp plain flour
seasoning
bunch of fresh mixed herbs or
    bouquet garni
275 ml (½ pint) water
150 ml (½ pint) red wine

Garnish
12 small onions, parboiled, and then
    cooked gently in butter
3–4 stuffed olives, sliced
croûtes (see page 93)

Heat the oven to 220°C (425°F) mark 7. Rub salt into the skin of the duckling and prick all over especially around the legs and back. Place in a roasting tin and roast for 45 minutes.

While the duck is cooking, prepare the sauce. Melt the butter in a saucepan and lightly brown the giblets. Add the vegetables and bacon and cook for 5–7 minutes to soften the vegetables. Add the flour and cook gently until golden brown. Add the water, herbs and seasoning. Cover and simmer for 30 minutes. Add the wine, and allow to reduce in volume by one-third, removing any scum as it rises.

Remove the duck from the roasting tin, and cut it into joints. Place the joints in a shallow ovenproof dish, and strain the sauce over. Cover the dish and cook in the oven at 180°C (350°F) mark 4 for 30 minutes, or until the duck is tender.

Garnish with the onions, stuffed olives and croûtes, and serve with new potatoes and peas.

Salmis is the term given to a rich brown stew of duck (or game). It is usual for the duck to be roasted for about three-quarters of the cooking time. It is then finished in a rich brown sauce made from the giblets, with red or white wine added.

# ROAST DUCK WITH APRICOTS

Serves 6–8

*2 plump ducks, each 1.8–2 kg*
  *(4–4½ lb)*
*salt*
*giblets*
*1 small carrot, diced*
*1 small onion, diced*
*small bunch of herbs*
*seasoning*
*575 ml (1 pint) water*
*1 large can apricot halves*
*juice of 1 lemon*
*1 tbsp cornflour*
*2 tbsp redcurrant jelly*
*2 tbsp apricot brandy*

Heat the oven to 200°C (400°F) mark 6. Prepare and roast the ducks (see page 39). Place the giblets in a pan with the carrot, onion, herbs, seasoning and water. Bring to the boil, cover and simmer gently for about 1 hour. Strain.

Drain the juice from the apricot halves, and make the juice up to 575 ml (1 pint) with the strained giblet stock and lemon juice. Blend the cornflour with a little cold water in a basin, add a little of the juice and mix well. Pour into a saucepan, and bring to the boil, stirring continuously. Add the redcurrant jelly and stir to dissolve; add the apricot brandy. Check the seasoning.

Approximately 10 minutes before the ducks are cooked, place the apricot halves in the roasting tin to heat.

To serve, place the ducks, jointed, on a serving dish, arrange the apricot halves around, and glaze the ducks with a little of the sauce. Serve the rest of the sauce separately.

# CASSEROLED DUCK WITH PORT

Serves 4

*1 duck*
*1 medium onion, whole*
*5–6 sage leaves*
*seasoning*
*duck giblets*
*2 medium onions, chopped*
*bunch of fresh herbs or bouquet garni*
*1 tbsp each diced carrot and diced*
  *celery*
*425 ml (¾ pint) water or water and*
  *wine*
*1 tbsp plain flour*
*150 ml (¼ pint) port*
*lemon slices and croûtons (see*
  *page 93) to garnish*

Heat the oven to 150°C (300°F) mark 2. Place the whole onion and the sage leaves in the cavity of the duck and season well. Place the giblets in a saucepan with the chopped onions, herbs, carrot, celery and seasoning with the water. Bring to the boil, cover and simmer for ¾–1 hour. Strain. Place the duck in a casserole and pour the giblet stock around. Cover, bring to the boil and cook in the oven for 1½–2 hours or until the meat is tender.

Joint the duck, place on a serving dish, and keep warm. Remove the excess fat from the cooking juices. Mix the flour with a little cold water, add a few tablespoonfuls cooking juices, mix well, and pour into the casserole with the port. Bring to the boil; adjust the seasoning as necessary. Pour the sauce over the duck and garnish with lemon slices and fried bread croûtons.

This recipe is suitable for an older duck.

# ROAST GOOSE

Serves 8

*4.5-kg (10-lb) goose*
*double recipe quantity sage and*
  *onion stuffing (see page 85)*
*salt*
*25 g (1 oz) butter or dripping*
*watercress to garnish*
*apple sauce (see page 88)*

Heat the oven to 220°C (425°F) mark 7. Prepare the stuffing. Prepare the goose as for chicken (see page 13), but cut the wings off at the first joint before trussing. Place the stuffing in the cavity from the tail end. Prick the skin of the goose all over to allow the excess fat to run out during cooking. Sprinkle the breast with salt.

Melt the fat in a roasting tin, place the goose in the tin, and put it in the oven. Cook for 30 minutes. Reduce the oven temperature to 180°C (350°F) mark 4; continue cooking, basting regularly with the

fat which comes from the goose. Allow
35 minutes per kg (15 minutes per lb), but
if the goose is old, and perhaps a little
tough, allow 45 minutes per kg (20 minutes
per lb) and reduce the oven temperature to
170°C (325°F) mark 3.

When the goose is cooked, place it on a
serving dish and keep warm. Pour off most
of the fat from the roasting dish, and use the
residue to make gravy.

Garnish the goose with watercress and
serve gravy and apple sauce separately.

To carve, cut off the legs. Remove the
wings by slicing a piece of breast meat with
each wing. Cut the breast in slices parallel to
the breast bone.

*Variations*
(1) Prune and apple stuffing (see page 86).
(2) Potato stuffing (see page 85).
(3) For garnish, serve fried apple rings or
fried pineapple rings.
(4) The gravy is improved if a sour apple is
cooked in the roasting tin with the goose.

*Using up leftover goose*
(1) Slice and eat cold with jacket potatoes,
Waldorf salad, or a green salad,
accompanied by a damson or quince cheese.
(2) Curried: mince the leftover meat and
mix with any stuffing left, plus
1 teaspoonful curry powder, 2 teaspoonfuls
plain flour and sufficient gravy to moisten.
Season to taste. Place in a greased shallow
dish and cook in the oven at 200°C (400°F)
mark 6 for 20–25 minutes. Serve with
croûtes (see page 93) and any green
vegetable.

# GAME BIRDS

Game birds, once food for kings, are now
available to all from specialist shops and are a
tasty alternative to poultry for that special
occasion dinner. In this chapter recipes for
different varieties of game bird are given, from
pheasant to the tiny snipe.

# ROAST PHEASANT

See page 6 for servings

1 pheasant, trussed
50 g (2 oz) butter
1 medium onion or ½ apple or
    ½ small lemon
salt and pepper
3–4 rashers streaky bacon
150 ml (¼ pint) red wine (optional)
bread sauce (see page 89)
game chips (see page 93)

Heat the oven to 220°C (425°F) mark 7. Place 25 g (1 oz) of the butter in the cavity of the bird, together with the onion, apple or lemon. Rub the remaining butter over the surface of the bird, and sprinkle with salt and pepper. Cover the breast with the bacon. Place the bird in a roasting tin and put in the oven. Cook for ¾–1¼ hours, depending on size, basting regularly. The red wine may be poured into the roasting tin half-way through cooking and although most of it may disappear during cooking, it will give flavour when stock is added to the pan for making gravy.

The giblets should be placed in a pan with water, seasoning and small onion or carrot and cooked gently. The resulting stock should be used with the pan juices from the roasting tin to make a thin gravy.

Garnish the pheasant with watercress, with two tail feathers placed vertically between the legs. Serve with bread sauce, game chips and a green vegetable. Carve as for chicken.

# GIPSY PHEASANT

Serves 3–4

25 g (1 oz) butter
1 clove garlic, crushed
1 pheasant, jointed
350-g (12-oz) piece of bacon, cubed
2 large onions, sliced
4 ripe tomatoes, peeled and sliced
150 ml (¼ pint) sherry
salt and pepper
¼–½ tsp cayenne pepper

Melt the butter in a flameproof casserole. Add the garlic. Fry the pheasant joints and the bacon until lightly browned. Transfer to a plate. Place the onions in the casserole, and fry gently until soft. Add the tomatoes and cook for 2–3 minutes. Replace the pheasant joints, and pour the sherry over. Season lightly. Cover tightly and simmer gently for about 1 hour, or until the meat is tender. Just before serving, add the cayenne pepper to the sauce.

# PHEASANT IN RED WINE

Serves 3–4

1 tbsp oil
50 g (2 oz) butter
1 large pheasant, jointed
2 shallots, finely chopped
275 ml (½ pint) red wine
12 button mushrooms
salt and pepper
1 tbsp plain flour

Glazed onions
12 small onions
25 g (1 oz) butter
1 tbsp granulated sugar
150–275 ml (¼–½ pint) stock (see
    page 91)

Heat the oven to 170°C (325°F) mark 3.
Heat the oil and 25 g (1 oz) of the butter in
a flameproof casserole, add the pheasant
joints and sauté gently until golden brown.
Remove the joints to a plate. Add the
shallots to the casserole and cook gently
until soft. Pour in the red wine and combine
with the pan juices. Replace the joints in the
casserole and add the mushrooms and
seasoning. Cover, and cook in the oven for
approximately ¾–1 hour, or until the meat
is tender. Meanwhile knead together the
remaining butter with the flour. When the
bird is tender, use the kneaded flour to
thicken the sauce as required. Remove any
fat from the surface.

While the bird is cooking, prepare the
onions. Place them in a pan with the butter
and sugar and sufficient stock to barely
cover. Cook gently in an open pan until the
onions are tender and the stock is reduced
to a glaze. Garnish the pheasant with the
glazed onions. Serve with creamed potatoes
or rice.

# NORMANDY PHEASANT

Serves 2–3

1 tbsp cooking oil
25 g (1 oz) butter
1 pheasant
1 small onion, finely chopped
2 tbsp calvados or brandy
150 ml (¼ pint) game or chicken
    stock(see page 91)
2 medium dessert apples, peeled,
    cored and sliced
salt and pepper
150 ml (¼ pint) double cream

Garnish
2 dessert apples, cored and sliced
    into rings
icing sugar
1 tbsp cooking oil
25 g (1 oz) butter

Heat the oil and butter in a flameproof casserole. Gently brown the pheasant, then remove it to a plate. Add the onion to the casserole and fry until softened. Drain off surplus fat. Replace the pheasant in the casserole.

Pour the calvados or brandy into a heated ladle, set alight and pour over the pheasant.

Allow the flame to die, then add the stock and the apples. Cover the casserole tightly, and simmer gently for approximately 45 minutes, or until the pheasant is tender. Remove the pheasant, carve as for chicken .

Strain the sauce, stir in the cream, reheat, check the seasoning and pour over the pheasant.

Garnish with apple rings that have been liberally sprinkled with icing sugar and fried in the oil and butter.

# PEPPERED PHEASANT WITH ALMONDS

Serves 2–3

1 pheasant
50 g (2 oz) butter
1 tsp freshly ground black pepper
1 small onion, chopped
75–100 g (3–4 oz) piece of fat
    bacon
50 g (2 oz) flaked almonds

Heat the oven to 170°C (325°F) mark 3. Mix together the butter and black pepper, and spread over the bird. Place the onion and bacon inside the bird.

Place the bird on a piece of foil, and cover the breast with the almond flakes. Seal the foil, place the bird in a roasting tin and cook for 1½–2 hours. 15 minutes before the end of cooking time, open the foil to allow the breast and almonds to brown.

Serve with an orange and watercress salad.

# PHEASANT IN MADEIRA

Serves 4

25 g (1 oz) butter
1 pheasant
4 slices fat bacon, cut small
2 slices ham, cut small
1 medium onion, finely chopped
1 stick celery, finely chopped
1 carrot, finely diced
1 tsp chopped fresh parsley
salt and pepper
pinch of nutmeg
150 ml (¼ pint) Madeira
150 ml (¼ pint) game or chicken
  stock (see page 91)
croûtes (see page 93) to garnish

Melt the butter in a flameproof casserole and fry the pheasant, bacon and ham until lightly browned. Transfer to a plate. Fry the onion, celery and carrot until soft. Replace the meats in the casserole. Add the parsley and seasonings. Pour in the Madeira and stock. Cover tightly and cook gently for approximately 1 hour or until the meat is tender.

Place the bird on a serving dish. Liquidize or sieve the sauce, adjust the seasoning and pour over the bird. Garnish with croûtes.

# PHEASANT CASSEROLE WITH ORANGE

Serves 3–4

1 tbsp cooking oil
25 g (1 oz) butter
1 pheasant, jointed
225 g (8 oz) mushrooms, sliced
2 tbsp plain flour
275 ml (½ pint) game or chicken
  stock (see page 91)
150 ml (¼ pint) orange juice
150 ml (¼ pint) dry white wine
salt and pepper
1 orange

Heat the oven to 180°C (350°F) mark 4. Heat the oil and butter in a frying pan, and add the pheasant joints; fry until browned all over. Transfer the joints to a flameproof casserole. Add the mushrooms to the frying pan and fry for 4–5 minutes, then transfer to the casserole. Sprinkle the flour into the remaining fat, and cook for 2–3 minutes. Mix together the stock, orange juice and wine, and gradually add to the fat and flour. Bring to the boil, stirring all the time, season to taste, and pour into the casserole. Cover tightly, and cook in the oven for approximately 1 hour, or until tender.

Meanwhile peel the zest from the orange and cut into fine strips. Place these in a pan with a little water and simmer gently until soft. Strain. Remove the rest of the peel from the orange and divide it into segments.

When the pheasant is cooked, adjust the

seasoning. Sprinkle the orange strips over the top of the joints, and garnish with the orange segments.

This dish is suitable for an older bird.

# ROAST GUINEA-FOWL

Serves 4–5

1 guinea-fowl
4–6 streaky bacon rashers
1 tbsp plain flour
seasoning
275 ml (½ pint) stock using the
    giblets (see page 91)
150 ml (¼ pint) sour cream or
    yoghurt

Stuffing
6–8 olives, stoned and chopped
4 tbsp fresh breadcrumbs
freshly ground black pepper
25 g (1 oz) melted butter
beaten egg

Heat the oven to 190°C (375°F) mark 5. Make the stuffing by mixing the ingredients together, and adding sufficient beaten egg to bind. Place the stuffing in the cavity of the bird. Cover the breast with the bacon rashers and roast for approximately 1 hour, or until the meat is tender, basting frequently.

When cooked, place the bird on a serving dish and keep warm. Sprinkle the flour in the roasting tin and stir into the pan juices. Cook for 2–3 minutes. Gradually stir in the stock, bring to the boil, simmer for 3–4 minutes and add seasoning to taste. Stir in the cream or yoghurt, reheat carefully, and strain into a sauce-boat.

Garnish the guinea-fowl with watercress and serve with game chips (see page 93) and a green vegetable. Carve as for chicken.

# ROAST PARTRIDGE

Allow 1 partridge for 1–2 persons

For each bird
*a knob of butter*
*seasoning*
*1 tsp lemon juice*
*1 rasher streaky bacon*
*1 vine leaf (optional)*

Garnish
*croûtes (see page 93)*
*lemon wedges*
*watercress*

Heat the oven to 220°C (425°F) mark 7. Clean and truss the bird, and place the butter, seasoning and lemon juice in the cavity of the bird. If available, tie a vine leaf next to the skin of the bird with a rasher of bacon over it. Place in a well-buttered tin and roast in the oven for 20–25 minutes. (Alternatively, it may be spit-roasted.)

Serve on a croûte with the pan juices poured over, garnished with lemon wedges and watercress.

As accompaniments, serve fried breadcrumbs, or bread sauce (see page 89), clear gravy and game chips (see page 93).

To carve, cut in half.

# COLD PARTRIDGE IN VINE LEAVES

Serves 4

*4 young partridges, dressed and*
  *trussed (see page 8)*
*salt and pepper*
*4 rashers streaky bacon*
*8–12 vine leaves (fresh or tinned) or*
  *cabbage leaves*

Season the partridges with salt and pepper. Wrap a rasher of bacon around each. Rinse any brine off the vine leaves, and simmer in a little water for 5 minutes. Wrap each bird tightly in 2–3 vine leaves and tie securely. (Cabbage leaves may be used if vine leaves are not available – these need blanching in boiling water, then refreshing in cold water.)

Place the wrapped partridges in a pan, cover with water, bring to the boil, then simmer for 35 minutes.

Plunge immediately into ice-cold water and leave to cool for approximately 10 minutes. Remove the vine leaves and bacon. Serve with a plain green salad, or apple sauce (see page 88), game chips (see page 93) and watercress.

# PARTRIDGE WITH CABBAGE

Serves 3–4

1 hard green cabbage, about 900 g
 (2 lb)
salt and pepper
175 g (6 oz) streaky bacon in one
 piece
25 g (1 oz) butter
2–3 partridges (according to size)
8 small onions
2 medium carrots, sliced
225 g (8 oz) pork sausages
bunch of fresh herbs, including
 parsley, thyme and a bay leaf
275–575 ml (½–1 pint) stock (see
 page 91)
2 tsp arrowroot, mixed with 2 tbsp
 cold water

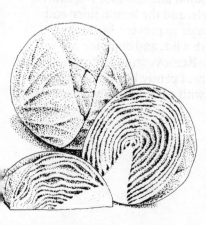

Heat the oven to 170°C (325°F) mark 3. Cut
the cabbage into quarters, and cook it in a
pan of boiling salted water for 6 minutes.
Drain, and refresh in cold water. Divide
each quarter into 2–3 pieces. Season lightly.

Place the bacon in cold water, bring to
the boil, drain and refresh. Melt the butter
in a flameproof casserole and gently brown
the partridges, then remove them to a plate.
Place half the cabbage in the casserole, and
place on top of it the bacon, onions, carrots,
sausages and the partridges, with the bunch
of fresh herbs. Add some seasoning. Cover
with the remaining cabbage, and moisten
with stock. Cover tightly, using foil under
the lid.

Place in the oven, and cook for
1½–2 hours. If the partridges are young,
take them out after 35 minutes; also remove
the sausage. Keep covered, whilst the
cabbage continues cooking. Check
occasionally to make sure it does not
become too dry.

Replace the sausages (and partridges if
removed) approximately 10 minutes before
the end of cooking time to ensure that they
are hot.

To serve, cut each partridge in half, the
bacon into strips and the sausages into
slices. Drain the cabbage, having removed
the herbs, and thicken the strained juice
with a little slaked arrowroot.

Place the cabbage in a serving dish,
arrange the partridges on top, and decorate
with the bacon, sausage and onions. Spoon
a little of the sauce around the cabbage and
serve the rest separately.

This *perdrix aux choux* is a famous French
recipe for cooking older birds.

# PARTRIDGE WITH MUSHROOMS

Serves 4–6

4 partridges, dressed (see page 8)
50 g (2 oz) butter
225 g (8 oz) mushrooms, sliced
salt and pepper
1 tbsp oil
1 small onion, finely chopped
1 tbsp plain flour
150 ml (¼ pint) dry sherry
425 ml (¾ pint) stock (see page 91)
100 g (4 oz) button mushrooms
chopped fresh parsley to garnish

Melt 25 g (1 oz) butter in a saucepan and cook the sliced mushrooms slowly. Add seasoning. Divide the mushrooms into 4 and stuff the partridge cavities. Melt the oil and the remaining butter in a flameproof casserole and gently brown the partridge. Add the chopped onion and cook for a further 3–4 minutes. Sprinkle in the flour; cook for 2 minutes. Gradually add the sherry and stock and bring to the boil. Season to taste.

Cover and simmer gently for ¾–1 hour, or until the meat is tender. 15 minutes before the end of cooking time, add the button mushrooms. Serve garnished with chopped parsley.

# PARTRIDGES IN CREAM

Serves 4–6

4 young partridges
salt and pepper
juice of 2 lemons
25 g (1 oz) butter
1 small onion, chopped
4 slices streaky bacon, chopped
½ tsp dried sage
275 ml (½ pint) single cream

Heat the oven to 170°C (325°F) mark 3. Season the birds inside and outside, and sprinkle with the lemon juice. Melt the butter in a flameproof casserole. Add the partridges and brown all over. Add the bacon and onion and cook for 5 minutes. Add the herbs and the lemon juice and sufficient water to prevent burning.

Cover with a lid, and cook for 30 minutes. Remove from the oven, stir in the cream, heat gently but do not allow to boil. Serve with game chips (see page 93).

# PARTRIDGE CASSEROLE

Serves 4

1 tbsp oil
25 g (1 oz) butter
2 partridges, cut in half
4 shallots, chopped
2 carrots, finely diced
small wedge of turnip, finely diced
2 rashers streaky bacon, chopped
150 ml (¼ pint) red wine
275 ml (½ pint) stock (see page 91)
seasoning
beurre manié (see page 92)

Heat the oven to 150°C (300°F) mark 2.
Heat the oil and butter in a flameproof
casserole and lightly brown the partridges.
Transfer to a plate. Gently fry the shallots,
carrot and turnip with the bacon. Return
the partridges to the casserole, and add the
red wine and stock.

Cover and cook in the oven for ¾–1 hour
or until the birds are tender. Thicken the
sauce with a little beurre manié. Serve with
creamed potatoes and pickled red cabbage.

# POT-ROASTED PARTRIDGES IN MILK

Serves 4–6

1 tbsp oil
4 partridges (reserve the livers)
2 large onions, quartered
8 small tomatoes
150 ml (¼ pint) sherry
275 ml (½ pint) water
275 ml (½ pint) milk
salt and pepper
2 tbsp capers
2 tbsp parsley
2 tbsp stoned olives

Heat the oven to 150°C (300°F) mark 2.
Heat the oil in a flameproof casserole and
carefully brown the birds. Add the onions
and the whole tomatoes. Cook gently for a
further 5 minutes. Pour in the sherry, water
and milk. Season with salt and pepper.
Bring to the boil and simmer gently. Pound
the livers with the capers, parsley and olives
in a mortar, and add to the casserole. Cover
tightly with foil under the lid, and cook in
the oven for approximately 2 hours, or until
the birds are tender.

Serve straight from the casserole,
accompanied by plain boiled potatoes and
Brussels sprouts.

This recipe is suitable for older birds.

# ROAST GROUSE

Serves 4

50 g (2 oz) butter
juice of ½ lemon
salt and black pepper
2 young grouse
2 rashers streaky bacon
4 croûtes (see page 93)
1 tbsp oil

Heat the oven to 220°C (425°F) mark 7. Combine the butter and lemon juice and season well with salt and black pepper. Place the mixture inside the birds, and cover the breast of each with streaky bacon.

Stand the birds on the croûtes and place on a roasting tin in the oven. Roast for 25–30 minutes, basting occasionally with oil. Serve on the croûtes, garnished with watercress and slices of lemon.

To carve, cut into joints.

# CASSEROLED GROUSE

Serves 4

2 grouse
2 rashers streaky bacon
25 g (1 oz) butter
1 tbsp oil
4 shallots, chopped
2 carrots, chopped
2 tbsp brandy
1 bouquet garni
275 ml (½ pint) red wine
275 ml (½ pint) game stock (see
page 91)
salt and black pepper
beurre manié (see page 92)
chopped fresh parsley to garnish
lemon slices to garnish

Heat the oven to 150°C (300°F) mark 2. Tie a rasher of bacon around each bird. Heat the oil and butter in a flameproof casserole and lightly brown the birds. Transfer to a plate. Fry the shallots and carrots until soft. Return the birds to the casserole. Heat the brandy and ignite it; whilst it is flaming, pour over the birds. Add the bouquet garni, wine and stock. Season well. Cover and cook slowly for 1½–2 hours, until the birds are tender.

Thicken the sauce with beurre manié. Adjust the seasoning. Garnish with chopped parsley and lemon slices.

# ROAST WILD DUCK

Serves 2–4

2 wild duck (any variety)
piece of apple, onion or orange
butter
salt and black pepper
a little red wine, port or orange juice
watercress to garnish

Heat the oven to 220°C (425°F) mark 7. Place a piece of apple, onion or orange in the cavity of each bird, with a knob of butter and seasoning. Season the outside of the bird and smear the breasts with softened butter. Place in a roasting tin and cook for 30–50 minutes for mallard, 30–40 minutes for wigeon, 20–30 minutes for teal. Baste frequently with butter and red wine, port or orange juice. Wild duck is usually served underdone, although this is a matter of taste.

Place on a warmed serving dish and garnish with watercress. Serve with a thin gravy made from the pan juices, having removed the excess fat, or with orange sauce (see page 38). Depending on size, either cut in half or into joints.

# POT-ROASTED WILD DUCK

Serves 4

2 wild duck (any variety)
salt and pepper
50 g (2 oz) butter
2 shallots, chopped
1 clove garlic, crushed
1 bouquet garni
1 wine-glass port
juice of 1 orange

Garnish
8 small dessert apples, peeled and
  cored
50 g (2 oz) butter
3–4 tbsp redcurrant jelly
2 tbsp wine vinegar

Heat the oven to 180°C (350°F) mark 4. Season the ducks. Melt the butter in a flameproof casserole and brown the birds. Add the shallots, garlic and bouquet garni. Cover tightly and place in the oven. Cook for 50–60 minutes, basting occasionally.

Meanwhile bake the apples in the oven with the butter until golden brown. Melt the redcurrant jelly in the vinegar and coat the apples.

When the ducks are tender, cut in half and arrange on a serving dish. Keep warm. Skim the fat from the casserole, add the port and orange juice to the juices in the casserole. Bring to the boil and adjust the seasoning. Pour a little sauce over the ducks to glaze, and serve the rest separately.

# TEAL WITH ANCHOVIES

Serves 4

4 teal
butter
salt and pepper
75 g (3 oz) cheese, finely grated
8 anchovy fillets
150 ml (¼ pint) stock
(see page 91)
lemon slices to garnish

Sauce
1 tsp mustard
1 tsp Worcestershire sauce
1 tsp anchovy essence
1 tbsp brown sugar
1 tsp mushroom ketchup
1 tbsp stock (see page 91)
2 tbsp port

Heat the oven to 220°C (425°F) mark 7. Season the teal well, and smear with the butter. Place in a roasting tin in the oven for 20 minutes. Cut each teal in half and place in a casserole. Sprinkle with cheese and place an anchovy fillet on each piece. Moisten with stock, cover and cook at 170°C (325°F) mark 3 for 45 minutes. Meanwhile mix together the rest of the ingredients in a bowl.

When the birds are cooked, transfer them to a serving plate. Pour the sauce ingredients into the casserole and mix with the liquid. Bring to the boil and pour over the birds. Garnish with lemon slices.

# PLAIN ROAST WOODCOCK OR SNIPE

1 woodcock or snipe
butter
salt and pepper
fat bacon (one piece per bird)
pieces of bread (one piece per bird)
lemon juice
watercress to garnish

Press the legs and wings together, draw the head around and run the beak through the point where the legs and wings cross. Brush the bird with melted butter, season well and tie a piece of fat bacon around each bird. Spit or oven roast at 220°C (425°F) mark 7. Toast pieces of bread on one side only, and place one under each bird, untoasted side upwards, to catch the juices as they run out from the bird.

Woodcock require cooking for 25–30 minutes, whereas the snipe, being a very small bird, should, as the saying goes, 'fly through the kitchen' and be cooked for 12–15 minutes.

Serve with clear gravy flavoured with lemon juice, and game chips (see page 93).

# WOODCOCK WITH ORANGE

Serves 4

4 woodcock
melted butter
salt and pepper
4 rashers fat bacon
4 croûtes (see page 93)
150 ml (¼ pint) white wine
3–4 tbsp concentrated game stock
  (see page 91)
rind and juice of 1 orange
1 tsp melted butter
orange segments to garnish

Prepare and cook the birds as in the previous recipe. Arrange on the croûtes, on a serving dish. Keep warm.

Add the wine and game stock to the pan juices and simmer for 5 minutes. Add the rind and juice of the orange and stir in the melted butter and seasoning. Pour the sauce over the woodcock and garnish with orange segments.

# SNIPE WITH MADEIRA

Serves 4

8 snipe, cooked as in recipe opposite
croûtes (see page 93)

Sauce
15 g (½ oz) butter
50 g (2 oz) bacon, finely chopped
3 shallots, finely chopped
2 tsp plain flour
1 tsp tomato purée
50 g (2 oz) mushrooms, chopped
275 ml (½ pint) stock (see page 91)
small bunch of fresh herbs
salt and pepper
75 ml (2 fl oz) Madeira

Cook the snipe as in the recipe opposite. While it is cooking, make the sauce. Melt the butter in a pan, add the bacon and shallot and fry until golden. Stir in the flour, and cook over a low heat until it turns a golden brown colour – stir during this time otherwise the flour will burn. Add the tomato purée, mushrooms and stock. Carefully bring to the boil, stirring; add the seasoning and herbs. Cover and simmer for 15–20 minutes. Strain, add the Madeira and simmer for another 3 minutes.

Serve the snipe on croûtes with a little sauce poured over each, and the remainder of the sauce served separately.

# ROAST QUAIL

1 quail per person for a starter, 2
   per person for a main course

*quail*
*fat bacon, one rasher per bird*
*butter*
*watercress to garnish*

Brush the birds with melted butter, and
wrap a rasher of fat bacon around each.
Place in a shallow casserole with butter and
cook at 220°C (425°F) mark 7 for
20 minutes, basting frequently. Serve with
a thin gravy made from the pan juices, and
garnish with watercress.

If available, vine leaves, wrapped around
the birds, will improve the flavour.

# QUAIL IN WHITE WINE WITH OLIVES

Serves 4

*8 quail*
*salt and pepper*
*25 g (1 oz) butter*
*2–3 rashers streaky bacon, chopped*
*1 small onion, finely chopped*
*1 carrot, finely diced*
*2 tbsp brandy*
*425 ml (15 fl oz) stock (see page 91)*
*275 ml (½ pint) white wine*
*½ tsp dried sage*
*12 green olives, pitted*

Season the quail with salt and pepper. Heat
the butter in a pan and brown the quail.
Transfer them to a place. Add the bacon,
onion and carrot to the pan and fry gently
until the vegetables begin to soften. Replace
the quail in the pan.

   Warm the brandy, ignite it and while it is
still flaming, pour it over the birds. Add the
stock, wine, sage and some seasoning, bring
to the boil and simmer gently for
15 minutes. Add the olives and simmer for
a further 10 minutes.

   Remove the quail to a serving dish,
return the pan to the heat and boil to reduce
the liquid by half. Pour over the quail.

   Serve with plain boiled rice and a
green salad.

# QUAIL WITH MUSHROOMS

Serves 2

4 quail
seasoned plain flour
25 g (1 oz) butter
1 tbsp oil
3 rashers streaky bacon, chopped
1 shallot, finely chopped
2 tbsp brandy
100 g (4 oz) mushrooms, sliced
425 ml (15 fl oz) stock (see page 91)
1 bouquet garni or bunch of fresh
    mixed herbs
salt and black pepper
juice of 1 orange
beurre manié (see page 92)

Cut the quail in half and toss in seasoned flour. Heat the oil and butter in a pan and gently brown the quail; transfer them to a plate. Place the bacon and shallot in the pan and fry for 5 minutes.

Return the quail to the pan. Warm the brandy, ignite it and, while it is flaming, pour it over the quail.

Add the mushrooms, stock, herbs and seasoning. Bring to the boil, cover tightly and simmer for 20–25 minutes, until the birds are tender. Add the orange juice.

If necessary thicken the sauce with a little beurre manié. Serve with duchesse or creamed potatoes and glazed carrots.

# QUAIL WITH HERBS

Serves 4

8 quail
100 g (4 oz) butter
1 tbsp chopped fresh parsley
1 tbsp chopped fresh summer savory
1 tsp chopped fresh mint
½ tsp chopped fresh thyme
salt and black pepper
8 rashers streaky bacon
150 ml (¼ pint) white wine
150 ml (¼ pint) chicken stock (see
    page 91)
1 tbsp plain flour
croûtes (see page 93)

Heat the oven to 180°C (350°F) mark 4. Place a knob of butter in each quail. Place the birds in a roasting tin, and brush with melted butter. Mix together the herbs and seasoning and sprinkle over the quail. Cover each bird with a rasher of bacon. Mix together the wine and stock and pour it around the birds. Cook in the oven for about 45 minutes, basting occasionally. Remove the bacon rashers. Raise the oven temperature to 200°C (400°F) mark 6, and continue to cook the quail until they are browned and tender.

Place the quail on a serving dish and keep warm. Strain any surplus fat from the roasting tin. Stir the flour into the pan juices. Cook on top of the stove, stirring continuously, until it thickens. Boil for 1 minute. Pour the sauce over the quail and serve with croûtes.

# RAISED PIGEON PIE

Serves 6–8

breasts from 2 pigeons
1 tbsp oil
2 medium carrots, diced
1 onion, diced
1 stick celery, sliced
1 bouquet garni
seasoning
275 ml (½ pint) stock (see page 91)
350 g (12 oz) pork sausagemeat
225 g (8 oz) veal or fillet steak cut
    up finely
2 pickled walnuts, chopped
beaten egg
jelly (made from 275 ml/½ pint
    stock, heated with 1 heaped tsp
    powdered gelatine)


Hot water crust pastry
225 g (8 oz) plain flour
75 g (3 oz) lard
¼ tsp salt
scant 150 ml (¼ pint) boiling water

Remove the breasts from the pigeons. Heat the oil in a flameproof casserole and sauté the prepared vegetables until soft. Place the pigeon breasts on top of the vegetables and add stock to come to the top of the vegetables. Add the bouquet garni and seasoning. Braise the breasts until tender. Allow to cool. Heat the oven to 220°C (425°F) mark 7. Grease a raised pie mould, or prepare a collar of doubled greaseproof paper 10 cm (4 inches) deep and 15 cm (6 inches) in diameter. Grease well. Place on a greased baking sheet.

Make the hot water crust pastry by sieving together the flour and salt. Rub in the lard and add most of the boiling water to make a soft dough, mixing well with a knife. Knead gently until smooth. Line the mould or collar with three-quarters of the pastry.

With three-quarters of the sausagemeat, line the inside of the pastry. Mix the veal (or steak) with the walnuts and season well. Place half the mixture in the base of the mould, and lay the pigeon breasts on top. Cover with the remaining veal or steak mixture, and moisten with 3–4 tablespoonfuls stock. Cover with the remaining sausagemeat.

Roll out the last piece of pastry and cover the pie, sealing the edges well. Decorate with pastry leaves as desired. Bake at 220°C (425°F) mark 7 for 15 minutes. Reduce the heat to 170°C (325°F) mark 3 and cook for a further 1¼ hours. Approximately 20 minutes before the end of cooking time, carefully remove the mould or collar and brush the pastry with beaten egg. After removing the pie from the oven, fill with hot, well-seasoned jelly.

# PAPRIKA PIGEON

Serves 2–3

2 pigeons
1 tbsp plain flour
2 tsp paprika
salt
50 g (2 oz) dripping
1 onion, sliced
1 clove garlic, crushed
275 ml (½ pint) stock (see page 91)
150 ml (¼ pint) wine
bunch of fresh herbs (parsley, thyme, bayleaf) or 1 bouquet garni
2–3 tbsp soured cream or yoghurt
chopped fresh parsley to garnsh

Heat the oven to 170°C (325°F) mark 3. Cut the pigeons in half and toss in the flour mixed with the paprika and salt. Heat the dripping in a flameproof casserole, and fry the pigeons until golden brown. Transfer them to a plate.

Add the onion and garlic to the pan and fry for 5 minutes. Gradually stir in the stock and wine, add the herbs and replace the pigeons in the casserole. Bring to the boil, cover and cook in the oven for 1½–2 hours or until the pigeons are tender. Just before serving, stir in the soured cream or yoghurt. Adjust the seasoning. Sprinkle with chopped parsley.

# PIGEON CASSEROLE WITH STEAK

Serves 4

2 pigeons
25 g (1 oz) butter
1 tbsp oil
225 g (8 oz) chuck steak, cubed
2 rashers streaky bacon, diced
275 ml (½ pint) stock (see page 91)
100 g (4 oz) mushrooms, sliced
salt and pepper
1 tbsp redcurrant jelly
1 tbsp lemon juice
1 tbsp plain flour, slaked with 1 tbsp water
chopped fresh parsley to garnish

Cut the pigeons in half. Heat the butter and oil in a pan and fry the pigeons, steak and bacon until lightly browned. Add the stock, mushrooms and seasoning. Cover tightly and simmer slowly for approximately 2 hours or until the pigeons are tender.

Stir in the redcurrant jelly and lemon juice. Thicken the sauce with the slaked flour. Bring to the boil, cook for 2 minutes, and adjust the seasoning. Sprinkle with chopped parsley to serve.

# BRAISED PIGEON WITH ORANGE

Serves 4

4 pigeons
4 small oranges
4 rashers streaky bacon
50 g (2 oz) dripping or butter
4 shallots, chopped
1 tbsp plain flour
150 ml (¼ pint) port or red wine
275 ml (½ pint) stock (see page 91)
salt and pepper
bunch of fresh herbs (parsley, thyme,
   bayleaf, etc.) or 1 bouquet garni
½ tsp crushed coriander
beurre manié (see page 92)
1–2 tbsp Cointreau or Grand
   Marnier (optional)

Heat the oven to 170°C (325°F) mark 3. Remove some thin slices of zest from half the oranges with a potato peeler or zester and place on one side. Place an orange in the cavity of each bird, and wrap a rasher of bacon around each. Secure with string. Heat the dripping in a flameproof casserole, and fry the birds until golden brown. Transfer to a plate. Fry the shallots until golden brown. Stir in the flour and cook for 3 minutes. Gradually stir in the wine and stock and bring to the boil. Add the seasoning. Return the pigeons to the casserole and add the herbs and coriander. Cover tightly and cook in the oven for 1½–2 hours or until the pigeons are tender.

Meanwhile cut the orange zest into strips, place in a small pan with a little water and simmer gently for 15–20 minutes. Strain and reserve the strips.

When the pigeons are cooked, transfer them to a serving dish. Strain the sauce into a saucepan and thicken as necessary with a little beurre manié. Adjust the seasoning and add the orange liqueur. Pour a little over the pigeons and serve the rest separately. Sprinkle the orange strips over the pigeons. Serve with creamed potatoes and broccoli.

# CIDER-BRAISED PIGEON

Serves 4–6

1 tbsp oil
25 g (1 oz) butter
4 pigeons
4 rashers bacon

Heat the oven to 180°C (350°F) mark 4. Heat the oil and butter in a flameproof casserole and fry the pigeons. Transfer to a plate. Cut the bacon into 1-cm (½-inch) strips. Add the bacon, onion and carrots, and fry until the vegetables begin to soften.

225 g (8 oz) small onions
2 carrots, sliced
1 tbsp plain flour
275 ml (½ pint) stock (see page 91)
150 ml (¼ pint) dry cider
salt and pepper
225 g (8 oz) mushrooms, sliced

Garnish
2 eating apples
icing sugar
50 g (2 oz) butter
watercress

Stir the flour into the pan and cook for 2–3 minutes; gradually add the stock and cider, stirring until the mixture boils. Season well. Return the pigeons to the casserole, and cover and cook in the oven for 45 minutes.

Add the sliced mushrooms and continue cooking for a further 45 minutes or until the pigeons are tender. Place the pigeons on a serving dish, drain the vegetables and place around the pigeons. Keep hot. Adjust the seasoning of the sauce, and if necessary thicken with a little more flour. Pour the sauce over the pigeons.

During the latter stage of cooking, prepare the garnish. Core the apples, slice into 5-mm (¼-inch) slices. Dust thickly with icing sugar. Melt the butter in a frying pan, and gently fry the apple slices. Garnish the pigeons with apple slices and watercress.

# GAME ANIMALS

The meat of wild rabbit, hare and venison has less fat on it than that of domesticated animals and can be dry. This chapter shows how to make many delicious dishes which make the most of the succulent juices and distinctive flavour of these game animals.

# ROAST RABBIT

Serves 3–4

1 young rabbit, paunched and
  skinned
6–8 rashers streaky bacon
100 g (4 oz) dripping
25 g (1 oz) plain flour
275 ml (½ pint) stock (see page 91)
bacon rolls (see page 94)

Stuffing
4 heaped tbsp fresh breadcrumbs
50 g (2 oz) shredded suet
salt and pepper
1 tbsp chopped fresh parsley and
  fresh mixed herbs
a little grated lemon rind
a little grated nutmeg
2 tbsp milk

Heat the oven to 200°C (400°F) mark 6.
Make the stuffing: mix the dry ingredients
together and bind with the milk. Place the
stuffing in the rabbit and sew it up. Tie the
streaky bacon rashers over the back. Heat
the dripping in a roasting tin and place the
rabbit in it; covered with greased,
greaseproof paper or foil. Roast for 1 hour,
basting regularly with the fat.

When cooked, remove the paper or foil,
and sprinkle with flour; return to the oven
for about 10 minutes to brown. Transfer to
a serving dish, remove the trussing strings
and keep warm.

Drain most of the fat from the roasting
tin, leaving about 1 tablespoonful. Sprinkle
in the remaining flour, and cook for a few
minutes. Gradually stir in the stock,
ensuring that all the pan juices have been
incorporated. Boil for 4–5 minutes then
strain into a sauce-boat.

Garnish the rabbit with bacon rolls, and
serve, accompanied by redcurrant or quince
jelly, with roast potatoes and green beans.
To carve, cut into joints.

# RABBIT IN BEER

Serves 4–5

1 rabbit, about 900 g (2 lb), jointed
1 tbsp seasoned plain flour
25 g (1 oz) dripping
100 g (4 oz) streaky bacon, chopped
1 medium onion, sliced
275 ml (½ pint) pale ale
275 ml (½ pint) stock (see
  page 91)
1 tsp sugar
1 tbsp vinegar
1 bayleaf
1–2 tsp French mustard
12 soaked prunes

Toss the rabbit joints in the seasoned flour. Heat the fat in a heavy saucepan or flameproof casserole, and fry the joints until golden brown. Remove them from the pan.

Add the bacon and onion to the pan and fry until the onion is soft. Pour off any excess fat. Replace the joints in the pan.

Add the ale, stock, sugar, vinegar, bayleaf and mustard. Bring to the boil, cover tightly and simmer gently until almost cooked (1–1½ hours).

Season to taste, add the prunes, and cook for a further 20 minutes. Serve with jacket potatoes and green beans.

# RABBIT TENERIFE-STYLE

Serves 4

1 medium-sized rabbit, jointed
salt

Marinade
275 ml (½ pint) dry white wine
100 ml (3 fl oz) vinegar
2 sprigs fresh thyme
2 tsp fresh oregano
1 bay leaf

Salmerejo sauce
4 tbsp oil
white wine
2 large cloves garlic
2 tsp paprika
small piece of hot red chilli pepper,
  or ½ tsp cayenne pepper

Place the rabbit joints in a dish and sprinkle with salt. Mix together the ingredients for the marinade and pour over the joints. Allow to stand for a few hours, preferably overnight. Remove the joints and dry thoroughly, reserving the marinade.

Heat the oil in a pan, and gently cook the joints until golden brown all over. Pour the marinade over, adding more wine if necessary to cover the joints. Partially cover the pan and simmer gently.

Meanwhile crush the garlic in a mortar with the paprika, chilli (finely chopped) or cayenne, and a little salt. Add this to the pan and check the seasoning – it should be slightly hot but not over-hot. Continue the cooking for approximately 1 hour or until the meat is tender, adding more wine if necessary. Check the seasoning again before **serving.**

This tasty dish is one found in any local restaurant in Tenerife. It is a well-flavoured, spicy dish which improves if it is cooked the day before it is required, and then reheated. It is sometimes served with fried potatoes, but more often with fresh crusty bread, and of course, red wine.

# RABBIT HOT-POT

Serves 4–6

1 rabbit, jointed
50 g (2 oz) dripping
350 g (12 oz) onions, sliced
225 g (8 oz) carrots, sliced
25 g (1 oz) plain flour
850 ml (1½ pints) stock (see page 91)
450 g (1 lb) potatoes, thickly sliced
bunch of fresh herbs
salt and pepper
melted butter
chopped fresh parsley to garnish
bacon rolls (see page 94)

Heat the oven to 170°C (325°F) mark 3. Place the rabbit joints in cold salted water and leave for 30 minutes to remove the blood. Remove and dry well.

Heat the dripping in a frying pan, and fry the joints until golden brown, then transfer to a casserole. Fry the onions and carrots gently until beginning to soften, and then place on top of the rabbit in the casserole. Add the flour to the remaining fat in the frying pan, and cook for 2–3 minutes. Gradually stir in the stock and bring to the boil.

Place the sliced potatoes in the casserole, season well, pour the sauce from the frying pan over, and add the herbs. Cover tightly and cook in the oven for approximately 2 hours or until the rabbit is tender.

30 minutes before serving, the lid may be removed and the potatoes brushed with melted butter. Return the casserole to the oven without the lid, to brown the potatoes. Check the seasoning. Serve garnished with chopped parsley and bacon rolls.

# CASSEROLED RABBIT

Serves 4–5

1 rabbit, jointed
175 g (6 oz) streaky bacon, cut into
    strips
350 g (12 oz) onions, finely chopped
1 tbsp chopped fresh parsley
salt and pepper
stock (see page 91)
1 tbsp plain flour
forcemeat balls (see page 87
    variation)

Heat the oven to 150°C (300°F) mark 2.
Layer the bacon, rabbit and onions in a
deep casserole, sprinkling the parsley and
seasoning between the layers. Add sufficient
stock to just cover. Cover with a tightly
fitting lid and cook in the oven for
approximately 2 hours or until the meat is
tender.

Mix the flour with a little water in a basin,
add several tablespoonfuls gravy from the
casserole. Pour it all into the casserole and
bring to the boil.

Adjust the seasoning and serve with
forcemeat balls and redcurrant jelly,
accompanied by jacket potatoes and carrots.

# TASTY RABBIT

Serves 4–5

1 rabbit, jointed
salt and pepper
1 small onion, finely chopped
2 tsp dried or fresh mixed herbs
2 bay leaves
4 cloves
575 ml (1 pint) water and vinegar
    mixed
25 g (1 oz) butter
1 tbsp oil
225 g (½ lb) onions, finely chopped
plain flour

Place the rabbit joints in a deep dish and
sprinkle with salt and pepper and add the
onion, and the herbs. Cover with the water
and vinegar mixture, and leave to soak
overnight. Remove from the liquid, and dry
the joints thoroughly. Reserve the liquid.

Heat the butter and oil in a strong
saucepan or a flameproof casserole, lightly
brown the rabbit joints, add the remaining
onions and gently fry. Pour over the
marinade in which the rabbit was soaked.
Cover tightly and simmer gently for
1½ hours. Just before serving, thicken the
gravy with a little flour, and adjust the
seasoning. If the flavour is a little sharp, a
teaspoonful sugar will rectify this.

This is good served with jacket potatoes
and a green vegetable.

# RABBIT & SAUSAGE CRUMBLE

Serves 4–5

1 rabbit, jointed
375 g (12 oz) sausagemeat
225 g (8 oz) onions, chopped
1 tbsp chopped fresh herbs
stock (see page 91)
75–100 g (3–4 oz) fresh
    breadcrumbs
salt and pepper
25 g (1 oz) butter

Heat the oven to 150°C (300°F) mark 2. Place half the sausagemeat in a casserole and lay the rabbit joints on top. Sprinkle with the chopped onion and herbs, and some salt and pepper. Place the remaining sausagemeat on top. Half-fill the dish with stock.

Cover with the breadcrumbs, pressing down well, and put small knobs of butter on top. Cover with foil, and cook for 1½ hours or until the rabbit is tender. 15 minutes before the end of cooking, remove the foil to allow the top to brown.

Serve with creamed potatoes and a green vegetable.

# CURRIED RABBIT

Serves 4

1 rabbit, jointed
25 g (1 oz) butter
1 tsp oil
2 large onions, chopped
1 large apple, chopped
½–1 tbsp curry powder
1½ tbsp plain flour
575 ml (1 pint) stock (see page 91)
1 tbsp sultanas
1 tsp chutney
1 tsp redcurrant or gooseberry jelly
seasoning

Heat the oven to 170°C (325°F) mark 3. Heat the butter and oil in a frying pan and fry the rabbit joints until golden brown, then transfer them to a casserole. Add the chopped onion to the pan and fry until soft, then sprinkle over the rabbit, together with the chopped apple.

Put the curry powder and flour in the frying pan and fry for 1–2 minutes. Add the stock gradually, and bring to the boil. Add the remaining ingredients and pour into the casserole. Cover tightly and cook for 1½–2 hours, or until the meat is tender. Adjust the seasoning and, if too sweet, a little lemon juice will rectify this.

Serve with boiled long grain rice.

# ROAST HARE

Serves 4–6

1 leveret
6 rashers fat bacon
100 g (4 oz) dripping
1 tbsp plain flour
575 ml (1 pint) strong stock (see
    page 91)
1 wine-glass port
1 tbsp redcurrant jelly
salt and pepper
watercress and lemon slices to
    garnish

Stuffing
175 g (6 oz) fresh breadcrumbs
1 medium onion, finely chopped
50 g (2 oz) shredded suet
the liver, parboiled and finely
    chopped
1 tbsp chopped fresh parsley
½ tbsp chopped fresh thyme, or
    marjoram
grated rind and juice of 1 lemon
grated nutmeg
salt and pepper
1 egg

Heat the oven to 200°C (400°F) mark 6.
Prepare the hare (see pages 11–12). Mix the
stuffing ingredients together and add
sufficient beaten egg to bind. Place in the
cavity of the hare. Sew up and truss. Tie the
rashers of bacon around the hare.

Place the hare in a roasting tin with the
dripping. Cover and place in the oven.
Roast for 1½–2 hours, basting regularly.
When the hare is nearly cooked, remove the
bacon rashers and sprinkle with the flour.
Return to the oven, uncovered, and cook
for a further 20 minutes, basting
occasionally, until well browned. Transfer
the hare to a hot serving dish, and remove
the trussing strings.

Strain off any fat from the roasting tin,
add the stock, port and jelly, and simmer
for about 5 minutes. Adjust the seasoning.
If the sauce is too sweet, a little lemon juice
may be added. Strain the sauce into a
sauce-boat.

Garnish the hare with watercress and
lemon slices. Serve with roast potatoes,
fresh green vegetables and redcurrant jelly.
To carve, cut into joints.

*To roast hare of doubtful age*
Prepare and truss the hare so that it will fit
into a steamer. Steam until tender, leaving
unstuffed. Place the hare in a roasting tin
and cook as in the recipe above. Serve with
forcemeat balls (see page 87) which may be
roasted with the hare for the last
15 minutes.

# JUGGED HARE

Serves 8

1 hare, paunched, skinned and cut
   into neat pieces
2 tbsp bacon fat
2 large onions, each stuck with
   1 clove
4–5 peppercorns
1 stick celery, sliced
1 carrot, quartered
1 tsp whole allspice
bouquet garni of fresh herbs
juice of 1 lemon and a strip of rind
salt
½–1 litre (1–2 pints) stock (see
   page 91)
beurre manié (see page 92)
1 large glass port or glass of the
   marinade
blood of the hare
2 tsp redcurrant jelly

Marinade
150 ml (¼ pint) red wine
1 tbsp oil
1 shallot, sliced
2 bay leaves
freshly ground black pepper
6 juniper berries, crushed
salt

Prepare the marinade: place all the ingredients in a pan, bring to the boil, remove from the heat and allow to cool. Place the hare in a deep dish, and pour over the cold marinade. Leave to stand several hours, or preferably overnight.

Remove the hare pieces from the marinade and dry well. Heat the oven to 140°C (275°F) mark 1. Heat the bacon fat in a frying pan and quickly brown the hare pieces. Pack into a deep casserole with the vegetables, spices, bouquet garni, lemon rind, juice and salt. Barely cover with stock. Either cover tightly with foil before closing the lid of the casserole, or seal the edges of the lid with a flour and water paste. Place the casserole in a deep pan of hot water and cook in the oven for 3 hours.

Remove the lid, pour off the gravy into a pan, and remove the vegetables and bouquet garni. Thicken the gravy with sufficient beurre manié to produce a thin creamy consistency, bring to the boil and remove from the heat.

Add several spoonfuls of gravy to the hare's blood then carefully pour it back into the pan; add the port (or strained marinade) and redcurrant jelly. Adjust the seasoning. When the jelly has melted, pour the gravy over the hare and reheat gently.

Serve hot with forcemeat balls (see page 87 main recipe), accompanied by braised red cabbage.

This is a classic dish which was originally cooked slowly in a deep earthenware 'jug', standing in a deep pan of hot water, in a slow oven.

# HARE IN BEER

Serves 5–6

*1 small hare, jointed*
*blood of the hare*
*1 tbsp plain flour*
*1 tsp paprika*
*50 g (2 oz) dripping*
*1 clove garlic, crushed with salt*
*2 medium onions, each stuck with*
   *2 cloves*
*575 ml (1 pint) brown ale*
*1 wine-glass port*
*salt*

Heat the oven to 150°C (300°F) mark 2.
Toss the hare joints in the flour mixed with
paprika. Heat the dripping in a flameproof
casserole and fry the joints until evenly
brown. Add the crushed garlic, onions and
brown ale. Bring to the boil, cover tightly
and place in the oven. Cook slowly for
3–4 hours or until the meat comes off the
bone. Remove the onions. Add several
spoonfuls of the gravy to the blood in a
basin, mix well and pour back into the
casserole. Add the port, and heat gently
without boiling. Adjust the seasoning.

Serve with reducurrant jelly, boiled
potatoes and broccoli.

# SADDLE OF HARE WITH CREAM

Serves 4

*1 good plump hare, paunched and*
   *skinned*
*French mustard*
*25 g (1 oz) butter*
*150 ml (¼ pint) strong stock (see*
   *page 91)*
*150 ml (¼ pint) cream*

*Marinade*
*3 tbsp oil*
*2 small onions, sliced*
*2 small carrots, sliced*
*275 ml (½ pint) red wine vinegar*
*150 ml (¼ pint) red wine*
*large sprig fresh thyme*
*2 bay leaves*
*small sprig fresh rosemary*
*6 peppercorns*
*salt*

To prepare the marinade, heat the oil in a
pan, add the vegetables and cook gently
until soft. Add the remaining marinade
ingredients, bring to the boil and simmer
for 7 minutes. Pour into a large bowl and
leave to cool.

Joint the hare (see page 17), leaving the
back (saddle) whole. Place all the hare in the
marinade and leave for 36 hours, basting
and turning occasionally. Remove the
saddle – the rest of the hare should be put
on one side and dealt with separately.
Spread the saddle with mustard.

Heat the oven to 170°C (325°F) mark 3.
Melt the butter in a flameproof casserole,
and gently brown the saddle. Strain the
marinade and pour over the saddle, then
simmer until the marinade is reduced by
about one third. Pour on the stock – the
saddle should be barely covered. Bring to

the boil, cover tightly and cook in the oven until absolutely tender (about 1¾ hours).

Remove the saddle to a serving dish. Add the cream to the remaining contents of the casserole and boil up well for a few minutes. Adjust the seasoning. Strain the sauce, pour a little over the hare, and serve the rest separately in a sauce-boat. Serve with game straws (see page 93) and green beans.

# HARE & GROUSE PIE

Serves 4–6

1 casserole grouse
225 g (8 oz) stewing beef
2–3 joints of hare (fore-legs)
1 lamb's kidney, halved and sliced
50 g (2 oz) mushrooms, chopped
1 small onion, finely chopped
100 g (4 oz) streaky bacon, diced
stock (see page 91)
salt and pepper
225 g (8 oz) flaky pastry
forcemeat balls (see page 87
   variation)

Heat the oven to 220°C (425°F) mark 7. Make the forcemeat balls (see page 87).

Divide the grouse into 4 portions, cut the beef into strips, and cut the hare joints into smaller pieces. Layer the meats, mushroom, onion and bacon in a 1½-litre (2½-pint) pie-dish. Season well between the layers. Barely cover with stock. Place the forcemeat balls on top.

Roll out the pastry and cover the dish, decorate the edges, and make 4–6 pastry leaves with the trimmings for the top. Brush with beaten egg. Bake in the oven for 15 minutes. Reduce the heat to 170°C (325°F) mark 3, and bake for a further 1½ hours or until the meat feels tender. If the pastry browns too quickly, cover the pie with a piece of greased greaseproof paper. Serve hot or cold.

# ROAST HAUNCH OF VENISON

Serves 6–8

1 haunch of venison
olive oil
100 g (4 oz) butter
350 g (12 oz) fat bacon rashers
plain flour and water paste to cover
    the joint
1 tbsp plain flour

Marinade
275 ml (½ pint) red wine
275 ml (½ pint) water
1 clove garlic, crushed
1 tbsp onion, chopped
1 tbsp carrot, chopped
1 stick celery, chopped
50 g (2 oz) mushrooms, sliced
6 peppercorns
bay leaf

Sauce
1 tbsp plain flour
seasoning
juice of ½ orange

Make the marinade by placing all the ingredients in a saucepan, bring slowly to the boil, boil for 2 minutes and allow to cool. Place the venison haunch in a deep dish and pour the cold marinade over. Marinate for 1–3 days, basting and turning the joint 2–3 times a day. When ready, remove the joint from the marinade and dry well. Reserve the marinade.

Heat the oven to 230°C (450°F) mark 8. Rub the joint with olive oil, and cover with pats of butter. Wrap the bacon around the joint. Cover with the flour and water paste, or wrap in cooking foil. Place the joint in a roasting tin, and put in the oven for 15 minutes. Reduce the temperature to 150°C (300°F) mark 2 and roast the joint, allowing 55 minutes per kg (25 minutes per lb) for red deer, and 35 minutes per kg (15 minutes per lb) for roe or fallow deer.

15 minutes before the end of cooking time, crack the paste open, or unwrap the foil. Remove the bacon rashers, sprinkle the joint with flour, and baste well. Raise the oven temperature to 200°C (400°F) mark 6 and return the haunch to the oven for 15 minutes to brown.

Place the haunch on a serving dish. Pour the cooking juices out of the paste case or foil into a pan and skim off some of the fat.

Mix the flour with salt and pepper and a little of the strained reserved marinade. Add to the pan juices, with more marinade as required, and the orange juice. Stirring, bring to boil, and simmer for 3–4 minutes. Adjust the seasoning and serve in a sauce-boat.

Serve the venison accompanied with redcurrant jelly, roast potatoes and a purée of celeriac. Carve as for a leg of lamb.

# ROAST SADDLE OF VENISON

Serves 6–8

1 saddle of venison, 2–2.5 kg
(4–6 lb)
8–12 rashers streaky bacon
150 ml ( ¼ pint) port (optional)
beurre manié (see page 92)

Marinade
425 ml ( ¾ pint) red wine
150 ml ( ¼ pint) red wine vinegar
275 ml ( ½ pint) water
4 tbsp oil
2 sprigs fresh thyme
6 juniper berries, crushed
2 bay leaves
1 blade of mace
piece of orange rind (zest only),
about 2.5 cm (1 inch) square

Trim the saddle, removing any hard skin. Place the saddle in a deep dish. Mix together the ingredients for the marinade, and pour it over the saddle. Allow to marinate for about 2 days, turning and basting 2–3 times daily.

Heat the oven to 200°C (400°F) mark 6. Remove the saddle from the marinade and dry well. Strain and reserve the marinade.

Place the bacon rashers over the top of the saddle and tie in place. Put the saddle in a roasting tin and cover tightly with foil. Place in the oven. After 30 minutes, reduce the temperature to 180°C (350°F) mark 4 and continue cooking (55 minutes per kg/25 minutes per lb for red deer, and 35 minutes per kg/15 minutes per lb for fallow deer). During the cooking period, baste the saddle every 15 minutes with the marinade.

15 minutes before the end of cooking time, remove the foil, and remove the bacon rashers, reserving them for garnish. Sprinkle the port over the saddle and raise the oven temperature to 200°C (400°F) mark 6 and allow the saddle to brown.

Transfer the saddle to a serving dish. Add more marinade or water to the juices in the roasting tin, to make up to about 575 ml (1 pint). Stir over the heat to blend and thicken with beurre manié. Strain the sauce and serve separately.

To carve, slice the meat across the ribs, parallel to the backbone, carving from the narrow end of the joint to the wide end (i.e. tail to head).

Serve the saddle with redcurrant jelly, game chips (see page 93) and a purée of celery or chestnuts.

# VENISON STEAKS WITH RED WINE SAUCE

Serves 4

4 slices (1–2 cm/½–¾ inches thick)
  from the loin or haunch
salt and freshly ground pepper
25 g (1 oz) butter
1 tbsp oil
4 juniper berries, crushed
1 good sprig fresh rosemary
150 ml (¼ pint) soured cream or
  yoghurt
salt and pepper
lemon slices to garnish

Marinade
2 shallots, finely chopped
strip of lemon rind
pinch of celery salt
200 ml (7 fl oz) red wine

Lay the venison slices in a dish and season well with salt and freshly ground pepper. Add the ingredients for the marinade, and pour the wine over. Cover and leave to marinate for up to 2 days. Remove the meat from the marinade and dry thoroughly. Reserve the marinade.

Heat the oil and butter in a large frying pan and gently brown the steaks on each side. Add the juniper berries and rosemary, and cover the pan. Lower the heat and cook gently until the meat is tender (for about 30–40 minutes).

Remove the steaks from the pan, place on a serving dish and keep warm. Strain the marinade into the pan, and dissolve the pan juices. Boil up to reduce the liquid a little. Add the soured cream (or yoghurt) and simmer for 2–3 minutes. Check the seasoning. Pour the sauce over the meat and garnish with lemon slices.

Serve with potatoes (sautéed in butter) and a tossed green salad.

# VENISON STEAKS WITH CHERRIES

Serves 5–6

700 g (1½ lb) loin of venison
  (without bone) or slices from the
  top of the haunch
3 tbsp oil
120 ml (4 fl oz) red wine or port
freshly ground black pepper
225 g (8 oz) canned cherries, stoned

Slice the venison into 2-cm (¾-inch) steaks, and place them in a shallow dish. Sprinkle over 1 tablespoonful oil and the port or wine, with a liberal grinding of pepper. Cover and leave for a minimum of 1 hour.

To make the sauce, heat the oil in a saucepan, add the vegetables and venison trimmings and cook gently until the vegetables start to soften and brown lightly. Add the flour and continue to cook gently until the flour becomes a golden brown colour. Gradually stir in two-thirds of the

Sauce
75 g (3 oz) onion, diced
75 g (3 oz) carrot, diced
1 small stick celery, diced
trimmings from the venison
2 tbsp oil
1 tbsp plain flour
575 ml (1 pint) game stock (see
    page 91)
25 g (1 oz) mushrooms, chopped
½ tsp tomato paste
small bunch of fresh herbs
120 ml (4 fl oz) red wine
2 tbsp red wine vinegar
1 tbsp redcurrant jelly

stock, and add the mushrooms, tomato paste, herbs and wine, bring to the boil, partially cover and simmer for 25 minutes. Remove any scum as it rises. Add half the remaining stock and bring to the boil, skimming again. Add the rest of the stock, reboil, and skim. Strain the sauce into a clean pan, add the vinegar and the redcurrant jelly, bring to the boil, and simmer for 5–6 minutes until the jelly is dissolved. Add the cherries.

Meanwhile, remove the venison from the marinade, and dry thoroughly. Heat 2 tablespoonfuls oil in a frying pan, and fry the venison in it for about 4 minutes on each side.

Reboil the sauce. Arrange the venison steaks on a flat serving dish, with cherries at each end, pour a little sauce over the steaks and serve the rest separately.

Serve with game chips (see page 93) and artichoke hearts.

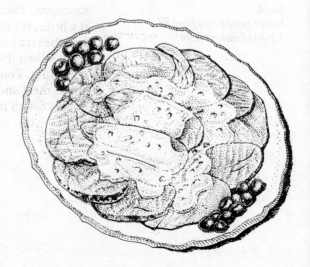

# BRAISED VENISON

Serves 5–6

1.5–2 kg (3–4 lb) haunch or loin of
   venison

Marinade
4 tbsp oil
100 g (4 oz) carrots, sliced
100 g (4 oz) onions, sliced
50 g (2 oz) celery, sliced
1 clove garlic, sliced
575 ml (1 pint) red wine or wine
   and water
6 juniper berries, crushed
sprig of fresh rosemary, sprig of fresh
   thyme and 3–4 fresh parsley
   stalks, tied together
1 bay leaf

Mirepoix
1 tbsp oil
225 g (8 oz) carrots, diced
225 g (8 oz) onions, diced
100 g (4 oz) celery, sliced
100 g (4 oz) turnip, diced

Stock
beurre manié (see page 92)
1 tsp redcurrant jelly

To make the marinade, heat the oil in a pan,
add the vegetables and cook gently to
soften. Add the remaining ingredients,
bring to the boil and simmer for
30 minutes. Leave until cold.

Place the venison in a deep dish, pour the
marinade over, leave up to 3 days, basting
and turning the venison 2–3 times daily.

Heat the oven to 190°C (375°F) mark 5.
Remove the venison from the marinade,
and dry well. Strain and reserve the
marinade.

Heat the oil for the mirepoix in a pan, add
the vegetables, and gently sauté them until
softened. Place the vegetables in a deep
casserole and moisten them with some of
the marinade. Place the venison joint on top
and add sufficient stock to come a quarter of
the way up the joint. Cover tightly and place
in the oven. Cook for 1½–2 hours or until
the meat is tender. Remove the meat, carve
into slices, and place on a serving dish, and
keep warm.

Strain the gravy from the casserole into a
saucepan. Place it over the heat and reduce
it a little, skimming off any fat. Thicken
with beurre manié and add the redcurrant
jelly. When the jelly is dissolved, check the
seasoning. Pour some of the gravy over the
sliced meat and serve the rest separately.

Serve with potato and celeriac purée and
green beans.

# RAISED GAME PIE

Serves 6–8

*350 g (12 oz) shoulder or neck*
  *venison*
*2 tbsp sherry*
*450 g (1 lb) hot water crust pastry*
  *(see page 64)*
*4 rashers streaky bacon*
*beaten egg to glaze*

Filling
*225 g (8 oz) pig's liver, minced*
*1 medium onion, finely chopped*
*225 g (8 oz) pork sausagemeat*
*1 hard-boiled egg*
*1 tsp chopped fresh parsley*
*½ tsp chopped fresh thyme*
*2–3 juniper berries, crushed*
*seasoning*

Prepare a collar of doubled greaseproof paper, 10 cm (4 inches) deep and 18 cm (7 inches) in diameter. Grease well. Place on a greased baking sheet. Cut the venison into fine strips and sprinkle with the sherry. Cover and leave to marinate for at least 1 hour.

Heat the oven to 190°C (375°F) mark 5. Make the hot water crust pastry (see page 64). Use three-quarters of the pastry to line the base and sides of the collar, ensuring there are no thin places. Line with the streaky bacon. Mix the ingredients for the filling together. Place one-third of the filling in the base of the mould and cover with half the venison. Continue filling the mould with alternate layers, finishing with a layer of the filling. Cover the pie with the remaining pastry, ensuring that the edges are well sealed. Use any trimmings to make pastry leaves for decoration. Make a 1-cm (½-inch) hole in the centre of the top. Bake in the oven for approximately 1½–2 hours. If the pastry appears to be browning quickly reduce the temperature after ¾–1 hour to 170°C (325°F) mark 3. 20 minutes before the end of cooking, remove the paper collar and brush the pastry well with beaten egg.

# STUFFINGS, SAUCES AND GARNISHES

This chapter shows how to make a variety of
tasty sauces and stuffings for both poultry and
game as well as traditional accompaniments
such as game chips and bacon rolls.

# SAGE AND ONION STUFFING

75 g (3 oz) onion, chopped
175 g (6 oz) fresh breadcrumbs
2 tsp fresh chopped sage
3 tbsp melted butter (or margarine)
　　or 50 g (2 oz) grated suet
salt and pepper
beaten egg

Place the onion in a pan with a little water and simmer gently until soft. Drain well and mix with the dry ingredients. Add sufficient beaten egg to bind.

Both this stuffing and the parsley and thyme one (page 88) may be shaped into balls, rolled in seasoned flour and baked in the roasting tin around the bird, or in a separate tin for 40–45 minutes, basting and turning occasionally.

# SAUSAGE AND CHESTNUT STUFFING

25 g (1 oz) butter
1 tbsp oil
1 turkey liver
100 g (4 oz) streaky bacon, chopped
100 g (4 oz) onion, chopped
225 g (8 oz) chestnuts, peeled and
　　chopped
450 g (1 lb) pork sausagemeat
1 tbsp fresh chopped parsley
salt and pepper

This stuffing is suitable for turkey. Heat the oil and butter in a frying pan and fry the turkey liver until firm and the bacon until crisp. Remove from the pan. Chop the liver into small pieces. Fry the onion until soft.

Place all the ingredients in a large bowl and mix well to thoroughly combine. Allow to get cold before using to stuff the neck end of a turkey.

Any remaining stuffing may be formed into balls and cooked as in the recipe for sage and onion stuffing (above).

# POTATO STUFFING

225 g (8 oz) onions, finely chopped
550 g (1¼ lb) potatoes
75 g (3 oz) butter or double cream
1 tbsp fresh chopped sage
salt and pepper

This stuffing is good for goose. Place the onion in a pan with sufficient water to cover and simmer gently until soft. Drain well. Boil the potatoes, and drain well. Mash the potatoes and blend in the butter or cream. Stir in the sage and onions, mix well and season to taste.

# ANCHOVY AND HERB STUFFING

175 g (6 oz) fresh breadcrumbs
1 rasher streaky bacon, chopped
1 medium onion (or 4 shallots),
   finely chopped
2 tsp chopped chives
1 tsp fresh thyme
2 tsp fresh chopped parsley
4–6 anchovy fillets, chopped
grated rind and juice of ½ lemon
6 tbsp melted butter or 50 g (2 oz)
   shredded suet
beaten egg

This stuffing is good for roast hare. Mix all the dry ingredients together, add the lemon juice and melted butter (if used) and bind with beaten egg.

# PRUNE AND APPLE STUFFING

15–20 prunes (depending on size)
575 ml (1 pint) red wine, or water,
   or wine and water mixed
700 g (1½ lb) cooking apples

This stuffing is good for goose. Soak the prunes in the wine or water overnight. Remove the stones. Peel, core and quarter the apples. Use to stuff the cavity of a goose after it has been seasoned.

# PORK AND HERB STUFFING

1 medium onion (or 4 shallots),
   finely chopped
25 g (1 oz) butter
450 g (1 lb) shoulder pork, minced
100 g (4 oz) fresh breadcrumbs
1 tbsp fresh chopped parsley
1 tsp fresh thyme and 1 tsp fresh
   marjoram, or 1 tsp mixed dried
   herbs
½ tsp ground nutmeg
beaten egg
salt and pepper

This stuffing is suitable for turkey. Melt the butter in a pan and gently fry the onion until soft. Mix all the ingredients together, season well and bind with the beaten egg.

# OATMEAL STUFFING

50 g (2 oz) butter
1 small onion, chopped finely
100 g (4 oz) medium oatmeal
1 tbsp fresh chopped parsley
salt and pepper
milk to mix

This stuffing is suitable for chicken. Heat the butter in a pan and gently fry the onion until soft. Add the oatmeal, parsley and seasoning. Mix well. Add milk to moisten further if necessary, but do not make it too wet. Allow to cool before using.

# CELERY STUFFING

4 sticks celery, finely chopped
1 small onion, chopped
25 g (1 oz) butter
1 tbsp oil
175 g (6 oz) fresh breadcrumbs
salt and pepper

Heat the butter and oil in a pan and gently cook the celery and onion for 5 minutes. Add the breadcrumbs and seasoning, mix well, adding a little melted butter, if necessary, to bind.

# FORCEMEAT BALLS

1 small onion, finely chopped
1 rasher bacon, chopped
4 tbsp fresh breadcrumbs
1 tbsp suet
1 tbsp fresh chopped parsley
1 tbsp fresh lemon thyme or
    marjoram
beaten egg
breadcrumbs and butter for frying

Cook the onion with the bacon until soft. Add the rest of the ingredients, mix well and bind together with beaten egg. Shape into balls, coat in egg and breadcrumbs and fry in butter until golden brown.

*Variation*
Omit the onion and bacon, and do not coat in egg and breadcrumbs or fry in butter.

# PARSLEY AND THYME STUFFING

*100 g (4 oz) fresh breadcrumbs*
*1 tbsp chopped fresh parsley or 2 tsp*
  *dried parsley*
*2 tsp fresh thyme or 1 tsp dried*
  *thyme*
*½ tsp grated lemon rind*
*salt and pepper*
*2 tbsp melted butter (or margarine)*
  *or 40 g (1½ oz) grated suet*
*beaten egg*

Mix the ingredients together in a bowl, and add sufficient beaten egg to bind – take care not to add too much otherwise the stuffing will be hard.

# APPLE STUFFING

*700 g (1½ lb) cooking apples,*
  *peeled, cored and diced*
*50 g (2 oz) butter*
*salt and pepper*
*1 tsp grated lemon rind*
*2 tbsp sugar*
*225 g (8 oz) fresh breadcrumbs*

Prepare the apples and cook gently in the butter until soft. Add the remaining ingredients, and moisten with a little water if necessary.

# APPLE SAUCE

*450 g (1 lb) cooking apples*
*25 g (1 oz) butter*
*2–3 tbsp water*
*strip of lemon rind*
*sugar to taste*

Peel, core and thickly slice the apples. Place in a pan with the butter, water and lemon rind. Cover and cook gently until soft (a good cooking apple should fluff up during cooking and it should not be necessary to sieve it). Remove the lemon rind, and beat well with a wooden spoon until smooth (or pass through a coarse sieve). Add sugar to taste.

# BÉCHAMEL SAUCE

*275 ml ( ½ pint) milk*
*1 small onion, stuck with 4 cloves*
*1 piece carrot*
*sprig of fresh parsley*
*blade of mace*
*6 peppercorns*
*25 g (1 oz) butter*
*25 g (1 oz) plain flour*
*salt*

Place the milk in a saucepan with the onion, carrot, parsley, mace and peppercorns and bring slowly to the boil. Remove from the heat, cover and allow to infuse for 20–30 minutes, then strain. In a clean pan, melt the butter, add the flour and cook for 2–3 minutes. Gradually add the milk, stirring constantly, bring to the boil, and simmer for 2 minutes. Check the seasoning. Use as required.

# CRANBERRY SAUCE

*450 g (1 lb) cranberries*
*100 g (4 oz) sugar*
*2 tbsp port (optional)*

Place the cranberries in a pan, add sufficient water to cover, bring to the boil and simmer gently, bruising the cranberries with a wooden spoon, until reduced to a pulp. Stir in the sugar and port, and cook until the sugar is dissolved.

# BREAD SAUCE

*275 ml ( ½ pint) milk*
*1 small onion, stuck with*
    *3–4 cloves*
*blade of mace*
*1 bay leaf*
*75–100 g (3–4 oz) fresh*
    *breadcrumbs*
*salt and pepper*
*pinch of ground nutmeg*
*25 g (1 oz) butter*

Place the milk in a saucepan with the onion, mace and bay leaf and bring slowly to the boil. Remove from the heat, cover and leave to infuse for 15–20 minutes. Remove the onion, blade of mace and bay leaf. Stir in the breadcrumbs with the seasoning and butter, and beat well.

# ESPAGNOLE SAUCE

1 rasher bacon, chopped
25 g (1 oz) butter
1 tbsp oil
100 g (4 oz) onion, chopped
100 g (4 oz) carrot, chopped
25 g (1 oz) plain flour
575 ml (1 pint) stock (see page 91)
50 g (2 oz) mushrooms, chopped
1 tbsp tomato purée
bunch of fresh mixed herbs or
    bouquet garni
salt and pepper
1 glass sherry

Heat the butter and oil in a pan and fry the bacon, add the onion and carrots and fry gently to soften. Sprinkle in the flour and cook gently to a golden brown colour. Gradually add the stock and bring to the boil, stirring constantly. Add the mushrooms, tomato purée and herbs. Cover and simmer for approximately 30 minutes. Strain into a clean pan, add the sherry and season to taste.

# POIVRADE SAUCE

Make as for espagnole sauce (see above) but use marinade and red wine vinegar for part or all of the stock.

The zest and juice of 1 orange may be added together with 1 tablespoonful redcurrant jelly.

# DEMI-GLACE SAUCE

Make as for an espagnole sauce (see above), but add half the stock to start with, bring to the boil and simmer for 30 minutes, skimming as necessary. Add half the remaining stock, boil for 5 minutes, skim, add the remaining stock and repeat the process. Strain into a clean pan, add the sherry, and cook to a consistency which will coat the back of a spoon.

# GIBLET GRAVY

giblets (heart, liver, gizzard and
    neck)
1 small onion
1 small carrot
small piece of celery
bunch of fresh herbs or bouquet garni
6 peppercorns
salt and pepper
575–850 ml (1–1½ pints) water
cooking juices from the roasting tin
1 tbsp plain flour

Place the giblets in a pan with the onion, carrot, celery, herbs, peppercorns and salt and 575 ml (1 pint) of the water in a pan. Bring to the boil, cover and simmer for at least 1 hour, or for the duration of the bird's cooking time.

Strain the stock and make up to 575 ml (1 pint) with water. Pour a little into the roasting tin in which the bird was cooked (excess fat having been removed) and stir around well to ensure that all the pan juices have been incorporated. Blend the flour with a little cold water in a basin, add some of the stock and pour into a saucepan. Add the remaining stock. Stir until it boils, adjust the seasoning and simmer for 2–3 minutes.

This gravy is suitable for any bird.

# STOCK

carcase of chicken (or other poultry
    to suit recipe) plus giblets if
    available, or carcase of game
1 medium onion, sliced
2 medium carrots, sliced
1 matchbox-sized piece of swede,
    diced
1 stick of celery, sliced
1 bouquet garni, or bunch of fresh
    herbs
seasoning

Place the ingredients in a saucepan with sufficient water to cover. Bring to the boil and remove any scum as it rises. Simmer for 1½–2 hours. Strain into a bowl and use as required. Should a strong stock be required for a recipe, the stock should be placed in a saucepan and boiled to reduce the volume and concentrate the contents.

Stock may be frozen or stored in a refrigerator. If not required the day of making, cool quickly and freeze or store. Reboil the next day if not required.

# MAYONNAISE

*1 egg yolk*
*½ tsp salt*
*¼ tsp pepper*
*½ tsp dry mustard*
*2 tbsp white wine vinegar or*
  *distilled malt vinegar*
*150 ml (¼ pint) salad oil*

Place the egg yolk with the seasonings in a basin, add half the vinegar and mix well with a wooden spoon. Dribble in the oil, a little at a time, beating well. When all the oil has been incorporated, add more vinegar as necessary. Season to taste.

# VINAIGRETTE DRESSING

*2 tbsp white wine vinegar, or*
  *distilled malt vinegar*
*½ tsp salt*
*¼ tsp dry mustard*
*¼ tsp pepper*
*4 tbsp salad oil*
*1 small whole clove garlic,*
  *(optional)*

Place all the ingredients in a screw-top jar and shake vigorously to form an emulsion.

*Variations*
2 shallots, very finely chopped or
2 tablespoonfuls finely chopped fresh parsley or 1–2 teaspoonfuls finely chopped chives may be added to the basic dressing.

# BEURRE MANIÉ (KNEADED BUTTER)

*butter*
*plain flour*

This is a liaison for thickening sauces.
   Use twice as much butter as flour, and work them together to form a paste. Add small pieces to the contents of a pan or casserole, off the heat. The butter melts and draws the flour into the liquid.

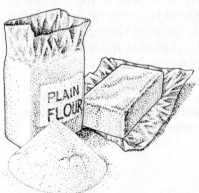

# CROÛTES AND CROÛTONS

*slices of bread*
*butter for frying (optional)*

Croûtes are thick slices of bread, cut in squares or circles, either fried in butter or toasted. Small game may be served with and/or cooked on croûtes.

Croûtons are small dice or fancy shapes of bread, usually fried, but may be toasted. The fancy shapes are used to garnish savoury dishes. The small dice are used to garnish soup.

# GAME CHIPS

*potatoes*
*deep fat/oil for frying*
*salt*

Peel the potatoes, and shape into cylinders. Slice very finely into wafers (the use of a mandolin slicer would be advantageous). Soak in cold water to remove the surface starch. Heat the oil to 190°C (375°F).

Drain the potato wafers, and dry thoroughly. Lower them gently into the hot oil, and keep them moving to prevent them sticking. After 1–2 minutes, the wafers will rise to the surface of the oil, indicating that they are nearly cooked. Watch carefully as they change colour. They should be golden brown and crisp. Drain the wafers and sprinkle with salt.

# GAME STRAWS

*potatoes*
*deep fat/oil for frying*

Peel the potatoes, and cut into 3-mm (⅛-inch) slices. Cut each slice into 3-mm (⅛-inch) sticks. Soak in cold water to remove the surface starch. Heat the oil to 190°C (375°F).

Drain the straws and dry thoroughly. Lower the straws into the hot oil and keep shaking the basket gently to keep the straws separate. Fry for 3–4 minutes, then remove from the oil. Reheat the fat, and again lower the straws into the oil, and cook for approximately 1 minute until the straws are golden brown and crisp. Drain, and serve immediately.

# BACON ROLLS

Allow 1–2 rolls per person

*rashers of streaky bacon*

Take rashers of streaky bacon, place on a board, hold one end of a rasher with the left hand, and with a firm palette knife, working from left to right, stroke the bacon to stretch it. Cut into 7.5-cm (3-inch) lengths, roll up each length and secure with a skewer. Grill or cook in the oven until crisp.

# MEAT

For centuries meat has been the centre of culinary art in many different cultures, and is closely linked with many customs and traditions. 'Roast beef of old England' is famed abroad, and research shows that over 90 per cent of the population still feel that a 'proper meal' should contain meat, and for a great number that meal will be 'meat and two veg'. In Britain the average family spends 30 per cent of its total food bill on meat. With such a financial investment, it obviously makes sense to use meat to its best advantage. Knowing more about meat and its potential may be of assistance in economising while still providing interesting, nutritionally good meals for the family, or in creating a culinary masterpiece for a special occasion. This book should help to achieve both.

Today there is probably a greater awareness of nutritional values and product quality than ever before. More and more people are concerned with the importance of maintaining a healthy diet and are eager for information and advice. Unfortunately there is a great deal of conflicting material published and the consumer is often very confused about the issues. The recent nutritional guidelines, which have emerged in several reports from various medical and scientific committees, are that, as a nation, we would be much healthier, if we modified our diet. The recommendations are that we should eat less fat overall, and reduce the percentage of saturated fat (from animal sources), using unsaturated fats and oils (vegetable sources) instead; reduce our sugar and salt intake and increase the dietary fibre in our diet. A further recommendation is that we should increase the percentage of vegetable protein we eat; this would automatically increase the fibre intake as the main sources of vegetable protein (nuts, pulse vegetables, beans and wholegrain cereals) are all high in fibre and low in vegetable oil content. How do these recommendations fit in with meat eating?

Meat does not contain sugar or salt, so providing we do not add a great deal during cooking this is not a problem. Salt is not required in cooking, except for flavour (other than in bread making, where it is necessary for a good texture). Increasingly people are finding that they can cut down slowly on the amount of salt in their food, eventually leaving it out altogether. It is amazing what a delicious flavour some foods have when not masked by salt.

The recipes in this book do not require salt, unless stated, although all can be seasoned to taste, which may include salt, pepper or your favourite flavourings. Other flavouring is often required to compensate for the lack of salt; herbs, spices, tomato ketchup and many others can be used for this purpose.

When cutting down on fat, especially animal fat, meat consumption must be considered although it accounts for only a quarter of the saturated fat in our diets. Over the last few years the meat industry has appreciated the consumer's requirement for leaner meat, and the breeding of quickly maturing animals, slaughtering at a younger age, better butchery techniques with presale trimming, have all contributed to much leaner meat being available. It is up to the consumer to look around and choose the meat required. With greater demand the meat industry will continue to respond and produce a product that will sell.

The farmers, producers and butchers are playing their part, but there is plenty the consumer can do. If the meat is not already trimmed, this should be done before cooking. Add little or no fat during cooking; this may mean adapting your usual methods to prevent drying out, but foil or covered containers can help. Prefrying is not necessary before making stews etc, and can be left out, or a minimum of vegetable oil used. The recipes in this book tend to do the latter; readers can opt for leaving that stage out if they wish. Mince and bacon can be cooked in their own fat provided they are heated slowly at the beginning. Leaving out the browning stage may require added flavouring to compensate. Wherever possible, grill rather than fry and drain food well if fried or roasted.

## What is meat?

Meat is the flesh or muscle of animals, with its associated fat, and in its wider meaning includes any part of an animal normally consumed. In Britain this usually means the produce from cattle, giving veal and beef, from sheep, giving lamb and mutton, and from pigs, giving pork and bacon, along with offal such as liver, kidney etc from these animals.

## Methods of cooking meat

Meat is cooked to add distinctive flavour, to make it more tender and to make it look more appetising. The choice of cooking method depends largely on the amount of fine gristle contained in the muscles of the cut of meat. In order to get tender meat from muscles with a high proportion of gristle, it is necessary to use long, moist cooking such as stewing, braising or pot roasting. However, cuts with little gristle do not need prolonged, moist cooking and are cooked by the dry methods of roasting, frying and grilling.

*Oven roasting.* This is in fact baking. The food is cooked in an enclosed space, the oven, and is heated mainly by the convection of hot air. If the joint is very lean, extra fat can be added before roasting, alternatively a roasting bag or foil will prevent drying. An average oven temperature setting is 180°C (350°F) mark 4, which is hot enough to give good browning, but not too much shrinkage. Some people roast at a higher temperature for a shorter time. If potatoes and Yorkshire pudding are to be cooked at the same time, raise the temperature, but cook the meat low in the oven.

Weigh the joint, including stuffing, to calculate the cooking time. The size, shape and percentage of fat all affect cooking time and if using foil or film, will require a little longer.

> Beef, rare allow 20 minutes per ½ kg plus 20 minutes over (15 minutes per 1 lb plus 15 minutes over)
>
> Beef, medium allow 25 minutes per ½ kg plus 25 minutes over (20 minutes per 1 lb plus 20 minutes over)
>
> Pork, allow 35 minutes per ½ kg plus 30 minutes over (25 minutes per 1 lb plus 30 minutes over)
>
> Lamb, allow 30 minutes per ½ kg plus 30 minutes over (25 minutes per 1 lb plus 25 minutes over).

The only accurate way to roast meat is to use a meat thermometer, ensuring that the tip is in the centre of the joint and not touching a bone. When the thermometer registers the following temperatures, the meat is cooked.

> 60°C (140°F) for rare meat
> 65°C (150°F) for underdone
> 70°C (160°F) for medium
> 80°C (180°F) for well done.

Pork should be medium or well done.

Meat, particularly if lean, can be basted during cooking. This is unnecessary with foil or roasting film, which gives a result more like pot-roasting, but is very succulent and juicy.

*Spit roasting.* In olden times the meat was roasted by being impaled on a rotating spit in front of a glowing fire. This was true roasting, cooking by radiant heat. Nowadays many grills have a rotisserie attachment where the meat is placed on a mechanically operated spit and cooked over or under a direct source of heat. Allow 20 minutes per ½ kg plus 20 minutes over (15 minutes per 1 lb plus 15 minutes over). Pork may require a little longer.

*Grilling.* This is a quick method of cooking by radiant heat from a preheated gas, electric or charcoal fire or grill. As the heat is fierce, the meat needs to be brushed with oil or butter to prevent drying. Grilling times vary according to the thickness of the meat and the desired degree of cooking. Grilling is only suitable for small tender cuts. As a general guide, for a 2.5 cm (1 in) steak or chop, allow for rare 5 minutes per side, for medium 7 minutes per side and for well done 12 minutes per side.

*Frying.* As with grilling, frying is only suitable for small tender cuts. Shallow or dry frying, rather than deep-fat frying is used for meat. The fat should be preheated, to avoid greasy results. Turn the meat from time to time and drain well on absorbent paper before serving. Cooking time varies according to the thickness of the meat. Allow 7–10 minutes for 2.5 cm (1 in) steaks, and 4–5 minutes for 1 cm (½ in) steaks.

*Stewing.* This is the cooking of pieces of meat in liquid, such as water, stock, wine or cider, with added flavourings and/or vegetables, herbs or spices, with or without a thickening agent.

The meat is cooked in 275–575 ml (½–1 pint) of liquid and should only simmer. Stewing can be done in a covered pan, or in a casserole dish in a slow oven, 170°C (325°F) mark 3, when it is usually called casseroling. Joints and large pieces of meat, when covered with liquid and simmered are cooked by boiling. This is in fact stewing.

Stews should be stirred from time to time and not allowed to boil dry. Ensure the lid fits well and top up with stock or water if necessary. Time the cooking from when the stew or cooking liquor comes to the boil, and allow a minimum of 1½ hours. For larger joints, allow 30 minutes per ½ kg (25 minutes per 1 lb) plus an extra 30 minutes. Cuts with a lot of gristle may require longer.

If the meat is covered with water and brought to the boil, it produces a white stew. If the meat and vegetables are fried first, a brown stew is the result.

*Braising.* After initial browning in hot fat, the meat is

placed on a bed of fried vegetables (called a mirepoix) with just enough water, stock or wine to cover the vegetables. Braising can be done on top of the cooker or in the oven, but the pan must have a tightly fitting lid to prevent loss of moisture. Meat should be braised in a slow oven, 180°C (350°F) mark 4, or over a low heat on top of the cooker, for 50 minutes per ½ kg (45 minutes per 1 lb). With a minimum of 2 hours for joints, 1½–2 hours for steaks and ¾–1 hour for chops.

After cooking, the meat is removed and the cooking liquor reduced by boiling, and used to glaze the meat. The vegetables can be served with the meat, but as they are very well cooked it is usually more satisfactory to liquidise them, and use them as a basis for a sauce or gravy. If the braise is chilled overnight, any fat can be skimmed off before reheating.

*Pot roasting.* This is really a combination of frying and steaming. The meat is browned all over, then covered and cooked slowly with a minimum amount of liquid either in the oven or on top of the cooker.

The joint should be turned every 30 minutes, but do not remove the lid at other times, or the steam will be released. Allow 50 minutes per ½ kg (45 minutes per 1 lb) in an oven at 180°C (350°F) mark 4.

Using a pressure cooker for the moist cooking methods will reduce the cooking time to a third, in most cases. Consult the manufacturer's instructions for details. The amount of liquid required is usually a third less.

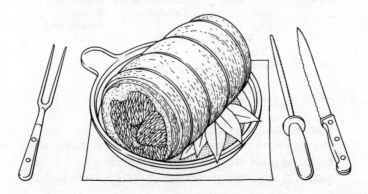

## Cuts suitable for different cooking methods

| Cooking method | Beef | Pork | Lamb |
|---|---|---|---|
| Frying & Grilling | Rump ⎫<br>Fillet ⎬ Steaks<br>Sirloin ⎭ | Fillet<br>(tenderloin)<br>Loin chops<br>Spare rib chops<br>Belly – sliced | Best end of<br>neck cutlets<br>Loin ⎫<br>Chump ⎬ Chops |
| Roasting | Topside<br>Sirloin<br>Fore rib<br>Silverside<br>Thick flank | Neck end<br>(spare rib &<br>blade bone)<br>Loin<br>Leg<br>Hand & spring<br>Belly | Loin<br>Best end of<br>neck<br>Leg<br>Shoulder<br>Breast |
| Braising | Chuck & blade<br>Brisket<br>Thin flank<br>Thick flank<br>Topside<br>Silverside<br>Thick rib | Spare rib chops<br>Belly | Middle neck<br>Breast<br>Shoulder<br>Scrag |
| Pot Roasting | Silverside<br>Thick flank<br>Topside<br>Thick rib<br>Thin rib<br>Brisket | | |
| Boiling | Brisket<br>(salted)<br>Silverside<br>(salted) | Belly (can be<br>salted)<br>Hand & spring<br>(can be salted) | |
| Stewing | Thin flank<br>Shin<br>Leg<br>Neck & clod<br>Chuck & blade<br>Skirt | Hand & spring<br>Shoulder | Scrag<br>Breast<br>Middle neck |

NB: All cuts of pork and most lamb cuts can be roasted.

## Carving and serving
Carving is no problem given a few simple rules. The essential tools are a two pronged fork with a finger guard, a large sharp carving or cook's knife and an

effective means of sharpening the knife at regular intervals. Boned and rolled joints are simply cut through. The butcher will usually bone a joint if asked, however with a good sharp knife and practice, it is easy to do yourself. Start from where the bone can be seen, work along it, cutting the meat away and follow the bone through. Any slips of the knife can be sewn up with cotton before cooking, provided it is removed before serving. Carving bone-in joints varies according to the position and shape of the bone. As a general rule, meat is carved down on to the bone, and the slice then cut off the bone.

Where a joint contains a backbone, chining by the butcher will aid carving. Ensure that the meat is stable, on a wooden board or spiked meat dish, which should be on a non-slip surface.

Wherever possible cut across the grain to shorten the muscle fibre length. When carving a leg or shoulder, it is often easier to hold the shank bone with one hand, using a tissue or paper towel. When doing this, the cutting edge of the knife must be angled away from the hand. With legs and shoulders, cut the meat down to the bone on one side and remove, then turn the joint over and repeat, or cut slices horizontally from the other side.

Inexperienced cooks may prefer to carve in the kitchen and reheat the meat to serve. Learning to carve can be a slow business, and the meat and vegetables can be cold by the time everything is ready. New cutting techniques and boneless joints, which are becoming more popular, will make carving and serving very much easier. Cold meat cuts up more economically than hot, and overcooked meat far less economically.

If meat is carved cold for reheating, it is imperative that the reheating must be quick and thorough, the meat must be served immediately and any not consumed discarded. All meat once cooked must be kept protected from contamination by dirt and pests, and refrigerated as quickly as possible. Warm meat is an ideal breeding ground for the bacteria that are responsible for food poisoning.

# Accompaniments when serving meat

| Meat | Sauces | Stuffing | Accompaniments |
|------|--------|----------|----------------|
| Beef | Horseradish cream | Sausage meat | Yorkshire pudding |
| | Horseradish in white sauce | Cooked rice and bacon | Batter popovers |
| | | Mashed chestnuts | Roast parsnips |
| | Mustard sauce | Chopped cooked celery | Suet or oatmeal dumplings |
| | Brown onion sauce | Mushroom and herbs | |
| | Red wine sauce | | |
| Veal | Thick gravy, sherry-flavoured | Lemon and thyme | Bacon rolls |
| | Tomato sauce | Cooked rice and ham | Baked ham or bacon |
| | Cumberland sauce | Chopped parsley and bacon (cooked) | Risotto noodles or spaghetti |
| | Sherry or Marsala sauce | Walnut orange and coriander | |
| Lamb & Mutton | Mint sauce | Garlic, cooked rice and capers | Suet or oatmeal dumplings |
| | Onion sauce | | |
| | Caper sauce | Rosemary and/or onions | Braised onions |
| | Madeira sauce | Mint or watercress | Potato and onion casserole |
| | | Lentil | Red currant or mint jelly |
| Pork | Thin gravy, cider-flavoured | Sage and onion | Pease pudding |
| | Apple sauce | Chopped apples and raisins | Sauerkraut |
| | Gooseberry purée | | Baked apples |
| | Cranberry sauce or jelly | Chopped cooked celery and onions | Cucumber salad |
| | | | Baked beans |
| | | Prunes and walnuts | Red cabbage |
| | | Apricot and walnut | Apple cake |

| Meat | Sauces | Stuffing | Accompaniments |
|------|--------|----------|----------------|
| Bacon & Gammon | Parsley sauce Cumberland sauce Mustard sauce Gravy with cider Clove and brown sugar coating Raisin sauce | Prunes Sage and onion Chopped apples and walnuts Almond and raisin Apricot | Apple or pineapple rings Half peaches Butter beans in parsley sauce Pease pudding |

# BEEF AND VEAL

An interesting selection of beef and veal
recipes ranging from Pot Roast Beef with
Whisky to Veal Orloff – to suit every
taste and budget

## Beef

When buying beef, it will be bright red when it is first cut, but goes darker on exposure to air. Look for fine even graining and firm fat. The colour of the fat depends on the breed and its feed, but is usually creamy white. Avoid meat which is dried or discoloured, and if it has too much marbling fat within the lean.

*Principal cuts of beef* In some areas regional names may be found.

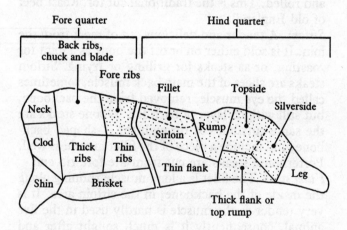

The shaded areas show cuts with small amounts of gristle which are suitable for roasting, grilling and frying (the dry methods).

Unshaded areas have more gristle and need to be cooked by a moist method (stewing, casseroling and braising) to make the meat tender.

## Cuts of beef

*Shin (foreleg) and leg (hindleg).* This is lean meat with a high proportion of gristle. It requires long slow moist cooking and can be used for stews, casseroles, stocks, soup and brawn.

*Neck and clod.* Normally cut up as stewing steak or minced.

*Chuck and blade steak.* A large, fairly lean cut of meat, removed from the bone and sold as chuck steak for braising, stewing and pies.

*Brisket.* Brisket is sold in pieces, on the bone, or boned and rolled, and is suitable for braising or boiling. It can be salted and is excellent boiled and served cold. It is recognised by its layers of fat and lean.

*Thin and thick ribs.* These are usually sold boned and rolled, for braising or pot roasting.

*Fore ribs.* A good roasting joint on the bone or boned and rolled. This is the traditional cut for 'Roast beef of old England'.

*Sirloin.* A tender and delicious cut of meat from the loin. It is sold either on or off the bone as a joint for roasting, or as steaks for grilling or frying. Sirloin steaks are slices of the main back muscle, sometimes called the eye muscle, removed from the backbone, but still with its layer of back fat. T-bone steaks are the same cut, but cut through the T-shaped backbone, and include a piece of the fillet muscle as well. Porterhouse steaks are cut from the fore rib end.

*Fillet steak.* The fillet is a long muscle running along the inside of the backbone, in the sirloin area. It is very tender as the muscle is hardly used in the live animal, consequently it is much sought after and therefore very expensive. Although tender, it often does not have as much flavour as other cuts of beef. It is sold whole, or in large pieces for such classic dishes as Beef Wellington (fillet steak in a puff pastry case) or in slices as fillet steak. It can be tied to keep it round, and steaks cut from this are called tournedos. Cut into strips, it is the basis for Beef Stroganoff, and minced, for Steak Tartare. The Châteaubriand steak is cut from the place where the fillet divides to join the muscles of the rump.

*Rump steak.* This is an excellent lean and tender cut,

usually sold in slices for grilling and frying. Steaks are cut down, through the back fat to the hip bone, and have a characteristic, oblong shape, with the fat at one end. One slice of rump steak, depending on the area from which it comes, is often enough to serve two.

*Thin flank*. Ideal for braising or stewing, it is often salted or pickled, and frequently sold as mince.

*Thick flank*. A lean cut suitable for roasting, pot roasting and braising, or when sliced for braising or frying.

*Topside*. A lean cut, with little or no naturally occurring fat, it is usually sold in rolled joints, which have had a layer of fat tied round them. It roasts and pot roasts well.

*Silverside*. A very lean joint, often treated like topside. If roasting, baste while cooking to prevent drying out. Silverside is traditionally salted and sold for boiling, and is used for boiled beef and carrots. Uncooked salted beef is grey, but turns its characteristic pink during cooking.

## Veal

The cuts of veal correspond in name and position with those of lamb (see page 126). However, the shank end of the leg is more usually called the knuckle end and the fillet end is often cut in thin slices, which are beaten out to produce escalopes. The animal is larger than the lamb, so joints, chops etc are correspondingly bigger. Cuts can be cooked in the same way, the lower part of the legs and necks are best stewed, the remainder can be roasted, grilled or fried according to cut. Take care if the veal is very thin that it does not dry out during cooking. Cover with a sauce, foil or a lid if necessary. Veal cooks very quickly, and spoils if overcooked. Marinading will often add flavour, and help to keep the meat moist during cooking.

# BEEF CARBONNADE

Serves 4

450–700 g (1–1½ lb) chuck steak in
   large cubes
1 tbsp flour
2 tbsp oil
seasoning
1 large onion, sliced
4 celery stalks, chopped
2 carrots, sliced
275 ml (½ pint) beer or stout
1 tbsp vinegar
1 bouquet garni
1 tbsp chopped parsley to garnish

Heat the oven to 170°C (325°F) mark 3 or
simmer the carbonnade on top of the stove.
Toss the meat in the flour and then fry in oil
to brown. Season to taste and add the onion,
celery and carrots and fry for a few minutes.
Add the beer, vinegar and bouquet garni.
Stir well and transfer to a warm casserole
with lid, or cook on a very low heat in a
covered pan.

Cook for 2–2½ hours or until the meat is
tender. Add a little water to the casserole if
it becomes dry during cooking. Discard
bouquet garni and adjust seasoning.
Garnish with chopped parsley.

Serve with creamed or jacket potatoes.

# STEAK, KIDNEY AND MUSHROOM PIE

Serves 4–6

225 g (8 oz) flaky or mixer pastry
   using plain flour
450 g (1 lb) stewing steak in 2.5 cm
   (1 in) cubes
100–225 g (4–8 oz) young ox
   kidney
1 tbsp flour, seasoned
½ tsp mixed herbs
1 onion, finely chopped or left whole
   and spiked with cloves
100 g (4 oz) mushrooms, sliced
water or stock
egg for glazing

If time is short, the filling can be cooked in a
pressure cooker, as for a stew, but for the
best flavour, and most delicious pie, the
meat should be cooked from raw, under the
pastry crust.

Heat the oven to 220°C (425°F) mark 7
for flaky and 200°C (400°F) mark 6 for
mixer pastry.

Make the pastry and leave in a cool place
to relax. Toss the steak and kidney in
seasoned flour. Mix in the herbs, onion and
mushrooms. Place in a 1 litre (2 pint) pie
dish (with a flat rim). Ensure the dish is full,
if necessary pad out with raw potato. Add
sufficient stock or water to come half way
up the meat.

Roll out the pastry to the shape of dish
plus about 1 cm (½ in) extra all round. Cut
out the shape of the pie dish. Use the
trimmings to cover the rim of pie dish. Use

water to stick the pastry to the dish. Cover
with pastry, pressing down the edges to
seal. Knock up the edges, making
horizontal cuts with the back of a small
knife, then flute around rim of pie by
bringing up the back of a knife, every 5 cm
(2 in). Decorate with pastry leaves, and cut
a hole in the middle to release the steam.
Glaze with beaten egg. Bake for 30 minutes,
then reduce heat to 180°C (350°F) mark 4
for a further 1½–2 hours until meat feels
tender when tried with a skewer through
the hole in the top. If necessary cover pastry
with greaseproof paper to prevent burning.
Top up with stock if required.

Serve with extra gravy.

# PEPPERED BEEF

Serves 4

25 g (1 oz) flour
1 tsp ground ginger
seasoning
450–700 g (1–1½ lb) braising steak
3 tbsp oil
225 g (8 oz) tomatoes, skinned
1–2 tsp chilli or Tabasco sauce
1 tbsp Worcester sauce
2 tbsp wine vinegar
2 cloves garlic, crushed
150 ml (¼ pint) tomato juice or stock
1 small red pepper, decored, in rings
1 small green pepper, decored, in
   rings
1 yellow pepper, decored, in rings (if
   available)
100 g (4 oz) mushrooms

Heat the oven to 170°C (325°F) mark 3. Mix
the flour, ginger and seasoning and rub into
the steak. Fry in the oil to brown both sides.
Transfer to a casserole dish.

In a liquidiser, combine the tomatoes,
chilli sauce, Worcester sauce, vinegar,
garlic and tomato juice. Pour over meat,
cover and cook for about 1½ hours. Add the
peppers and mushrooms and cook for a
further 30 minutes or until meat is tender
and pepper cooked but not too soft.

A can of red kidney beans can be added
with the peppers if desired. This will stretch
the meal to serve 6, and provide vegetable
protein and fibre.

Serve with rice, pasta or jacket potatoes.

# BEEF STROGANOFF

Serves 4

450–700 g (1–1½ lb) fillet steak in
   thin strips
ground black pepper
½ tsp basil
25 g (1 oz) butter
1 tbsp oil
50 g (2 oz) streaky bacon in strips
1 onion, finely chopped
225 g (8 oz) mushrooms, sliced
½ tsp ground mace
1 tbsp parsley, chopped
150–275 ml (¼–½ pint) soured
   cream or natural yoghurt
chopped parsley to garnish

Season the steak with the pepper and basil.
Heat the butter and oil and stir fry the steak
and bacon for about 5 minutes until the
meat is browned all over. Remove the meat
from pan and keep warm. Add the onion to
the pan and fry gently until transparent;
add the mushrooms and fry for 3 minutes.
Return the meat to pan and add the mace,
parsley and cream. Heat through but do not
boil.

Serve garnished with parsley on a bed of
boiled rice.

# GOULASH WITH NATURAL YOGHURT

Serves 4

450–700 g (1–1½ lb) stewing beef
   (or veal) in 2.5 cm (1 in) cubes
3 tbsp oil
1 large onion, chopped
1 clove garlic, finely chopped
2 tbsp paprika
½ tsp caraway seeds
400 g (14 oz) can of tomatoes
425 ml (¾ pint) beef stock
1 red pepper, deseeded and cut in
   strips
450 g (1 lb) potatoes, scrubbed and
   sliced
100 g (4 oz) button mushrooms
black pepper to taste
150 ml (¼ pint) natural yoghurt (or
   soured cream)

Heat the oven to 150°C (300°F) mark 2 or
simmer on top of the stove in a pan. Brown
the meat in hot oil. Add the onion, garlic,
paprika and caraway seeds and fry for a few
minutes, stirring continuously. Add the
tomatoes and stock. Cook with a lid on, for
2–3 hours until meat is tender.

Add the pepper and potatoes for the last
45 minutes, and the mushrooms for the last
10 minutes. Adjust the seasoning, serve in a
heated dish, with yoghurt poured on top,
and swirled in.

Serve with a green or mixed salad. The
potatoes can be omitted and the goulash
served with dumplings, pasta or rice.

# POT ROAST BEEF WITH WHISKY

Serves 4–6

900 g (2 lb) joint (flank, top rib or
   chuck)
4 tbsp oil
2 carrots, sliced
2 small parsnips, sliced
1 stick of celery, chopped
75 ml (3 fl oz) whisky

Heat the oven to 180°C (350°F) mark 4. If possible, use a casserole in which the meat can be fried and roasted, or use a frying pan and then transfer the meat and fat to an earthenware casserole to pot roast.

Brown the joint well in oil. Add the vegetables around the joint and pour in the whisky. Cover with a well-fitting lid. Cook for about 2 hours, turning the joint once, until the meat is tender. Remove the meat to a heated serving dish. Use the cooking liquor, liquidised if preferred, diluted with water and suitably thickened, for a sauce or gravy.

# BEEF SLICES IN RED WINE

Serves 4

4 slices of topside or similar, about
   1 cm (½ in) thick
150 ml (¼ pint) red wine
1 onion, finely chopped
1 bay leaf
1 tsp parsley
¼ tsp marjoram
¼ tsp thyme
25 g (1 oz) flour
3 tbsp oil
275 ml (½ pint) beef stock
seasoning to taste
225 g (8 oz) button onions
225 g (8 oz) baby carrots
2 tbsp chopped parsley to garnish

Lay the meat in shallow dish, or in sealable polythene container. Pour over the wine, add the onion and herbs and marinade for several hours but preferably overnight.

Heat the oven to 150°C (300°F) mark 2. Drain the meat well, reserving marinade. Coat with flour and fry in oil to brown. Place meat in a casserole dish. Add any remaining flour to the fat, and cook to brown, but do not burn.

Slowly add the stock and marinade. Season to taste, and pour over meat. Cover and cook slowly for 1–1½ hours. Add onions and carrots and cook for a further hour until meat is tender.

Serve sprinkled with chopped parsley.

Other meats can be cooked in this way, using white wine with lighter meats.

# SLICED BEEF IN ASPIC

Serves 4

8 slices rare roast beef
cooked carrot, sliced
cooked button onions
fresh herb leaves

Aspic
425 ml (¾ pint) well flavoured stock
150 ml (¼ pint) Madeira wine
1 pkt or 4 tsp gelatine
1 tsp Worcester sauce
pinch cayenne pepper

Place the meat in a shallow serving dish and arrange in overlapping slices. Decorate by placing the carrot and onions between the slices. Arrange the herb leaves on top.

Heat the stock and Madeira. Sprinkle on gelatine and leave to dissolve. Add Worcester sauce and cayenne pepper. Cool until aspic is syrupy. Glaze the beef and chill. Place the remaining aspic in a shallow dish and, when set, cut into cubes. Use chopped aspic to decorate the meat by forming two rows on either side of it.

Serve with a salad or as part of a buffet table.

# BEEF AND HARICOT BEANS

Serves 4

100 g (4 oz) haricot beans, soaked
    overnight
450 g (1 lb) chuck or braising steak
    in 2.5 cm (1 in) cubes
100 g (4 oz) lean streaky bacon
    pieces
1 large onion, sliced
2 carrots, sliced
2 cloves garlic, crushed
225 g (8 oz) tomatoes, skinned
bouquet garni or 1 tsp herbs
275 ml (½ pint) stock
275 ml (½ pint) red wine or further
    stock
seasoning to taste
chopped parsley to garnish

Put all ingredients into a large pan and bring to the boil. Stir well and cover with a well fitting lid. Simmer for 2–2½ hours until meat is tender.

The casserole should not need thickening as the haricot beans will absorb excess liquid, but adjust consistency if necessary.

Serve sprinkled with chopped parsley.

This dish reheats well next day, and is delicious served with a chunk of granary bread.

# BEEF AND PRUNE RAGOUT

Serves 4

575 ml (1 pint) beef stock, beer or
    wine
225 g (8 oz) prunes
450–700 g (1–1½ lb) chuck steak in
    cubes or pieces
25 g (1 oz) seasoned flour
3 tbsp oil
1 tbsp tomato purée
2 bay leaves
225 g (8 oz) small tomatoes, skinned

Heat the stock and pour over the prunes. Leave to soak, if possible overnight. Coat the meat in flour and fry in oil to brown. Add the tomato purée, bay leaves and about 6 finely chopped prunes, with the drained stock. Simmer for 1¾ hours, until meat is tender. Add the remaining prunes and tomatoes, whole, and cook for approximately 20 minutes until the prunes are soft but prunes and tomatoes have not collapsed in shape.

Serve with potatoes, pasta or rice.

Prunes can be replaced with dried apricots, peaches or large raisins.

# BOILED SALT BEEF

Serves 6–8

900 g (2 lb) salt brisket
cold beef stock to cover
2 onions, quartered
4 carrots, sliced
1 small turnip, chopped
1 tsp black peppercorns
2 tsp mixed herbs

Soak the brisket overnight, then drain and discard soaking water. Place the meat in a large pan and cover with stock. Add the vegetables and seasonings (do not add salt). Cover and bring to the boil. Simmer, very slowly for about 1½ hours.

Served sliced with unthickened cooking liquor and vegetables, and boiled potatoes. If serving cold, allow to cool in cooking liquor, slice and serve with salads or in sandwiches, with horseradish sauce.

# STIR FRY BEEF

Serves 4–6

*1 tbsp cornflour*
*450 g (1 lb) rump steak in paper thin*
  *slices*
*3 tbsp oil*
*4 spring onions, finely chopped*
*100–175 g (4–6 oz) Chinese leaves*
  *or white cabbage, finely shredded*
*75 g (3 oz) bean sprouts*
*2 sticks celery, finely chopped*
*1 tbsp soy sauce or more to taste*

Mix the cornflour to a paste with 3 tbsp water and mix with steak. Heat the oil and stir fry the meat for about 3 minutes, over a high heat in a frying pan or wok. Remove from the pan, drain and keep hot.

Adding a little more oil if necessary, stir fry the vegetables, also over a high heat, for about 5 minutes or until cooked to taste. The vegetables should still be crisp. Pour over soy sauce, return the meat to the pan and stir well.

Serve immediately with boiled or fried rice, or as part of a Chinese meal.

# CARPET BAG STEAKS

Serves 4

*4 thick pieces of fillet or rump steak*
*24 prepared mussels (or 12 oysters),*
  *fresh, canned, frozen or smoked*
*50 g (2 oz) butter*
*2 tbsp parsley, chopped*
*1 clove garlic, crushed*
*2 tbsp lemon juice*
*seasoning*
*melted butter*
*ground black pepper*

Split the steaks to make pockets. Mix the mussels with butter, parsley, garlic, lemon and seasoning, and divide between the pockets in the steaks. Skewer or sew up. Brush with melted butter and sprinkle with ground black pepper.

Grill or fry until cooked to personal taste. The cooking time will depend on thickness of the steak and the heat of the grill or pan. Turn once during cooking, and serve immediately with tomatoes, mushrooms and potatoes.

# SWISS STEAKS

Serves 4

*1 tbsp seasoned flour*
*4 × 1 cm (½ in) thick slices of*
  *topside or similar*
*25 g (1 oz) butter or margarine*
*1 large onion, finely chopped*
*2 sticks celery, finely chopped*
*400 g (14 oz) can tomatoes, broken*
  *up*
*2 tsp tomato purée*
*½ tsp Worcester sauce*
*150 ml (¼ pint) stock or water*
*4 tbsp single cream or yoghurt*
  *(optional)*

Press flour well into slices of meat. Fry in butter to brown both sides. Add the onion and cook for a few minutes. Stir in celery, tomatoes, purée, Worcester sauce and stock, cover and simmer, or put into a casserole dish, and cook covered at 170°C (325°F) mark 3 for 2–2½ hours until meat is tender.

Serve topped with cream or yoghurt, with boiled or creamed potatoes and fresh green vegetables.

# STEAK DIANE

Serves 4

*450 g (1 lb) grilling or frying steak*
  *beaten out to ½ cm (¼ in) thick*
*25 g (1 oz) butter*
*3 tbsp oil*
*1 onion, very finely chopped*
*1 clove garlic, crushed*
*50 g (2 oz) bacon, finely chopped*
*100 g (4 oz) mushrooms, finely*
  *chopped*
*1 tbsp fresh chives, chopped*
*freshly ground black pepper*
*3 tbsp brandy, warmed*
*150 ml (¼ pint) single cream*

Cut the beaten steak into approximately 7.5 cm (3 in) square. Heat some of the butter and oil and when hot, fry the steak for 1½ minutes on either side. Drain and keep warm. Adding more fat if required, fry the onion for 2 minutes, add the garlic, bacon, mushrooms, chives and seasoning, and stir fry to cook, approximately 3 minutes. Return the meat to the pan.

Warm the brandy, pour over meat and ignite. Let the brandy burn until it extinguishes. Pour in the cream and warm but do not boil.

Serve on a warm platter with potato piped around as a border. This dish can be garnished with bacon rolls, sliced mushrooms or chopped parsley.

# CHINESE VEAL

Serves 4–8

1 tbsp cornflour
1 tsp ground ginger
seasoning to taste
450 g (1 lb) veal (or beef), well
    beaten and cut in strips
4 tbsp oil
1 onion, sliced
150 ml (¼ pint) light stock or water
1 tbsp soy sauce
1 tbsp sherry
½ red pepper, deseeded and in strips
50 g (2 oz) mushrooms, sliced
1 tbsp crystallised ginger, chopped
15 g (½ oz) cornflour

Mix the cornflour and ginger with the seasoning and coat meat strips well. Shallow fry in oil (or deep fat fry if preferred), stirring to prevent burning, until meat is cooked, about 7–10 minutes. Drain and keep warm.

Place the onion in a pan with the stock, soy sauce and sherry, and boil for 3–5 minutes. Add the pepper and cook for a further 2–3 minutes and add the mushrooms and cook for 1–2 more minutes. Stir in ginger. Vegetables should still be crisp. Blend the cornflour with a little water and use to thicken vegetable mixture.

Serve in a hot bowl, with fried meat added on top at the last minute. Vegetables can be cooked at the same time as the meat, but do not let vegetables stand or they will get soft.

Serve with boiled rice, or as part of a Chinese meal.

# ORANGE TARRAGON VEAL

Serves 4

4 veal chops or shoulder steaks
1 tbsp flour, seasoned
15 g (½ oz) butter
2 tbsp oil
1 large onion, sliced
175 g (6 oz) concentrated orange
    juice (usually frozen)
150 ml (¼ pint) chicken stock
1 tbsp dried tarragon leaves
15 g (½ oz) cornflour
150 ml (¼ pint) soured cream or
    natural yoghurt

Heat the oven to 180°C (350°F) mark 4 or simmer on top of the stove in a pan. Coat the meat in seasoned flour. Heat the butter and oil together and fry the meat to brown on both sides. Stir in the onion and fry for a few minutes. Add the orange juice and stock (if concentrated juice cannot be obtained, use 325 ml (12 fl oz) normal strength, and dissolve a stock cube in it instead of using stock). Stir in tarragon and simmer or cook in oven for 1–1½ hours until meat is tender.

Place the meat in a hot serving dish and keep warm. Thicken cooking liquor with cornflour to give a coating consistency. Stir

in the soured cream and heat but do not
boil. Pour over meat.

The dish can be garnished with fresh
tarragon, orange slices or orange rind
julienne strips.

# VEAL VERONIQUE

Serves 4

*4 veal (or pork) escalopes or chops,
    deboned*
*small onion, finely chopped*
*50 g (2 oz) mushrooms, finely
    chopped*
*40 g (1½ oz) butter*
*½ tsp herbs to taste*
*seasoning to taste*
*75 ml (⅛ pint) white wine*
*75 ml (⅛ pint) stock*
*150 ml (¼ pint) milk*
*25 g (1 oz) cornflour*
*100 g (4 oz) white grapes, skinned
    and deseeded*

Heat the oven to 190°C (375°F) mark 5 or
cook on top of stove. Beat the escalopes to
1 cm (½ in) thick or trim the chops and
make a pocket slit with a sharp knife. Fry
the onion and mushrooms in 15 g (½ oz) of
butter until cooked. Either spread the onion
and mushroom mixture on the escalopes,
roll up and secure with a cocktail stick, or
push the mixture into the slits in the chops.
Place in a casserole or pan with herbs,
seasoning, wine and stock and cook slowly
either in the oven or in a saucepan for 1–1½
hours until the meat is tender.

Remove the meat to a hot serving dish
and keep warm. Strain the liquor and make
up to 275 ml (½ pint) with milk. Heat the
remaining butter and cornflour together and
cook for 2–3 minutes. Gradually blend in
the milk and cooking liquor and bring to the
boil. Boil for 3–5 minutes until sauce is
thick and glossy. Pour over meat and
sprinkle grapes over the top. Return to the
oven for a few minutes if necessary, to heat
through.

The dish can be garnished with boiled,
sieved, or piped potatoes.

# VEAL AND BEAN RAGOUT

Serves 4

450–700 g (1–1½ lb) stewing veal
  (allow extra for bone)
2 tbsp oil
1 large onion, chopped
1 tbsp wholemeal flour, seasoned
½ tsp oregano
½ tsp grated nutmeg
225 g (8 oz) tomatoes, skinned and
  quartered
275 ml (½ pint) stock or wine and
  stock
225 g (8 oz) haricot or other beans,
  soaked overnight
chopped parsley to garnish

Brown the meat in the oil. Stir in the onion and cook for a few minutes. Stir in flour, oregano, nutmeg and tomatoes. Blend in the stock and wine, add the beans. Cover and simmer for 1½–2 hours until the meat is tender.

Garnish with chopped parsley and serve with boiled or baked potatoes in their jackets and fresh green vegetables.

# VEAL AND HAM PIE

Serves 4–6

225 g (8 oz) flaky or mixer pastry
450 g (1 lb) boneless veal in small
  cubes
175 g (6 oz) bacon, diced or pieces
2 hard-boiled eggs, sliced
1 tbsp parsley, chopped
1 tsp grated lemon rind
seasoning to taste
150 ml (¼ pint) stock, water or
  white wine
egg to glaze

Heat the oven to 230°C (450°F) mark 8. Roll out the pastry to the shape of the pie dish plus 1 cm (½ in) all round (use 1 litre (2 pint) size). Layer the veal, bacon, egg, parsley and lemon rind in pie dish and season. Add enough stock to come half way up the mixture.

To cover the pie, cut the pastry to the shape of the pie dish, and use 1 cm (½ in) trimming to make a ledge of pastry round the rim of the pie dish. Moisten this edge, and place on cut pastry shape. Press two layers together, knock up the edges with a small knife, and use the back of knife to flute round rim of pie, bringing it up every 4 cm (1½ in). Make a hole in the centre to allow the steam to escape. Use any trimmings to make leaves and rose for centre.

Glaze with beaten egg. Place on a baking tray and bake for 15 minutes, then turn down heat to 190°C (375°F) mark 5 for a further 1½ hours or until meat is tender when tested with a skewer through the hole in the top of the pie. If pastry is getting too brown, cover with greaseproof paper.

Serve hot with fresh vegetables, or cold with salad. If serving cold, stock can be topped up through the hole in the top, using veal bone stock, which will give a good set. For a picnic, use pastry below and above the meat, in order to cut out a good slice (double the quantity of pastry).

# BLANQUETTE OF VEAL

Serves 4

450–700 g (1–1½ lb) shoulder or
    knuckle veal, cubed
225 g (8 oz) small onions
2 carrots, sliced
2 bay leaves
1 lemon, rind and juice
seasoning to taste
100 g (4 oz) button mushrooms
40 g (1½ oz) butter or margarine
40 g (1½ oz) flour or cornflour
1 egg yolk
150 ml (¼ pint) single cream or
    natural yoghurt
grated nutmeg

Put veal in a pan, cover with water and bring to the boil. Strain and rinse scum off veal.

Replace the veal in the pan with onions, carrots, bay leaves, lemon rind and juice and seasoning. Add 850 ml (1½ pints) water (or very light stock could be used), bring to the boil, cover and simmer for 1½ hours, adding mushrooms for last 30 minutes. Strain meat and vegetables and place on a warm serving dish, cover with foil and keep warm. Reduce cooking liquor to 575 ml (1 pint) by boiling rapidly.

Heat the butter and flour together to make a white roux. Cook for a few minutes, but do not allow to brown. Slowly blend cooking liquor into roux and heat and then boil for 5 minutes. Adjust seasoning as required. (If sauce is not smooth, strain or liquidise).

Beat in egg yolk and cream and heat but do not boil. Pour sauce over meat, and sprinkle with grated nutmeg.

# VEAL OLIVES OR BIRDS

Serves 4

stuffing or forcemeat
4 veal (or pork or beef) escalopes,
    well beaten out
1 tbsp flour
15 g (½ oz) butter or 2 tbsp oil
150 ml (¼ pint) chicken stock
150 ml (¼ pint) dry white wine (red
    if using beef)
bouquet garni
seasoning to taste
beurre manié
75–150 ml (⅛–¼ pint) single cream
    or natural yoghurt
chopped parsley to garnish

Spread the stuffing evenly on the escalopes. Roll up and skewer or tie. Roll in the flour to coat and fry in butter to brown. Add the stock and wine and bring to the boil, stirring continuously. Lower heat to simmer, add the bouquet garni and seasoning and cook slowly for 45–60 minutes or until meat is tender when pierced with a skewer. Remove the skewers or string and the bouquet garni. Place veal olives in serving dish and keep warm.

Thicken the sauce to coating consistency using beurre manié or cornflour. Stir in cream and heat but do not boil. Coat the meat with the sauce, and serve garnished with chopped parsley. Potato can be piped around the dish, or served as duchesse potatoes.

# OSSO BUCCO

Serves 4

4 thick slices shin of veal with plenty
    of meat on
1 tbsp flour with seasoning
2 tbsp olive oil
2 cloves garlic, finely chopped
1 Spanish onion, sliced
150 ml (¼ pint) light stock
150 ml (¼ pint) white wine or more
    stock
3 tbsp tomato purée
4 anchovy fillets, finely chopped
4 tbsp chopped parsley
grated rind ½ lemon

To serve
225 g (8 oz) long grain rice
pinch of saffron or ¼ tsp turmeric

Dredge the meat with seasoned flour and fry in oil to brown on both sides. Add the garlic, onion, stock, wine and tomato purée and bring to the boil. Cover and simmer for 1½–2 hours until meat is tender. Add the anchovy fillets and cook for 5 minutes.

Boil the rice with saffron or turmeric until cooked but not soft, about 12 minutes for white rice and 20 for brown. Drain, rinse and dry for 15 minutes.

Serve the Osso Bucco sprinkled with parsley and lemon rind, on a bed of, or with, the saffron rice.

# VEAL ORLOFF

Serves 4–6

*1–1½ kg (2–3 lb) boned, rolled and*
*   tied joint of veal or lamb*
*3 tbsp oil*
*2 onions, 1 quartered, 1 chopped*
*2 carrots, sliced*
*1 stick celery, chopped*
*bouquet garni*
*150 ml (¼ pint) stock or water*
*175 g (6 oz) mushrooms, chopped*
*15 g (½ oz) butter*
*seasoning to taste*

Cheese sauce
*25 g (1 oz) butter or margarine*
*25 g (1 oz) cornflour*
*275 ml (½ pint) milk*
*¼ tsp mustard*
*75 g (3 oz) grated cheese*
*1 tbsp breadcrumbs*

Heat the oven to 200°C (400°F) mark 6. Fry the veal in oil to brown and transfer to a casserole dish. Add the quartered onion, carrot and celery with bouquet garni and stock. Cover and braise for 30 minutes. Lower the heat to 180°C (350°F) mark 4 and continue cooking for 1–1½ hours, until the meat juice runs clear when meat is pierced with a skewer.

Meanwhile fry the chopped onion and mushroom in the butter until soft and golden brown. Season as required.

Make the cheese sauce by heating the butter and cornflour together and cooking for 2–3 minutes. Slowly blend in milk and boil to thicken. Add the mustard, 50 g (2 oz) of the cheese and seasoning to taste. Stir to dissolve cheese.

Remove the meat from the braise and cut into 4 or 6 thick slices. Arrange on a serving dish with the mushroom and onion mix between slices. Coat with cheese sauce, sprinkle with 25 g (1 oz) grated cheese, and return to oven for 10–15 minutes to heat through and brown cheese.

This dish is fairly rich, so is best served with boiled rice or creamed potatoes and fresh, boiled vegetables.

The vegetables and liquor from the braise can be used as a basis for a gravy.

# VEAL CORDON BLEU

Serves 4

4 veal (or pork) escalopes beaten
  very thin
4 slices gruyère cheese (or Edam)
4 slices of ham
seasoning
beaten egg to coat
breadcrumbs to coat
lemon wedges and parsley to garnish

This dish can be assembled in three ways. For thicker escalopes lay a cheese slice on a veal slice, top with a ham slice and season. Press well together and coat with egg and breadcrumbs. Shallow fat fry for 3–5 minutes a side depending on thickness of the meat.

For thin escalopes, lay a cheese then a ham slice on an escalope and season, roll up and skewer. Coat with egg and breadcrumbs and deep fat fry for about 10 minutes, until cooked through and golden brown.

For very thin escalopes, lay a cheese and ham slice on half of a veal slice and season. Fold over and sew round with cotton to enclose ham and cheese. Coat with egg and breadcrumbs. Shallow fat fry on medium heat for 5–7 minutes a side. Remove the cotton and serve.

For all methods, drain well and serve piled on a hot serving dish, garnished with lemon wedges and sprigs of parsley.

# LAMB

British lamb is available fresh very nearly all the year round. It is cheapest and most plentiful from August until December. Britain imports frozen lamb from New Zealand. It is available all the year round, but has its 'new' season when British lamb is least available, from Christmas to Easter, when it can be a very economic buy.

When buying fresh lamb, look for firm, white fat, fine-grained, firm, pinky-brown lean, with very little gristle and a good proportion of lean to fat. Freshly cut surfaces should look slightly moist and the bones should be pinkish-blue.

*Principal cuts of lamb* In some areas regional names may be found

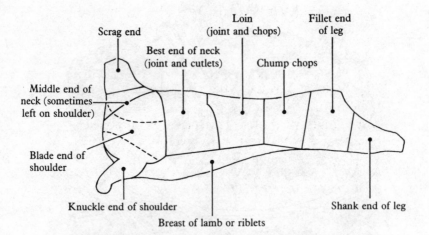

## Cuts of lamb

*Scrag and middle neck*. These are usually sold chopped into pieces and are used for stewing and braising. They are traditionally used for Irish stew and Lancashire hot-pot. Increasingly the meat is being cut off the bone and sold as neck fillet, it is sweet and easy to cook, and very reasonably priced with no wastage.

On small animals and frozen carcases (such as New Zealand lamb) these cuts are left on the shoulder, and more often sold in two halves.

*Shoulder.* A succulent, sweet, tender roasting joint, whether on the bone, or boned and rolled, with or without stuffing. Shoulders are sold whole or halved into blade and knuckle ends, both ideal for roasting or braising. Frozen carcases are often cut into slices with a band-saw, giving shoulder steaks, weighing about 150 g (5 oz) each. These can be grilled, braised, baked or casseroled.

*Best end of neck.* This can be purchased as a roasting joint with 6–7 rib bones. If chined by the butcher, it is easier to carve. It can be roasted on the bone, or boned and rolled, with or without stuffing. It is frequently cut into cutlets with one rib bone to each. Two best ends of neck (preferably a pair from a left and right side) joined together and curved, bones outwards, makes a Crown Roast, and facing each other, fat side outwards, they make a Guard of Honour. Allow 2 cutlets per person. When boned and rolled and then cut into slices, the slices are known as noisettes.

*Loin.* This is either roasted in a piece, on the bone, or boned and rolled, with or without stuffing, or cut into chops for grilling, frying or braising. A loin will cut into 6–7 chops. Allow 1 or 2 chops per person according to appetite and money available. Occasionally, valentine chops or steaks can be found. These come from a boned loin, cut into 2.5 cm (1 in) slices, and each one is cut nearly through, from the fatty side, and opened out to give a heart shape. Occasionally double loin chops are found, these are cut across the animal before the two sides are separated down the backbone. If a whole double loin is cut out it is known as a saddle, which traditionally includes the kidneys at one end and has a plait and bow or rose made from strips of fat down the centre back. It is an excellent roast when serving 8–10 people. To carve a saddle, cut down either side of the back bone, flatten the knife to loosen meat from bone, then cut slices as if carving a single loin.

*Chump.* This can be sold as a piece, but is normally cut into chump chops. They are larger than loin chops and vary according to where along the chump they are from. Chump chops are distinguished by a small round bone in the centre. Some also have a large piece of backbone.

*Leg.* The prime joint, excellent for roasting or for cutting up into cubes of succulent tender meat. It can be cooked on the bone, or boned and rolled, with or without stuffing. It is frequently cut in two and sold as fillet and shank end. Slices off the fillet end are ideal for frying or grilling.

*Breast.* A long thin cut of lean, streaked with fat. Choose one with plenty of lean. This can be boned and rolled, which with a tasty stuffing, provides an economical roast or braise. Cut into strips it can be roast or barbecued, this cut is known as riblets. If casseroling or stewing it is sometimes worth roasting for 15 minutes to remove some of the fat, or boiling and discarding the water.

*Boneless cutting methods.* Many traditional roasting cuts, sold on the bone are impractical for small families, and those wanting a quick meal with no left overs for the next day. New techniques have been developed whereby the carcase can be boned, the resulting meat butchered and cut into small boneless joints, steaks and slices which are suitable for quick cooking methods such as frying and grilling. Excess fat can be removed and the meat cut into suitably sized joints for the customer's needs. These are not likely to replace the traditional joints for those who still want them, but do make the animal more versatile.

# NOISETTES WITH RED CURRANT

Serves 4

marinade
4–8 noisettes, chops or cutlets
red currant jelly
slices of wholemeal bread for croûtes
150 ml (¼ pint) stock
watercress to garnish

Marinade the meat overnight if required. Heat grill on high. Place the meat on the grid of the grill pan, ensuring pan is clean. Place 1 tsp red currant jelly on each noisette or chop. Place under grill, lower the heat to medium. Grill for about 5–10 minutes depending on thickness. Turn over, add more red currant jelly and grill for further 5–10 minutes.

Cut out 7.5 cm (3 in) circles of bread and fry or toast to make croûtes. Place the croûtes on a serving dish, top with a noisette or chop on each, and keep warm. Add the stock to grill pan, mix well and pour over chops.

Serve garnished with watercress and duchesse potatoes.

# LAMB AND ORANGE RIBLETS

Serves 4

1 tbsp soy sauce
1 tbsp dry sherry
½ tsp ground ginger
25 g (1 oz) crystallised root ginger, finely chopped
2 oranges, rind and juice
450 g (1 lb) lean riblets or breast of lamb strips
1 onion, finely chopped
1 tbsp vegetable oil

Mix the soy sauce, sherry, gingers and the rind and juice of the oranges, and marinade meat overnight. Heat the oven to 180°C (350°F) mark 4. Fry the onion in oil until transparent. Add the onion to the meat. Turn the meat into a greased roasting tin and spread out. Bake for 1–1½ hours until meat is tender. Turn and baste meat frequently in the marinade.

Serve meat on a bed of rice or pasta.

If more sauce is required, add a little stock to meat at last basting, and this will form a gravy. Can be eaten with fingers like barbecued spare ribs in a Chinese meal and cooks well on a barbecue.

# LAMB PILAU (PILAFF)

Serves 4

450–700 g (1–1½ lb) cubed leg or
  shoulder of lamb
575 ml (1 pint) stock or water
1 cm (½ in) fresh root ginger in thin
  slices
5 cm (2 in) cinnamon stick
¼ tsp grated nutmeg
1 green chilli pepper, chopped
6 black peppercorns
150 ml (¼ pint) natural yoghurt
1 lemon, rind and juice
½ tsp cayenne pepper or tandoori
  spice mix
225 g (8 oz) long grain rice
50 g (2 oz) butter or margarine
2 tbsp oil
1 onion, finely chopped
4 cloves
4 cardamom seeds
1 onion, sliced and fried to golden
2 tbsp raisins
2 tbsp slivered almonds, toasted
2 hard-boiled eggs, quartered

Simmer the meat in stock containing ginger, cinnamon, nutmeg, chilli, and peppercorns for 40 minutes.

Remove the meat to a bowl. Discard the cinnamon but reserve the liquor for cooking the rice. Add the yoghurt, lemon rind and juice and cayenne to the meat, stir and leave to marinade for 2 hours.

Approximately half an hour before required, fry the rice in butter and oil for 3 minutes. Remove from the fat and put in a pan with the reserved cooking liquor, the chopped onion, cloves and cardamom seeds. Cover and simmer for about 12 minutes for white and 20 minutes for brown rice. All the liquid should be absorbed, if not drain.

While the rice is cooking, fry the marinaded meat in the remains of the butter and oil until browned, and cooked through. Mix the cooked meat and rice and pile into a warmed serving bowl, top with fried onions, raisins and almonds, with the egg around the edge of the bowl.

# BRAISED, ROLLED SHOULDER OF LAMB

Serves 6–8

1 shoulder of lamb, boned, rolled
   and tied (can be stuffed if
   preferred)
1 tbsp flour
1 tsp paprika
seasoning to taste
25 g (1 oz) butter or margarine
100 g (4 oz) dried apricots, soaked
50 g (2 oz) walnuts, broken in pieces
2 onions, sliced
2 large carrots, sliced
2 stalks celery, sliced
1 stock cube
275 ml (½ pint) water
3 tbsp tomato purée

Heat the oven to 180°C (350°F) mark 4. Dust the joint with a mixture of flour, paprika and seasoning. Melt the butter and fry joint to brown all round, remove and place in a casserole dish, with apricots and walnuts. Fry the onions, carrots and celery to lightly brown and then stir in the remaining flour mix. Blend the stock cube and water, add the tomato purée and mix. Add to the casserole dish. Cover and cook in the oven until the meat is tender, approximately 20 minutes per ½ kg (or 1 lb) weight of prepared joint.

Place the meat on a warmed serving platter and keep hot. Either strain the vegetables and use the liquor as the basis of a sauce by adding water and thickening with cornflour or beurre manié (see page 90), or liquidise vegetables with liquor, and serve, reheated, as a sauce.

# LAMB AND COURGETTE SAUTE

Serves 4

450 g (1 lb) boneless neck fillet of
   lamb
1 tbsp soy sauce
2 tbsp dry sherry
½ tsp caraway seeds
25 g (1 oz) butter
2 tbsp oil
4–6 spring onions in 2.5 cm (1 in)
   pieces
50 g (2 oz) button mushrooms
225 g (8 oz) small courgettes in 2 cm
   (¾ in) pieces

Mix the lamb with the soy sauce, sherry and caraway seeds. Heat the butter and oil and fry the meat until browned, add the remaining ingredients and fry, turning periodically until meat is cooked and courgettes browned.

Serve immediately.

# FRENCH LAMB CASSEROLE

Serves 4

700 g (1½ lb) stewing lamb, allow
  more if a lot of bone included
2 onions, quartered
1 tbsp oil
25 g (1 oz) wholemeal flour
2 cloves garlic, crushed
575 ml (1 pint) stock
1 bouquet garni
2 tbsp brandy (optional)
225 g (8 oz) pickling onions
25 g (1 oz) butter or margarine
100 g (4 oz) peas
1 tbsp chopped parsley to garnish

Heat the oven to 190°C (375°F) mark 5.
Trim as much fat off the meat as possible.
Put in large casserole. Cook the quartered
onions in oil until well browned. Stir in
flour and garlic and blend in stock, and
pour over meat. Add bouquet garni and
brandy (optional). Cover and cook in oven
for 1–2 hours, or until meat is tender.

Fry the onions whole in the butter until
golden brown. Drain well and add to the
casserole with the peas about 15 minutes
before the end of cooking time.

Serve with boiled potatoes and garnish
with chopped parsley.

# RAGOUT OF LAMB AND BUTTER BEANS

Serves 4

2 tbsp oil
1 tbsp wholemeal flour
1 tsp herbs, chopped
seasoning to taste
½ tsp paprika
450 g (1 lb) boneless or 700 g
  (1½ lb) with bone*, stewing lamb
100 g (4 oz) butter beans, soaked
225 g (8 oz) shallots or small onions
400 g (14 oz) can of tomatoes
150 ml (¼ pint) natural yoghurt

Heat the oil in a pan. Mix the flour, herbs,
seasoning and paprika together and put in
polythene bag with meat. Toss together
thoroughly.

Fry the meat in oil until browned. Add all
the ingredients except the yoghurt to the
pan and simmer, covered, for 1–1½ hours,
or until meat and beans are tender. If very
old or tough meat is being used, cook for ½
hour before adding the beans.

Just before serving, stir in the yoghurt,
and heat but do not boil. Serve garnished
with chopped parsley and boiled potatoes or
pasta.

If the meat is very fatty, cook the day
before, but refrigerate before adding the
yoghurt. The next day, remove the layer of
fat, reheat and finish as above.

# LAMB AND BEAN HOT POT

Serves 4

450 g (1 lb) boned or 700 g (1½ lb)
  with bone, stewing lamb or
  mutton
2 onions, sliced
3 carrots, sliced
1 small turnip or swede, cubed
100 g (4 oz) haricot or any other
  beans, soaked
1 tsp mixed herbs
seasoning to taste
2 tbsp Worcester sauce
575 ml (1 pint) stock
450–700 g (1–1½ lb) potatoes,
  scrubbed and sliced
15 g (½ oz) butter, melted

Heat the oven to 150°C (300°F) mark 2.
Trim the fat from the meat where possible.
If very fatty, just cover the meat with water,
bring to the boil and simmer for 10 minutes,
then drain, discarding the water with the
melted fat.

Layer all the ingredients except the
potatoes and butter in a deep casserole. Top
with sliced potato and melted butter. Cook
uncovered for 2–2½ hours or until meat is
tender. The oven can be turned up for the
last 20 minutes, if necessary, to brown
potatoes.

This dish can be cooked in a slow cooker,
follow manufacturer's instructions for time,
and brown under a grill to colour the potato
at the end. Stewing beef, veal and poultry
can be cooked in the same way.

# LAMB AND YOGHURT CASSEROLE

Serves 4

450–700 g (1–1½ lb) boneless
  lamb, cubed
1 tbsp flour
1 tsp chopped mint
ground black peppercorns
15 g (½ oz) margarine or butter
1 tbsp oil
1 onion, chopped
275 ml (½ pint) stock
1 tbsp capers
1–2 pickled dill cucumbers, sliced
1 lemon, rind and juice
1 tbsp chopped parsley or coriander
  leaves
275 ml (½ pint) natural yoghurt

Heat the oven to 170°C (325°F) mark 3.
Toss the meat in flour, seasoned with the
mint and pepper. Melt the margarine or
butter together with the oil and fry meat to
brown. Remove meat to a casserole. Fry the
onion until transparent and add to meat.
Mix in the stock, capers, cucumber, lemon
and herbs, cover and cook until meat is
tender, 1–2 hours, depending on cut used.

Remove from the oven and stir in the
yoghurt, adjust the consistency if required,
and heat through but do not boil. The dish
can be garnished with cucumber and lemon
slices.

Serve with rice, pasta or boiled potatoes
and fresh vegetables.

# LAMB AND CHICK PEA CURRY

Serves 4–6

100 g (4 oz) chick peas
1 tbsp curry powder
½ tsp each of ginger, turmeric,
  paprika and cayenne pepper
1 tbsp flour
450 g (1 lb) lean lamb cubed (any
  cut is suitable)
25 g (1 oz) butter or margarine
2 tbsp oil
1 large Spanish onion, sliced
2 stalks celery
1 green pepper, cored, seeded and
  diced
25 g (1 oz) dessicated coconut
150 ml (¼ pint) milk
575 ml (1 pint) stock or water
50 g (2 oz) raisins
150 ml (¼ pint) natural yoghurt

This dish should be started the day before required for eating. Put the chick peas to soak. Mix the curry powder, spices and flour with cubed meat and leave to stand in the refrigerator, for a few hours, or overnight.

Melt the butter and oil together and fry the spiced meat until browned all over. Remove meat, and fry the onion, celery and pepper for a few minutes. Return the meat to the pan.

Boil the coconut with the milk and leave to cool, then strain and add coconut milk to the meat and chick peas along with the stock. Cover and simmer until meat is cooked, 1–2 hours depending on cut of meat, and age of animal. Stir in the raisins and yoghurt. Adjust the consistency if necessary with water or stock. Heat through, but do not boil once yoghurt has been added.

Serve with boiled rice and traditional curry accompaniments such as pappadoms, naan bread, mango and apple chutney, preserved kumquats etc. If an overnight soak and spicing is not possible, the chick peas can be brought to the boil and left to stand for an hour instead of soaking. The flavour will not have permeated the meat as well, but will still be delicious.

# CITRUS LAMB CUTLETS

Serves 4

*2 limes, rind and juice*
*1 lemon, rind and juice*
*2 tsp clear honey*
*4–8 lamb cutlets*
*15 g ( ½ oz) cornflour or beurre*
  *manié*
*slices of lemon and lime to garnish*

Mix the rind and juices with the honey and use to marinade the cutlets for a few hours or overnight if possible.

Heat the grill and then grill cutlets until cooked, but still pink in the middle, about 5–7 minutes a side. Place on serving dish and keep warm.

Make remains of marinade up to 275 ml (½ pint) with stock or water and thicken with cornflour or beurre manié. Serve the sauce over cutlets, or separately. Garnish the meat with lemon and lime slices.

Serve with chipped, jacket or duchesse potatoes.

# SHISH KEBABS

Serves 4

Marinade
6 tbsp olive oil
4 tbsp dry sherry or vermouth
2 cloves garlic, finely chopped
¼ tsp cayenne pepper
¼ Spanish onion, finely chopped
2 tbsp fresh (1 tbsp dried) herbs
    (preferably marjoram, basil,
    oregano and parsley mixed)
ground black pepper

450–700 g (1–1½ lb) cubed lamb,
    from the leg
8 baby onions
1 green pepper, core and seeds
    removed
1 red pepper, core and seeds removed
4 medium or 8 small tomatoes
100 g (4 oz) button mushrooms

Combine the marinade ingredients and mix with meat overnight. If marinading is done in a water-tight, sealed polythene container, it can be turned periodically to mix.

Parboil or fry the onions. Cut the peppers into pieces, and tomatoes in half unless small.

After marinading, assemble the ingredients on skewers to give an attractive variety, evenly divide between skewers. Brush the skewers with marinade and grill or barbecue until cooked, about 15 minutes. Turn frequently and rebrush with marinade during cooking.

Serve with boiled rice or rice salad, chunks of granary bread, jacket potatoes or fresh vegetables and salad.

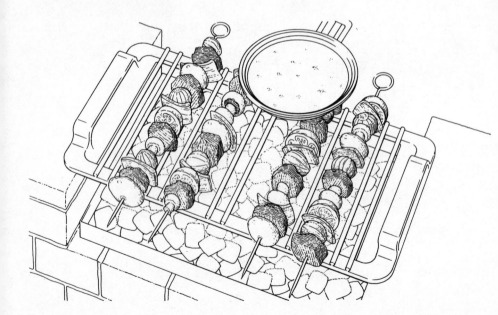

# PORK

This chapter includes a wide variety of
recipes from Chinese Sweet and Sour Pork to
Mendip Oggies

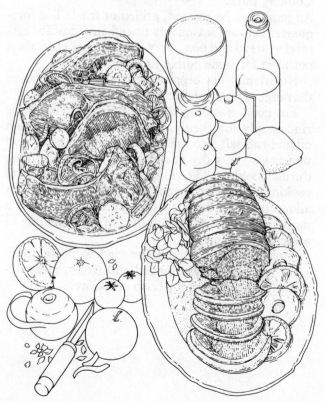

When buying, choose pork which is pale pink, firm, smooth and lean. Avoid pale watery looking meat. The fat should be firm and white. There is usually very little gristle, and increasingly the fat will have been trimmed away to give a lean product.

Although British pork is available all the year round, it becomes a particularly economical buy in the summer, when demand is traditionally at its lowest.

### Cooking pork.

All joints can be roasted, grilled or fried. The fore-quarter cuts are reasonably priced and ideal for casseroles, stews and pies. Very little of a pig's carcase is not used for some edible item.

No attempt has been made in this book to cover the range of pork products.

For good crackling, ask the butcher to score the rind deeply and evenly. Brush the cut surface with oil and rub salt into the scores. Roast with the rind uppermost, in a dry roasting tin, and do not baste during cooking. The rind can be removed prior to cooking and roasted separately in a hot oven. This allows the joint to be cooked more slowly, or by a moist method, but still producing the crackling to serve with the meat.

Moist methods require the rind to be removed prior to cooking. Marinaded and frozen meat frequently do not produce crisp crackling.

*Principal cuts of pork* In some areas, regional names may be found

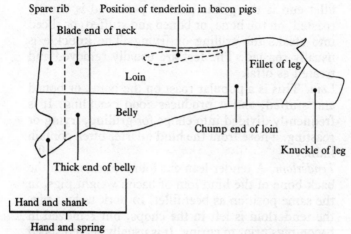

Spare rib
Position of tenderloin in bacon pigs
Blade end of neck
Loin
Fillet of leg
Belly
Chump end of loin
Knuckle of leg
Thick end of belly
Hand and shank
Hand and spring

## Cuts of pork

*Neck end* (spare ribs and blade bone). Sometimes called shoulder of pork, this large economical joint is particularly good when boned, stuffed and rolled. Often divided into blade and spare rib (not the cut used for barbecued spare ribs which is usually rib bones with a reasonable amount of meat left on). These small cuts can be roasted, braised or stewed. Spare rib is excellent for pies and spare rib chops are suitable for braising, grilling or frying.

*Hand and spring*. A large joint, often divided into hand and shank and thick end of belly. Suitable for roasting, casseroles and stews.

*Belly*. This is a long thin cut with streaks of fat and lean. Often thickly sliced as belly strips when it is ideally grilled or barbecued to remove some of the fat. Leaner belly can be used in casseroles and minced for pâtés and sausages. The thicker end can be stuffed and rolled for a very economical roast.

*Chump end of loin*. Usually sold in large, meaty chops, suitable for grilling, frying or roasting. It is sometimes sold as a roasting joint.

*Leg.* This is usually divided into *fillet end* and *knuckle end*, both of which can be cut into smaller joints. The fillet end is the prime joint of pork and is usually roasted, on the bone, or boned and stuffed, or sliced into steaks for grilling or frying. The knuckle is usually roasted. The feet are usually removed and treated as offal.

*Loin.* This is a popular roast on the bone, or boned and stuffed, and it produces good crackling. It is frequently divided into chops for grilling, frying or roasting. Those from the hind quarter often contain kidney.

*Tenderloin.* A tender lean cut found underneath the back bone of the hind loin of bacon weight pigs, in the same position as beef fillet. In pork weight pigs the tenderloin is left in the chops, but removed in bacon pigs prior to curing. It is usually served sliced or cubed for frying, or coating with a sauce. It needs little cooking. Although quite expensive per pound it has no wastage and no fat layer.

# PORK STIR FRY

Serves 4

450 g (1 lb) pork tenderloin or leg
  fillet, in thin strips
1 tbsp seasoned cornflour
1 clove garlic, finely chopped
4 tbsp oil
1 red pepper, cored and in strips
50 g (2 oz) mushrooms, sliced
100 g (4 oz) sweetcorn kernels,
  cooked
2 tbsp soy sauce

Toss the meat in the cornflour. Heat the garlic in oil in a frying pan or work, and when hot, stir fry meat until brown. Add the pepper and mushrooms, and continue stir frying until meat is cooked, approximately 10 minutes cooking altogether. Add the corn and fry to heat through.

Pour over the soy sauce and serve immediately with boiled brown rice or pasta.

# SWEET AND SOUR PORK

Serves 4

450 g (1 lb) lean cubed pork
2 tbsp cornflour
4 tbsp oil
1 onion, sliced
1 tbsp tomato purée
1 clove garlic, crushed
1 tbsp soy sauce
2 tbsp wine vinegar
2 tsp clear honey
1 tbsp dry sherry
275 ml (½ pint) light stock
25 g (1 oz) crystallised ginger,
    chopped
½ tsp allspice, ground
½ star anise (optional)
50 g (2 oz) dried apricots, soaked
50 g (2 oz) mushrooms, sliced
½ red pepper, cored and sliced

Coat the meat in cornflour. Heat the oil and fry the meat until browned. Remove and fry the onion until transparent. Return the meat to the pan and add all ingredients except the apricots, mushrooms and red pepper. Cover and simmer for 40 minutes. Add the remaining ingredients and simmer for a further 10–15 minutes until meat is cooked.

Serve with rice, or as part of a Chinese meal.

# PORK WITH RED CABBAGE

Serves 4

4 trimmed pork chops or shoulder
    steaks
450 g (1 lb) red cabbage, finely
    chopped
450 g (1 lb) cooking apples, peeled
    cored and sliced
225 g (8 oz) onions, sliced
2 cloves garlic, finely chopped
¼ tsp each nutmeg, allspice,
    cinnamon and thyme
black pepper
1 tsp orange rind, grated
juice of orange
2 tbsp wine vinegar
1 tbsp demerara sugar

Heat the oven to 180°C (350°F) mark 4. Grill the chops for a few minutes each side to brown. Layer the cabbage with apple, onions, garlic, spices and herbs, in a deep casserole. Add the pork chops on top.

Pour over the rind, juice and vinegar. Sprinkle sugar on top. Cover with a lid or foil and cook for 1 hour, or until meat and cabbage are cooked.

For a crisper top, remove cover for last 20 minutes cooking time.

# PORK CHOPS OR STEAKS WITH MUSTARD

Serves 4

1 tbsp dry mustard
1 tbsp demerara sugar
4 shoulder steaks, spare rib or loin
    chops
25 g (1 oz) shredded almonds,
    toasted
seasoning to taste
tomatoes and mushrooms grilled to
    garnish

Mix the mustard and sugar together and rub into chops, or blend with a little water, and spread over both sides of chops. Grill under a preheated grill until cooked, about 8 minutes a side.

Serve with almonds scattered on top, and halved tomatoes and mushrooms around.

# PORK AND PRUNE COBBLER

Serves 4–6

450 g (1 lb) lean, cubed pork
1 tbsp wholemeal flour
2 tbsp oil
1 onion, sliced
½ tsp ground allspice
½ tsp basil
275 ml (½ pint) dry cider
275 ml (½ pint) stock
225 g (8 oz) mixed root vegetables,
    diced (optional)
100 g (4 oz) prunes, soaked

Scone topping
225 g (8 oz) self-raising wholemeal
    flour (or add 1½ tsp baking
    powder to plain)
salt to taste
25 g (1 oz) margarine
bare 150 ml (¼ pint) milk or water

The stew can be made in the oven or simmered in a pan and transferred to a casserole dish to cook the 'cobbler' or scone topping. The same stew can be served with dumplings or in a pie.

Heat the oven if using to 180°C (350°F) mark 4. Toss the meat in flour and fry in oil until browned. Add the onion and fry a little longer. Stir in any remaining flour and blend in all other ingredients except the prunes. Either cover and simmer for 1½ hours or until meat is cooked, or turn into a casserole dish, cover and cook in the oven for a similar time. Add the prunes 20 minutes before the end of cooking.

Before making the topping, stir the meat well and ensure there is 5 cm (2 in) headroom in the casserole dish above the stew. Increase oven heat to 220°C (425°F) mark 7.

To make the scone mix, sieve the flour and baking powder (if used) with the salt, rub in the margarine and mix to a soft dough with the milk.

Knead lightly and using a floured board, roll out to 2 cm (¾ in) thick. Cut out 5 cm (2 in) rounds, and overlap these on top of the meat. Glaze with a little milk or beaten egg.

Bake for 30 minutes, or until scone mixture is risen and golden brown. If the meat was cold, cook for a little longer to heat the meat thoroughly. Cover scone topping with greaseproof paper to prevent overcooking.

# BRAISED PORK AND ORANGE

Serves 4–6

*1–1½ kg (2–3 lb) joint of pork,
  boned and rolled*
*25 g (1 oz) butter or margarine*
*1 onion, sliced*
*2 carrots, diced*
*2 parsnips, diced*
*1 chicken stock cube*
*275 ml (½ pint) orange juice*
*½ tsp mixed spice*
*¼ tsp Tabasco or Worcester sauce*

Garnish
*1 apple, cored and ringed*
*1 orange, peeled and sliced in rings*
*watercress*

Heat the oven to 170°C (325°F) mark 3. Fry the joint in butter, to brown. Remove and brown the onion, carrots and parsnips. Place vegetables in a large casserole dish and place meat on top.

Dissolve the stock cube in orange juice, add the spice and sauce. Pour over meat. Cover and cook slowly for 2–2½ hours until meat is tender. Check periodically that the liquor has not boiled away, topping up with a little water if necessary.

Poach the apple and orange for a few minutes, in orange juice or water. Serve the joint with the rings of fruit around it, and with watercress to garnish.

The vegetables and stock can be liquidised and used as a basis for a sauce or gravy, diluting and thickening with cornflour as required.

# PORK CHOPS IN FOIL

Serves 4

*butter or oil*
*450 g (1 lb) potatoes, thinly sliced*
*1 onion, finely sliced*
*4 pork chops or shoulder steaks*
*1 apple, cored and sliced*
*sage leaves, chopped*
*seasoning to taste*
*4 tbsp lemon juice*

Heat oven to 190°C (375°F) mark 5. Butter or grease with oil 4 pieces of foil approximately 25 cm (10 in) square. Divide the ingredients between the 4 pieces of foil, starting with a layer of potato, then onion, then the chop with apple on top. Add the sage, seasoning and lemon juice. Close up foil to form a parcel, and bake for 1 hour, or until meat is tender. For crisper, browner meat, foil can be opened up for last part of cooking.

Cooking can be speeded up by browning the meat first, parboiling potatoes and frying the onion. With this precooking, the parcels can be cooked on a barbecue in about 25–30 minutes, depending on its heat.

# PORK AND LIMES

Serves 4

*450 g (1 lb) cubed pork or 4 chops or*
*steaks*
*3 limes, rind and juice*
*1 chicken stock cube*
*1 tbsp soy sauce*
*bunch spring onions, cleaned*
*100 g (4 oz) button mushrooms*
*50–100 g (2–4 oz) bean sprouts*
*25–50 g (1–2 oz) cornflour to*
*thicken*
*1 lime, sliced to garnish*

Marinade the pork in lime juice and rind for several hours. Drain and measure lime juice. Make up to 575 ml (1 pint) with boiling water. Stir a stock cube into boiling water and lime juice. Add the stock and soy sauce to the meat, and simmer slowly for 1–1½ hours until meat is tender.

Fan the spring onions by cutting down the green part. Add the mushrooms, onions and bean sprouts, and simmer for a further 10–15 minutes so that the vegetables are just cooked, but still crisp. Thicken as necessary with cornflour, blended with a little water.

Serve garnished with sliced limes and accompanied with boiled rice.

# SOMERSET PORK TENDERLOINS

Serves 4

450–700 g (1–1½ lb) pork
    tenderloin
1 egg
2 tbsp breadcrumbs or flour
50 g (2 oz) butter or margarine
1 large onion, finely chopped
175 g (6 oz) mushrooms, sliced
275 ml (½ pint) dry cider
seasoning to taste
4 tbsp double cream
parsley to garnish

Cut the tenderloin into 8 pieces. Place each piece between greaseproof paper and beat with a mallet or rolling pin until ½ cm (¼ in) thick.

Coat the meat with egg and breadcrumbs. Heat the butter and fry the meat for about 4 minutes a side. Remove from the pan, drain well, and arrange on a serving dish and keep warm.

Add the onion and mushrooms to the pan and fry until soft. Stir in remaining flour or breadcrumbs and cook for 1 minute. Gradually blend in the cider and bring to the boil, season and adjust consistency if necessary.

Stir in the cream, heat but do not boil. Pour over the meat and garnish with chopped parsley.

Serve with boiled or jacket potatoes.

# PORK IN GINGER BEER

Serves 4

4 trimmed pork chops or steaks or
    450 g (1 lb) cubed pork
2 tbsp oil
1 onion, sliced
4 sticks celery, chopped
2 carrots, thinly sliced
25 g (1 oz) wholemeal flour
1 stock cube
425 ml (¾ pint) ginger beer
1 lemon, rind and juice
225 g (8 oz) tomatoes, skinned and
    quartered
seasoning to taste
2 tsp chopped crystallised ginger
    (optional)

Heat the oven to 180°C (350°F) mark 4. Fry the meat in the oil, to brown. Remove and place in a casserole dish. Fry the onion until transparent, stir in the celery, carrots and flour. Mix the stock cube with 4 tbsp of water. Blend in ginger beer, stock and lemon. Pour the mixture over the meat. Add the tomatoes, seasoning and ginger (optional). Cover and cook for 45–60 minutes until meat is tender.

Serve with boiled rice or potatoes.

# NORMANDY PORK

Serves 4

*4 thick slices of pork (shoulder
   steaks, chops)*
*1 tbsp flour*
*½ tsp sage leaves, chopped*
*3 tbsp oil or 25 g (1 oz) butter*
*3 onions, sliced*
*275 ml (½ pint) dry white wine,
   cider or stock*
*1 tbsp calvados or brandy*
*3 dessert apples, peeled, cored and
   sliced*
*seasoning to taste*

Heat the oven to 180°C (350°F) mark 4.
Coat the meat in flour mixed with sage. Fry
to brown in oil or butter and place in a
casserole dish. Fry the onions until
transparent. Add any remaining flour and
fry for a few minutes. Blend in the wine and
calvados. Pour over the meat. Add the
apples and seasoning. Cover and cook for 45
minutes or until meat is tender.

Serve with rice or boiled potatoes.

# STUFFED PORK CHOPS

Serves 4

*4 pork chops with bone removed*
*stuffing (see pages 87–89, apricot or
   apple go well)*
*450 g (1 lb) potatoes, scrubbed and
   sliced*
*1 small onion, finely chopped*
*¼ tsp ground mace*
*seasoning to taste*
*150 ml (¼ pint) single cream*
*100 g (4 oz) grated cheese (optional)
   or 15 g (½ oz) melted butter*

Heat the oven to 190°C (375°F) mark 5.
With a sharp pointed knife, slit chops
almost through, making a pocket. Divide
the stuffing between the 4 pockets. Part grill
or fry to brown the chops.

Parboil the potato slices for 2–3 minutes.
Arrange the potato slices in wide oven-proof
dish, sprinkling onion and mace between
layers. Season to taste. Pour over single
cream. Lay chops on top, pushing them
down into the potatoes. Sprinkle with
cheese (if cheese is not used, brush chops
with melted butter).

Bake for 1–1½ hours until meat is cooked
and the potato soft. If the meat gets too
brown, cover with foil.

# BACON AND HAM

A selection of bacon and ham recipes from
Bacon and Bean Bake to Boiled Ham and
Raisin Sauce.

Bacon is pork which has been treated with curing salts, a mixture of common salt (sodium chloride) and other permitted preservatives (saltpetre and other related substances), which give bacon its characteristic colour and flavour, and is essential for preserving the meat effectively.

*Storage.* Store loose bacon in the refrigerator, in 'cling-film', a polythene bag or rigid polythene container. Bacon can be kept like this for 10–14 days. Without a refrigerator, bacon will keep in a cool place for 4 days. Vacuum packs usually include a sell-by or best-before date and these should be adhered to. Once opened treat like loose bacon. Cooked ham, unless refrigerated, should be consumed within a day. With refrigeration and suitable packing, it can be kept for 2–3 days. Bacon can be frozen, although the salt in the meat accelerates the development of rancidity in the fat.

*Principal cuts of bacon.* In some areas regional names may be found and joints are sometimes subdivided.

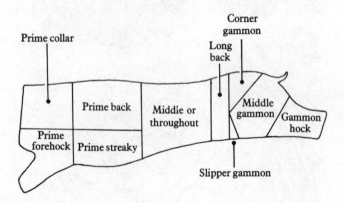

**Cuts of bacon** (weights where given are only approximate)

*Prime back.* This lean cut is normally sold as rashers, or boneless chops, which are usually grilled or fried. The chops can be baked or used in casseroles. A thick piece can be used for boiling or braising.

*Middle or through cut.* This is the back and streaky cut together, although in some localities it is cut into the two parts and sold separately. The through cut gives a long rasher with a mixture of lean and less lean meat and is an economical buy. It is used for grilling or a piece can be rolled and tied and used for boiling or baking, and is particularly good if stuffed before rolling.

*Long back.* Normally sold as fairly thin cut rashers, it is ideal for grilling or frying, but can be cubed for casseroles, pies and flans.

*Corner gammon.* This is a small, economical, triangular cut off the gammon, which is excellent boiled and served hot with a traditional sauce such as parsley. It is cheaper because of its rather awkward shape. It weighs about 1.8 kg (4 lb).

*Middle gammon.* A prime, lean and meaty cut for boiling, baking or braising whole, weighing about 2.25 kg (5 lb) but often sold as smaller joints. It can be cut into 1 cm (½ in) thick rashers for grilling or frying. *Slipper gammon* is sometimes cut from this joint and weighs about 700 g (1½ lb).

*Gammon hock.* Quite a high percentage of bone, especially at the lower end, but the meat is succulent and ideal for casseroles, soups and pies. Sometimes cut in half to give a reasonable boiling joint, ideal for a family meal. The hock is bought mainly for soup and stock. It weighs about 2 kg (4½ lb).

*Prime streaky.* These rashers combine lean with a percentage of fat in between. Look for a good proportion of lean. Excellent for grilling. Traditionally used to line pâté dishes and good for using in casseroles, pies, soups and rice dishes where carbohydrate helps to absorb the fat. A joint can be boiled and pressed. Streaky can be excellent value as it is the cheapest cut and with careful choosing can provide a filling meal, without necessarily having excess fat. Streaky usually contains little bits of cartilaginous bone, which should be cut out with scissors, along with the rind before cooking.

*Prime forehock*. This provides an economical meat to be cubed or minced for casseroles, meat loaves etc. It can be boiled, but is difficult to carve because of the position of the bones. Economical and weighing about 3.5 kg (8 lb) it is usually sold in smaller joints.

*Prime collar*. This makes an excellent joint boiled or braised as the bones are easily removed. It usually needs soaking as it can be rather salty. Collar is also sliced into rashers which are very lean. An inexpensive cut weighing about 2.5 kg (6 lb).

**Cooking with bacon**
Most joints are very versatile. When frying or grilling always remove the rind first. When boiling, some joints, notably the collar and hocks, may need soaking for a couple of hours to remove some of the salt. This is not always necessary with the larger, thicker joints, which today are usually less salty than was the taste a few years ago. The quick and mild cures definitely need no soaking. Where instructions are given these should be followed. Boiled joints are cooked with the rind on, this strips off easily when the meat is cooling. Baked joints usually benefit from a short period of boiling, so that the rind can be removed prior to baking. Slow baking with the meat wrapped in foil can produce a moist and succulent end result.

**Cooking times**

When baking, allow 20 minutes per 450 g (1 lb) and 20 minutes over for joints up to about 4.5 kg (10 lb). For larger joints only, allow 15 minutes per 450 g (1 lb).

When boiling, braising, casseroling or stewing, allow 20 minutes per 450 g (1 lb). Calculate the time from when the water comes to the boil. If using the oven, cover and cook at 180°C (350°F) mark 4.

When a combination of methods is used, the total time should be approximately 20 minutes per 450 g (1 lb). If meat has cooled down in between, allow a little for this.

# BACON STUFFED COURGETTES

Serves 4

8 medium courgettes, topped and tailed
1 large onion, chopped
25 g (1 oz) margarine or butter
450 g (1 lb) collar or forehock bacon, soaked
350 g (12 oz) tomatoes, peeled and chopped (or a tin of tomatoes)
1 tsp marjoram or mixed herbs
seasoning to taste

Heat the oven to 180°C (350°F) mark 4. Cut or scoop out flesh about halfway down into each courgette and use for soup or stew.

Fry the onion in the margarine until soft. Mince or finely chop the bacon, add to the pan and stir fry for about 10 minutes. Add the remaining ingredients and mix well. Divide the mixture equally and stuff the courgettes. If there is too much filling this can be put under the courgettes while baking. Place in an oven-proof dish and cover with a lid or foil. Bake for about 45 minutes until the courgette is cooked, but still crisp.

Serve with a tomato, pepper or cheese sauce and wholemeal bread or rolls.

A marrow or squash can be used in the same way, but allow about 1 hour for cooking.

# BACON AND BEAN BAKE

Serves 4

225 g (8 oz) rindless bacon, chopped
1 onion, sliced
1 clove garlic, crushed
2 tbsp tomato purée
2 tbsp parsley, chopped
2 tbsp soft brown sugar
225 g (8 oz) haricot beans, soaked
black pepper
stock

Heat the oven to 150°C (300°F) mark 2. Layer all ingredients in a deep casserole and add enough stock to cover them. Bake for about 4–5 hours until the beans are soft and the liquid has been absorbed. Check periodically and add more liquid if required.

The bake can be cooked overnight in an oven at 100°C (200°F) mark ½ or in a slow cooker (read manufacturer's instructions for time).

Serve with chunks of wholemeal, or granary bread and a side salad.

# HAM AND ASPARAGUS IN GRUYERE SAUCE

Serves 4

4 good slices of ham
225 g (8 oz) cooked asparagus

Sauce
25 g (1 oz) cornflour
25 g (1 oz) margarine or butter
275 ml (½ pint) milk
½ tsp powdered mustard
black pepper
¼ tsp paprika
2 tbsp cream (optional)
75 g (3 oz) gruyère cheese, grated
25 g (1 oz) wholemeal breadcrumbs
   to garnish

Heat the oven to 200°C (400°F) mark 6. Divide the asparagus between the ham slices and roll up. Place in an au gratin dish or other shallow oven-proof dish. Cover with foil. Put the rolls in the oven to heat through while the sauce is being made.

Make the sauce by heating the cornflour and margarine until the consistency is like that of a honeycomb, take off the heat then gradually add the milk. Return to the heat and boil for about 3 minutes until thick. Add all the other ingredients and stir until the cheese is melted. Do not boil once the cheese has been added or the cheese will go stringy and become indigestible.

Pour the sauce over the rolls and sprinkle with breadcrumbs. Return to the oven to brown.

The dish can be assembled and left and then heated and browned at the same time. This will take about 30–40 minutes.

# BACON, APPLE AND POTATO HOT POT

Serves 4

450 g (1 lb) bacon pieces or small
  joint, cubed
1 onion
450 g (1 lb) potatoes, scrubbed and
  quartered or sliced
225 g (8 oz) mixed root vegetables
  peeled and diced
2 eating apples, cored and thickly
  sliced
1 tsp sage leaves, chopped
275 ml (½ pint) stock
275 ml (½ pint) cider or more stock
chopped parsley to garnish

Heat the oven to 180°C (350°F) mark 4. Put all ingredients in a large casserole dish with well fitting lid and cook slowly until the meat is cooked, about 1½ hours. This recipe is ideal for a slow cooker (see manufacturer's instructions for times).

Serve garnished with the parsley.

An alternative way to assemble the dish is to mix all the ingredients together except the potatoes, and arrange these in a layer on the top. Remove the lid for last 30 minutes to brown the potatoes. Soaked butter or haricot beans can be substituted for the potatoes. No thickening is required with the potatoes or beans.

# BOILED HAM AND RAISIN SAUCE

Serving depends on joint size

bacon joint for boiling, soaked if
  necessary
1 onion, chopped
peppercorns and cloves

Sauce
25 g (1 oz) cornflour
425 ml (¾ pint) stock (water in
  which bacon was boiled may be
  too salty)
25 g (1 oz) seedless raisins
1 tsp Worcester sauce

Cover the joint with water and add the onion and spices. Bring to the boil and simmer for 20 minutes per ½ kg (or 1 lb) of bacon.

Just before the meat is cooked, make the sauce by blending the cornflour with the stock, adding the raisins and Worcester sauce and boiling until thickened. Remove the bacon when cooked, and remove the rind.

Serve separately as a joint with sauce, or carved in slices with the sauce poured over. One quantity of sauce serves up to 6 people. This dish is traditionally served with broad beans and carrots.

# HAM IN YOGHURT SAUCE WITH PASTA

*350 g (12 oz) wholemeal pasta*
*25 g (1 oz) cornflour*
*25 g (1 oz) margarine or butter*
*150 ml (¼ pint) milk or light stock*
*150 ml (¼ pint) natural yoghurt*
*¼ tsp ground mace*
*175 g (6 oz) cooked ham, in strips*
*½ green pepper in thin strips*
*50 g (2 oz) sweetcorn kernels, cooked*

Cook the pasta in slightly salted boiling water until soft, about 15 minutes. Drain well.

While the pasta is cooking, heat the cornflour and margarine together and cook for a few minutes until the mixture resembles a honeycomb. Slowly add the milk, yoghurt and mace. Add the ham, pepper and sweetcorn and heat through.

Spread the pasta around edge of a hot serving dish and heap the ham mixture in the middle. Garnish with grated cheese, breadcrumbs or a coloured salad vegetable. Serve immediately.

# BACON CHOPS WITH PINEAPPLE RINGS

Serves 4

*4 lean bacon chops (or gammon rashers)*
*1 small onion, finely chopped*
*15 g (½ oz) margarine or butter*
*1 level tbsp cornflour*
*1 small can pineapple rings, with juice*

With scissors, cut into fat around the chop or rasher, this prevents curling up during cooking. Grill or fry the chops until cooked, about 5–7 minutes per side.

Make the sauce by frying the onion in the margarine until soft, stirring in the cornflour and cooking for a few minutes, then gradually add the juice from the pineapple.

Just before the chops are cooked, add the pineapple rings to the pan and fry or grill to heat them through.

Serve the chops on a dish, garnished with the pineapple rings, with the sauce poured over. A watercress or grilled tomato garnish goes well with this dish.

Serve with fresh vegetables and chipped or jacket potatoes.

# COLD PARSLEYED HAM

Serves 4

450 g (1 lb) piece of ham, cubed
275 ml (½ pint) well flavoured stock
75 ml (3 fl oz) white wine
¼ tsp nutmeg
15 g (½ oz) 1 packet powdered
    gelatine
2 tbsp tarragon vinegar
3–4 tbsp parsley, finely chopped
cucumber and lettuce to garnish

Simmer the ham in stock, wine and nutmeg for 5 minutes, and leave to cool. Dissolve the gelatine in a little water by heating in a pan containing 2.5 cm (1 in) of water.

Strain the ham and add the stock to gelatine, followed by the vinegar. Use some gelatine mixture to paint the sides and bottom of a 1.2 litre (2 pint) mould or straight-sided dish. Sprinkle parsley liberally around the mould and leave to set. Leave the remainder of the gelatine until on the point of setting.

Mix the ham with the remainder of the parsley and tip into mould. Pour over the gelatine. Do not stir as this will disturb the coating. Leave in a cool place to set, preferably overnight.

When required, turn out and decorate with cucumber slices and twirls, or other appropriate garnish.

# PEAR, PRUNE AND HAM RISOTTO

Serves 4

225 g (8 oz) wholemeal rice
1 onion, chopped
2 tbsp oil
575 ml (1 pint) light stock
150 ml (¼ pint) white wine or more
    stock
½ tsp basil
1 eating pear
2 tbsp lemon juice
½ red or green pepper, deseeded and
    diced
225 g (8 oz) cooked ham, cubed
50 g (2 oz) prunes, soaked, destoned
    and halved

Fry the rice and onion in oil, in a strong based pan, until the rice begins to brown. Allow to cool slightly and add the stock, wine and basil. Bring to the boil and then lower the heat, cover with a lid and simmer for 20 minutes, or until rice is soft, but not collapsed.

Cut up the pear and toss in the lemon juice. Mix with the pepper. When the rice is cooked, add the ham, pear and prunes and heat through stirring all the time. Pile into a serving dish and decorate with rings of red or green pepper.

Serve hot or cold. Goes well with a green or mixed salad.

# MINCE

Mince is versatile and easy-to-use, make the
most of it using these recipes which include old
favourites and some that are more unusual

Always look for bright coloured, moist looking mince, avoiding that which is brown and dried with a lot of fat showing. The most usual type of mince to find is beef, but increasingly pork and, occasionally, lamb may be found. It is not necessary to buy meat ready minced. The increasing ownership of electric mixers with mincer attachments and food processors which chop the meat to mince in a few seconds, has encouraged many to buy the meat of their choice, and mince it at home. This appeals particularly to those who want very lean meat, or when less easily obtained meat such as veal or lamb are required. Purchased this way, mince is usually more expensive. The reason mince is normally so reasonably priced is that it utilises the trimmings from the carcase and the cheaper less popular cuts. This of course does not apply when you buy to mince it yourself.

Most recipes in this section can be made with any type of meat and experimentation is recommended. When a particular meat is more suitable, it is mentioned.

# BURGERS (WITH TOMATO SAUCE)

Serves 4–6

Burger
450 g (1 lb) minced beef or pork
50 g (2 oz) bacon, finely chopped
2 tsp capers, chopped
2 tbsp wholemeal breadcrumbs
pinch of cayenne pepper
1 tsp marjoram
1 egg

Combine all the burger ingredients together and form into a flat, circular shape. Fry in a little oil for about 10 minutes a side, or until well browned and cooked through. Keep hot until all the burgers are cooked.

Boil all the sauce ingredients together for 10–15 minutes or until the onion is cooked and the sauce is a suitable consistency.

Serve with the burgers piled down middle

Tomato sauce
450 g (1 lb) tomatoes, skinned and
    chopped, or large tin
1 onion, finely chopped
1 tsp sugar
1 tsp basil
1 tsp Worcester sauce

of serving dish, with the sauce poured over, or in a soft burger or picnic rolls with salad, tomato and chutney inside or to taste. Garnish with watercress and serve hot with salad (mixed bean goes very well) or fresh vegetables and jacket or chopped potatoes. The sauce can be used cold for picnics and packed lunches.

# LASAGNE

Serves 4

Sauce
575 ml (1 pint) milk
50 g (2 oz) cornflour
50 g (2 oz) grated cheese, preferably
    Edam or gruyère or cottage
¼ tsp nutmeg
seasoning

½ quantity bolognese sauce (see page
    81) with bacon and carrots
175 g (6 oz) lasagne or lasagne verdi
1 tbsp finely grated cheese
1 tbsp wholemeal breadcrumbs

To make the cheese sauce, heat the milk and blend the cornflour in a basin with a little water. When the milk is nearly boiling, pour onto the cornflour, stir well and return to pan and boil for about 3 minutes or until the sauce is thickened. The sauce should be a thin coating consistency. Add the cheese and nutmeg and season to taste. Heat the oven to 190°C (375°F) mark 5.

Ensure the bolognese mixture is fairly runny in consistency, adding a little water if necessary. The lasagne does not require previous cooking provided that the mixture has sufficient excess liquid for it to absorb. Arrange the meat, lasagne and sauce in layers in an oven-proof dish, starting with a layer of meat, and finishing with sauce. The dish should be fairly wide so that the mixture is not more than about 6 cm (2½ in) deep, but leave 1 cm (½ in) space at the top, or mixture will boil over.

Sprinkle on extra cheese and breadcrumbs and bake for 30 minutes or until brown and bubbling; garnish with sliced tomato. Serve with fresh vegetables or salad.

# STUFFED PANCAKES WITH CHEESE SAUCE

Serves 4–6

**Batter**
100 g (4 oz) wholemeal flour
¼ tsp salt
1 egg
275 ml (½ pint) milk or milk and
    water
vegetable oil for frying

**Filling**
1 small onion, finely chopped
1 tbsp oil
225 g (8 oz) lean mince
3 rashers bacon, chopped
3 tomatoes, skinned and chopped
100 g (4 oz) mushrooms, chopped
1 tsp marjoram
pinch cayenne pepper
ground black pepper to taste
½ red pepper, chopped

**Cheese sauce**
25 g (1 oz) wholemeal flour
25 g (1 oz) butter or margarine
275 ml (½ pint) milk
¼ tsp mustard
pinch of grated nutmeg
50 g (2 oz) grated cheese, preferably
    Edam, gruyère or cottage
wholemeal breadcrumbs

*Pancakes*
Sieve the flour and salt into a bowl and break the egg into a well in the centre. Gradually add half the milk, beating it into the flour with a wooden spoon. Beat for about 3 minutes then beat in the remaining milk. Leave to stand for 1 hour if possible. Cook the pancakes in a 20 cm (8 in) frying pan. Ensure the pan is well seasoned by heating it with a little oil, then rubbing well with salt and wiping out with a damp cloth. Run a little oil around the pan, and when hot run a little batter around the pan, to cover the bottom. The pancake should be thin and lacy. The mixture may need a few tablespoons of water added to thin it down. Cook over a high heat until the pancake comes away slightly from the edge. Carefully turn over using a palette knife, or by tossing. The second side needs only about 15 seconds. Remove the pancake from the pan, and keep warm in a pile if using immediately, or spread out until cold, if using later. Pancakes freeze very well.

*Filling*
Fry the onion in the oil until transparent. Add the mince and bacon, and fry to brown. Add the remaining ingredients and stir fry for about 7 minutes or until all the ingredients are cooked. Divide the mixture evenly between the pancakes and roll up, placing full rolls in an oven-proof dish.

*Sauce*
Cook the flour and fat for a few minutes. Gradually add the milk and cook until thick. Add the mustard, nutmeg and cheese, and stir until melted. Coat the pancakes with sauce, sprinkle with a mixture of cheese and breadcrumbs and

grill until golden brown. If the pancakes and filling are cold, reheat and brown at the same time in an oven at 190°C (375°F) mark 5 for 30 minutes.

# MINCE AND TOMATO PIE

Serves 4

225 g (8 oz) *wholemeal mixer pastry*
225 g (8 oz) *mince*
1 onion, *chopped*
25 g (1 oz) *wholemeal flour*
1 tsp *basil*
225 g (8 oz) *tomatoes, skinned and chopped*
black pepper
150 ml (¼ pint) *stock*
1 beaten egg

The pastry is best made well in advance and chilled. Mix the mince and chopped onion and heat gently in a pan to melt the fat in the meat. When the fat runs, turn up the heat and brown the meat. Stir in the flour and cook for a few minutes. Add the other ingredients apart from the egg and simmer for 45 minutes, taking care not to boil dry, adding more water if necessary (cooks well in a microwave oven in 10–15 minutes). Cool well. This dish can be made the day before if required.

Heat the oven to 200°C (400°F) mark 6. Divide the pastry in two and use half to line the bottom of a 20 cm (8 in) greased flan ring or foil dish. Pack in cold meat mixture. Cover with remaining pastry using water to seal. Knock up the edges by making horizontal cuts with the back of a knife, then scollop by bringing up the back of the knife every 4 cm (1½ in). Pierce the top, decorate with pastry leaves and glaze with beaten egg. Bake for 40 minutes or until pastry is golden brown and firm.

Serve hot or cold. Ideal for picnics and packed lunches.

# CHILLI CON CARNE

Serves 4–6

*100–175 g (4–6 oz) red kidney*
  *beans, soaked overnight*
*1 onion, chopped*
*1 tbsp vegetable oil*
*350–450 g (12–16 oz) minced beef*
  *or lamb*
*2 cloves garlic, crushed*
*1–2 tsp chilli powder (to taste)*
*400 g (14 oz) tin tomatoes, chopped*
*150 ml (¼ pint) beef stock*
*2 tbsp tomato purée*
*ground pepper to taste*

Boil the soaked beans in plenty of water for 20 minutes. Discard the water. Fry the onion in oil until transparent. Add the meat and fry to brown. Add the remaining ingredients and stir well. Add the cooked beans and simmer with the lid on for 30 minutes until the meat is cooked and the beans are soft but not collapsed. Adjust seasoning and serve on or with cooked wholemeal rice and a salad.

The flavour improves if it is made the day before and kept in the refrigerator. Tinned beans can be used and stirred in 5 minutes before the end of cooking.

Red kidney beans must be boiled for at least 10 minutes before eating, to ensure any mould that *might* be present is destroyed. Once this has been done, they are perfectly safe to eat, without further cooking, in salads. Tinned beans have already been cooked during the canning process.

# MINCE WITH CRANBERRIES AND ORANGES

Serves 4

*1 onion, chopped*
*1 tbsp vegetable oil*
*450 g (1 lb) lean mince*
*25 g (1 oz) wholemeal flour*
*275 ml (½ pint) stock*
*1 tsp oregano*
*1 orange, grated rind and juice*
*75 g (3 oz) cranberries, fresh or*
  *frozen*

Fry the onion in oil over a low heat, until it is transparent. Stir in the meat, turn up the heat and brown. Stir in the flour, gradually add the stock and remaining ingredients, except the cranberries. Cover and simmer for 20 minutes.

Add the cranberries and cook for a further 15 minutes or until the meat is tender. The cranberries should remain whole, but soft.

Serve with jacket potatoes as a filling, wholemeal rice or pasta, or as a pie filling.

# RISOTTO MILANESE

Serves 4–6

1 onion, chopped
2 cloves garlic, crushed
3 tbsp oil
225 g (8 oz) wholegrain brown rice
225 g (8 oz) beef mince
100 g (4 oz) bacon, chopped
400 g (14 oz) tin tomatoes, chopped
2 tbsp tomato purée
½ tsp oregano
½ tsp tarragon
100 g (4 oz) sweetcorn kernels
seasoning to taste
425 ml (¾ pint) stock or stock and
   white wine mixed
chopped parsley to garnish

Fry the onion and garlic in oil for 3–5 minutes until transparent. Add the rice and stir fry until brown, add the beef and fry for 5 minutes. Add all the ingredients and simmer until the rice is cooked, about 15 minutes. Alternatively the mixture can be cooked in an oven heated to 190°C (375°F) mark 5 for 40–50 minutes, depending on the thickness of the dish.

Serve hot or cold garnished with parsley.

Instead of mince any type of cooked meat can be used. Cut it up in cubes, and stir in just before rice is cooked, for 5 minutes cooking.

# BOLOGNESE SAUCE FOR PASTA

Serves 4

1 onion, chopped
1 tbsp vegetable oil
1–2 cloves garlic, crushed
450 g (1 lb) lean mince
2 tbsp tomato purée
400 g (14 oz) tin tomatoes, chopped
275 ml (½ pint) stock
1 tsp honey
1 tbsp wine vinegar
1 tsp basil
1 tsp oregano
black pepper
50–100 g (2–4 oz) streaky bacon,
   chopped (optional)
100 g (4 oz) carrots, finely diced
   (optional)
50–75 g (2–3 oz) spaghetti or pasta
   per person
Parmesan cheese, grated to garnish

Fry the onion slowly in oil to soften. Add the garlic and meat and fry to brown. Stir in the purée, tomatoes, stock and remaining ingredients. Simmer in a covered pan for about 30 minutes, adding more water if the mixture becomes too dry.

Meanwhile cook the spaghetti in plenty of boiling, slightly salted water for 12–15 minutes until it is tender but still firm to bite. Wholemeal pasta may take a few minutes more. Fresh spaghetti is usually cooked in about 5 minutes. The pasta may be tossed in a little butter.

Serve the meat piled in the centre of spaghetti or pasta, sprinkled with cheese; it is excellent with a side salad.

# CURRIED OR INDIAN MINCE FILLING

Serves 4–8

1 tart apple
lemon juice
1 onion, chopped
1 tbsp vegetable oil
450 g (1 lb) lean minced beef or
    lamb
25 g (1 oz) wholemeal flour
275 ml (½ pint) beef stock
1 tsp each turmeric, ground
    coriander and ground cumin
3–6 whole cardomon seeds
1 tbsp mustard pickle
25 g (1 oz) seedless raisins
1 tbsp red currant jelly
1 banana, sliced

Core and chop the apple and coat in lemon juice. Fry the onion in the oil until transparent, add the meat and brown. Stir in the flour, and blend in stock. Add the spices, pickle, raisins and jelly and simmer, with lid on for 45 minutes. If mixture gets too dry, add more water.

Ten minutes before the end of cooking, add the cored and chopped apple. When cooked, stir in banana and warm through.

Serve sprinkled with coconut in hot pitta bread; pancakes, optionally with a sauce to coat them; jacket potatoes; vol-au-vents; or as a pie filling; with side dishes such as sliced tomato, grated carrot and mango chutney.

# BEEF AND SPINACH MEATLOAF

Serves 4–6

225 g (8 oz) fresh spinach leaves,
    destalked
350 g (12 oz) mince (pork is
    excellent)
50 g (2 oz) mushrooms, finely
    chopped
50 g (2 oz) wholemeal breadcrumbs
1 onion, grated
1 clove garlic, crushed
1 tsp oregano
3 eggs, soft boiled (shelled) or
    poached

Heat the oven to 190°C (375°F) mark 5. Blanch the spinach in boiling water for 1 minute. Drain well. Grease a 1 kg (2 lb) loaf tin. Line the sides and base with spinach leaves, allowing them to hang over the edges, to be wrapped over when the filling is added.

Combine all ingredients except the eggs. Place half carefully in the tin, without disturbing the spinach. Make wells in the meat and place in eggs. Cover with the remaining meat, flatten the top, and fold over the spinach leaves to cover the meat.

Cover with foil or greaseproof paper. Bake for 1 hour until the meat is cooked. Turn out on to a serving dish and serve, sliced; this is delicious hot or cold and goes well with a tomato, spicy or curry sauce.

# MOUSSAKA

Serves 4–6

2 medium aubergines, sliced
2 tbsp vegetable oil
15 g ( ½ oz) butter
1 large onion, sliced
1 clove garlic, crushed
450 g ( 1 lb) minced meat (usually
    lamb)
1 tsp ground allspice or cinnamon
2 tbsp parsley, chopped
3 tbsp tomato purée
450 g ( 1 lb) potatoes, sliced and
    parboiled
150 ml ( ¼ pint) water or stock

Sauce
25 g ( 1 oz) butter or margarine
40 g ( 1 ½ oz) cornflour
425 ml ( ¾ pint) milk
seasoning
1 egg

Fry the aubergine slices in oil and butter until browned on both sides. Fry in batches, if necessary using a little more fat. Remove when browned and drain on absorbent paper.

Add the onion and garlic to the pan and fry for a few minutes. Add the meat and brown, then add the spice, parsley and purée.

Make the sauce by cooking the fat and cornflour together for a few minutes, gradually adding the milk and reheating and then boiling for 3–5 minutes until the sauce has thickened. Season and when cool, beat in the egg.

Heat the oven to 190°C (375°F) mark 5. Assemble the moussaka in a deep oven-proof dish with alternating layers of aubergine, meat and potato. Add the water. Pour over the sauce, and bake for 30 minutes until golden brown.

Serve hot or cold with fresh vegetables or a salad. It is particularly good with a sliced tomato and chive salad.

# MEATBALLS WITH SOURED CREAM

Serves 4–6

*75 g (3 oz) wholemeal bread*
*150 ml (¼ pint) milk or tomato juice*
*350 g (12 oz) mince*
*2 cloves garlic, crushed*
*2 tbsp parsley, chopped*
*2 tbsp curry powder or 1 tbsp*
  *anchovy essence or 2 tbsp tomato*
  *purée*
*flour for shaping*
*oil (if fried)*
*150 ml (¼ pint) soured cream*

Soak the bread in the milk or juice. Mash with all other ingredients except the soured cream. Form into balls approximately 2.5 cm (1 in) in diameter using flour to prevent sticking. Fry for 6–8 minutes or bake in an oven 180°C (350°F) mark 4 for 30 minutes. Pile on to a serving dish and top with soured cream.

Serve with chunks of wholemeal or granary bread and salad or fresh vegetables, or on a bed of buttered noodles.

# BOBOTIE

Serves 4

*2 onions, sliced*
*2 tbsp oil*
*450 g (1 lb) minced meat, beef or*
  *pork*
*1 tbsp curry powder*
*1 tsp mixed herbs*
*2 tsp soft brown sugar*
*½ tsp salt*
*1 tbsp vinegar*
*1 tbsp lemon juice*
*2 eggs*
*100 g (4 oz) wholemeal bread*
*275 ml (½ pint) milk*
*25 g (1 oz) flaked almonds, toasted*

Heat the oven to 200°C (400°F) mark 6. Fry the onions in oil until soft. Stir in the meat and fry until brown. Add the curry powder, herbs, sugar, salt, vinegar and lemon juice. Beat in *one* egg. Soak the bread in milk. Drain off excess milk and beat together with other egg. Beat the soaked bread with the meat mixture. Pour into a deep oven-proof dish. Pour the egg and milk mixture over the meat and sprinkle with almonds. Bake for 30 minutes, reduce oven to 180°C (350°F) mark 4 for a further 30 minutes.

Serve with fresh vegetables or a salad, with potatoes, rice or pasta.

This dish can be made with cooked meat, in which case only cook for 30 minutes.

# STUFFED CABBAGE OR VINE LEAVES

Serves 4–6

225 g (8 oz) minced cooked meat
225 g (8 oz) cooked rice (75 g/3 oz)
  uncooked)
2–3 spring onions, chopped
1 level tsp caraway seeds
25 g (1 oz) cashew or pine kernel
  nuts, chopped
1 tbsp tomato purée
1 egg
20–30 small cabbage or vine leaves
575 ml (1 pint) light stock or wine
  and stock mixture
4 tbsp oil

Heat the oven to 150°C (300°F) mark 2.
Combine all the ingredients, except for the
leaves, stock and oil, to form the stuffing.

Blanch the leaves in boiling water until
pliable, about 2 minutes. It is sometimes
easier to remove cabbage leaves without
them tearing if the whole cabbage is boiled
for a few minutes, then a few leaves
removed and the process repeated.

Divide the mixture between the leaves,
ensuring there is not too much in each so
that a good tight roll can be achieved. Roll
up the leaves, tucking the sides in to form
compact parcels. Pack closely together in an
oven-proof dish, forming a second layer if
necessary. Mix the stock and oil and pour
over the leaves. Cover with a lid or foil and
cook for 1 hour until the stock has been
absorbed.

Serve hot with a sauce such as tomato, or
well chilled as a starter or buffet dish.

# STUFFINGS AND ACCOMPANIMENTS

This chapter shows how to make a variety of
stuffings, marinades, sauces and pastries

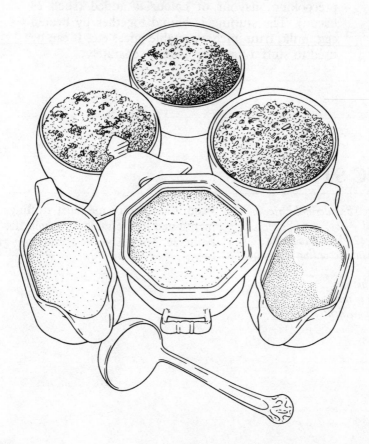

**Stuffings**

Stuffings, farces and forcemeats are usually based on either fresh breadcrumbs, which can be brown or white, cooked rice, oatmeal or rolled oats or starchy vegetables and nuts such as potatoes and chestnuts.

To this base can be added any ingredients to give flavour and/or succulence; these are frequently chopped onion, herbs and spices, savoury sauces and sometimes finely minced meat such as sausage meat, veal or pork, or chopped bacon rashers. Any combination can be tried. As a general rule, precook the ingredients which will not cook during the cooking time of the meat (this usually includes onion) or if by precooking, flavour or colour is added (such as bacon). The stuffing is bound together by beaten egg, milk, fruit juice, vegetable juices etc. It can be used to stuff a joint, or cooked separately.

# BASIC STUFFING

*100 g (4 oz) breadcrumbs, rice or
    oatmeal*
*50–100 g (2–4 oz) flavouring
    ingredients according to type of
    stuffing*
*1–2 tbsp herbs*
*seasoning to taste*
*binding ingredient*

From the basic recipe most stuffings mentioned in the table on pages 104–5 can be made. Some specific recipes are given below.

# BRAZIL AND DRIED PEACH STUFFING

*100 g (4 oz) Brazil nuts*
*100 g (4 oz) dried peaches or prunes*
*1 onion, finely chopped*
*25 g (1 oz) butter or margarine*
*100 g (4 oz) wholemeal breadcrumbs*
*1 tsp allspice, ground*
*1 tbsp parsley, chopped*
*1 tsp orange rind, finely grated*
*2 tbsp sherry*
*1 egg*

Finely chop or mill the Brazil nuts. Soak the peaches and then chop them.

Fry the onion in the butter until cooked. Combine all the ingredients.

This stuffing is suitable for all meats and poultry.

# APRICOT AND PINE KERNEL STUFFING

*100 g (4 oz) apricots, soaked and*
*   chopped*
*1 onion, grated*
*25 g (1 oz) pine kernels or cashew*
*   nuts*
*25 g (1 oz) sunflower seeds*
*1 tbsp fresh herbs, chopped*
*1 egg*
*seasoning to taste*
*25 g (1 oz) melted butter (optional)*

Combine all the ingredients together.

The pine kernels and sunflower seeds can be substituted by any other chopped unsalted nuts.

# VEAL FORCEMEAT (STUFFING)

*100 g (4 oz) fresh breadcrumbs*
*25 g (1 oz) butter, melted, or suet,*
*   shredded*
*1 tbsp parsley, chopped*
*½ tsp thyme*
*rind and juice of ½ lemon*
*¼ tsp ground nutmeg or mace*
*beaten egg to mix*
*100 g (4 oz) lean sausage meat,*
*   minced veal or pork (optional)*
*1 onion, finely chopped and fried*
*   (optional)*

Combine all the ingredients and use to stuff a joint, or escalopes of meat. The stuffing can be made into forcemeat balls and baked or fried to accompany meat.

This stuffing is very suitable for lighter meats.

# RICE STUFFING

100 g (4 oz) cooked rice
50 g (2 oz) sultanas
4 rashers streaky bacon, grilled and
    chopped
1 lamb's kidney, grilled and chopped
½ tsp rosemary, chopped
1 tsp lemon rind
seasoning to taste
egg or egg yolk to mix

Combine all the ingredients in a bowl with sufficient egg to bind them together.

Use to stuff joints and escalopes, or cook in a separate dish to serve with meat.

Stuffing balls coated in egg and breadcrumbs make an unusual starter when deep fat fried and served with a tomato or piquant sauce.

# WALNUT AND ORANGE STUFFING

1 onion, chopped
25 g (1 oz) butter or margarine
2 tsp ground coriander
grated rind of 1 orange
50 g (2 oz) walnuts, chopped
75 g (3 oz) raisins, chopped
75 g (3 oz) fresh breadcrumbs
1 tbsp parsley, chopped
seasoning to taste
2 tbsp orange juice
beaten egg to mix

Fry the onion in butter until soft and golden. Mix all ingredients in a bowl, with sufficient egg to bind together.

Use to stuff pork, veal or lamb, or to make stuffing balls.

# WATERCRESS OR MINT STUFFING

1 onion, chopped
25 g (1 oz) butter or margarine
50–100 g (2–4 oz) streaky bacon,
    chopped and fried (optional)
4 tbsp mint, chopped or 6 tbsp
    watercress, chopped
½ tsp ground allspice
100 g (4 oz) fresh breadcrumbs

Fry the onion in butter until soft and golden. Fry the bacon (optional). Mix all the ingredients together in a bowl, using a little milk if mixture will not bind together.

Use to stuff joints, or escalopes of meat, especially lamb.

# BEURRE MANIE (KNEADED BUTTER)

*25 g (1 oz) butter or margarine*
*50 g (2 oz) plain flour*

Knead the fat and flour together, and add small knobs to the casserole or pan, off the heat. Stir well and boil for a few minutes to cook the flour.

This is used as a liaison or thickener for soups, stews and sauces. It can be used instead of making a roux, or instead of using blended cornflour to adjust the consistency before serving.

# BASIC BROWN SAUCE

*1 onion, finely chopped*
*1 carrot, finely chopped or grated*
*40 g (1½ oz) cooking fat*
*40 g (1½ oz) flour*
*575 ml (1 pint) water*
*1 bay leaf*
*¼ tsp mixed herbs*
*seasoning to taste*

Fry the onion and carrot in the fat until well browned. Stir in flour and cook for 2–3 minutes. Slowly add the water and stir well.

Add the herbs and seasoning and simmer gently for about 30 minutes. Strain and use as required, thinning if necessary for gravy, and boiling to reduce if a thicker sauce is required.

# BASIC WHITE SAUCE

*25 g (1 oz) butter or margarine*
*25 g (1 oz) flour or cornflour*
*275 ml (½ pint) milk for a coating*
*sauce or 425 ml (¾ pint) for a*
*pouring sauce*

Melt the fat in a small pan. Stir in the flour and mix well. This mixture is called a roux. Cook gently for 2–3 minutes until the mixture appears to resemble a honeycomb. Remove from the heat and gradually add the milk, stirring well and heating between each addition. Boil gently for 3–4 minutes until the sauce is required consistency and smooth and glossy.

A roux can be stored in a refrigerator for a few weeks, and a little used as required to make sauces, or thicken soups and stews.

Use as a basis for such sauces as caper, mushroom, cheese, mustard, as well as sweet sauces, by the addition of the appropriate ingredients. Cream, yoghurt, sherry, brandy etc can all be beaten in just before using. Heat, but do not boil after the addition of cream or yoghurt.

# STOCK

*1 kg (2 lb) bones, sawn or chopped*
   *(do not use bacon bones)*
*1 onion, chopped*
*2 carrots, sliced*
*1 stick celery, chopped*
*small piece of turnip*
*1 bay leaf*
*bouquet garni, or bunch of herbs*
*4 peppercorns*

Put bones in a large lidded pan, cover with water and bring to the boil. Skim off any scum if necessary.

Add all the other ingredients, and simmer very slowly for 2–3 hours, or pressure cook for 45–60 minutes. Strain, discarding bones etc and use as required.

The stock must be cooled quickly and stored in a refrigerator, and reboiled for 10 minutes before use. It can be frozen in suitably sized containers.

For gravy and some sauces a strong stock is required. For this, boil to reduce the volume and concentrate the flavour. A darker stock may be obtained by frying the bones and vegetables to brown prior to stewing.

# MARINADE FOR RED MEATS

*150 ml (¼ pint) red wine*
*2–4 tbsp vegetable oil*
*1 onion, finely chopped*
*½ tsp marjoram*
*½ tsp basil*
*1 bay leaf*
*dash cayenne*
*salt and pepper to taste*
*1 clove of garlic, crushed or chopped*

Combine all the ingredients, and steep the meat in the marinade for at least 2 hours, turning frequently.

The remaining marinade can be used as a basis for the cooking liquor, or as an accompanying sauce. If this is to be the case, use the lesser amount of oil.

# MARINADE FOR WHITE OR LIGHT MEATS

*150 ml (¼ pint) white wine*
*2–4 tbsp vegetable oil*
*1 onion, finely chopped*
*1 carrot, in thin rings*
*½ tsp thyme*
*1 tbsp fresh, chopped parsley*
*1 bay leaf*
*½ tsp sugar*
*1 clove garlic, crushed or chopped*

Combine all the ingredients and steep meat in the marinade for at least 2 hours, turning frequently. It can be used to baste during cooking, in which case use the greater amount of oil.

# HOT LEMON AND HONEY MARINADE

*150 ml (¼ pint) lemon juice*
*2 tbsp white wine vinegar*
*1 heaped tbsp clear honey*
*1 onion, finely chopped*
*1 bay leaf*
*1 tbsp chopped verbena, if*
  *available, or mint*
*1 tbsp fresh parsley, chopped*
*freshly ground black pepper*
*2–4 tbsp oil*

Slowly heat all ingredients to boiling point. Use 4 tbsp of oil if using as a baste as well. Stir well to dissolve the honey. Pour over cubed meat and allow to cool.

This is an excellent marinade for pork or poultry which is to be barbecued. The hot marinade impregnates the meat with flavour quicker than does a cold marinade.

# FLAKY PASTRY

*175 g (6 oz) margarine and white*
  *vegetable fat mixed*
*225 g (8 oz) plain flour*
*¼ tsp salt*
*150 ml (¼ pint) cold water*

Blend the fats together and divide in four portions. If using polyunsaturated margarine and white fat, refrigerate well before using, or use straight from the freezer, and return the pastry to the refrigerator between each rolling, for 20 minutes.

Sieve the flour and salt and rub in one portion of the fat. Mix to a soft dough with the water, knead lightly until smooth. Leave, covered with a polythene bag, in the refrigerator for 10–20 minutes. Roll out to an oblong, about 30 cm × 10 cm (12 in × 4 in).

Flake on a portion of fat, to cover the top two-thirds of pastry leaving a good margin. Fold the pastry in three, folding first the unlarded third up, then the larded top third down. Press edges together to seal. Cool.

Give the pastry a half turn and roll out again, repeating the inclusion of fat and the rolling and folding process, so that the folded, closed edge is on your left. Continue until all fat is used, then repeat the rolling and folding, with no fat included.

After shaping, a better finished result will be obtained if the assembled dish is refrigerated for 10 minutes prior to cooking.

Cook at 220°C (425°F) mark 7 unless recipe states otherwise. Small items take about 15 minutes, larger ones longer, according to fillings.

# MIXER PASTRY

75 g (3 oz) polyunsaturated
  margarine
100 g (4 oz) plain wholemeal flour
100 g (4 oz) self-raising white or
  wholemeal flour
3 tbsp cold water

Using a small hand mixer, mix together the margarine with 2 tbsp of water and half of the flour. The mixture will resemble that of a cake rather than a usual pastry one. Cut and fold in the remaining flour with a little more water only if it is necessary to make a pliable consistency. Refrigerate well before using.

Use and bake as shortcrust pastry at 200°C (400°F) mark 6.

For cheese pastry fold in 50–75 g (2–3 oz) finely grated cheese, with ¼ tsp mustard and a dash of cayenne with the flour.

# FISH AND SEAFOOD

# INTRODUCTION

Fish is an important source of food. It is nourishing and very quick to prepare. In these health-conscious days, it is important to remember that fish is an excellent source of protein, vitamins and minerals, and that fish oil is polyunsaturated, which helps to lower the body's cholesterol level. Calorific value varies, with 100 g (4 oz) of herring having 190 calories compared to 90 calories in the same amount of sole, but this compares to 350 calories for the same quantity of lamb chop.

There are so many different varieties of fish that menus can be endlessly changed, and a couple of fish meals a week can scarcely be a hardship. Even those who prefer meat will not scorn a fish cocktail or pâté to start a meal, while flans and sandwiches may incorporate fish in a way which appeals to the young eater.

There is a fishmonger in most towns, while villages are often served by a travelling van. Supermarkets now often have a fresh fish department or a special chilled cabinet. However, we need never be deprived of fish in even the most remote areas, for there is now a wide variety of frozen fish available, as well as that traditional favourite – smoked fish. There is also canned fish which is nutritious and tasty and can be turned into some splendid meals.

In this book you will find more than a hundred recipes for fish and their accompanying sauces, about enough for two meals a week to last a whole year. It is hoped that you will want to cook some of them even more often because they will quickly become family favourites.

### Choosing and using fish

Frozen and canned fish will have been prepared to exacting standards, so there is no problem in choosing the required quality. Fresh fish, however, needs to be chosen with care and there are one or two easy points to remember.

*White fish fillets* should be a white translucent colour and a neat shape.

*Whole fish* should have clear bright eyes, shiny colourful skin, firm flesh and a fresh sea smell.

*Smoked fish* should have a fresh smoky smell, and the fillets should be neat and firm.

*Shellfish* should be undamaged in shells and closed tightly without cracks. Ready-cooked shellfish should be moist with a fresh look and smell.

### Preparation and storage

A good fishmonger will clean, bone and fillet fish if required, and will also skin fillets or whole fish if necessary. He has the expertise and the sharp knife to do the job, and will always be happy to co-operate with special preparation if you have an unusual dish in mind (but don't expect too much attention on a busy weekend morning).

Fresh fish should be used as soon as possible, but may be stored in the refrigerator overnight if washed, patted dry and covered.

Frozen fish should be stored at −18°C (0°F) or colder, as indicated on the packet. Usually frozen fish may be cooked immediately, but if it is to be defrosted, this is best done overnight in the refrigerator. It should not be thawed in water as it will quickly lose texture, flavour and nutritional value. Fish from the fishmonger should not be frozen, but fish straight from the sea or river may be frozen at home.

### Types of fish

One of the advantages of choosing fish is that many species are interchangeable. Whole fish may be bought, as well as fillets and steaks. Fish are basically divided into white and oily varieties. Some white and oily fish are also sold smoked or salted. Shellfish is now often known as 'seafood' and for culinary purposes may be recognised as being of the crustacea or mollusc type.

*White fish*. There are two types of white fish, divided into flat and round. Large round species such as cod and coley may be sold whole or prepared as fillets, steaks or cutlets. The smaller round fish such as whiting and haddock may be whole or filleted. All these round fish are interchangeable in recipes, varying slightly in flavour and texture.

Large flat fish like turbot and halibut are very special, and may be whole or in fillets and steaks, trimmed as required. The smaller flat fish include plaice, Dover sole and lemon sole, sold whole or in fillets.

Unusual flat fish include the monkfish (anglerfish) of which only the tail is eaten, tasting rather like scampi and with a similar texture. Skate is another delicious flat fish, of which the 'wings' are generally sold, ready-skinned. Odd round fish include the conger eel, the rather ugly John Dory, grey mullet, and red mullet which has a slightly 'gamey' flavour and is usually eaten uncleaned. If you do not recognise these fish, the fishmonger will be glad to tell you about them and to prepare them for cooking.

*Oily fish*. These tend to be smaller than other species, and are a particularly rich source of vitamins A and D. Herring, mackerel and sprat are the most commonly found, and they are sold whole, though often boned or filleted for cooking. Salmon also comes into this group.

*Smoked and salted fish*. Some white fish may be smoked, particularly cod, haddock and whiting, although smoked halibut is sometimes found, and is a great delicacy. Smoked salmon and trout are often regarded as special occasion fish. The herring is one of the most adaptable fish, being salted or marinated, but also being smoked and appearing as the kipper or bloater. The small sprat may also be smoked and served on special occasions. In recent times, mackerel has become a very popular smoked fish, and may be prepared in two ways. Cold smoked mackerel and kippers have a smoky flavour but are still raw and must be cooked. Hot smoked mackerel is prepared at a higher temperature so that the flesh cooks and the fish are ready to eat.

*Seafood (shellfish).* Scallops, mussels, oysters, cockles, whelks and winkles are distinguished by their very hard shells. Oysters are generally eaten raw and can be opened by the fishmonger (if you have to do the job yourself, the shell is opened by inserting a knife through the hinge of the shell). Scallops and the smaller Queens may be sold in the shell or loose, and the deep shell is used for serving the cooked dish. Mussels need to be scrubbed and the 'beards' removed before steaming open, but the fishmonger may have a supply of freshly cooked ones. The same applies to cockles and whelks. Winkles are sold ready cooked but still in the shell.

Lobsters, crabs, prawns, shrimps and scampi (Dublin bay prawns) are recognised by their bright pinky-red shells when cooked. Prawns, shrimps and scampi may be sold in the shell or ready peeled. Crabs and lobsters are generally sold boiled but not prepared, but some fishmongers sell dressed crabs.

*Canned fish.* A wide variety of fish is canned in oil, brine or tomato sauce. Popular varieties include sardines, salmon, tuna, pilchard and mackerel, but it is also possible to find kipper fillets, herring roes, prawns, shrimps, clams and oysters. All of these are useful for the store cupboard.

**Fish cookery**
Whichever method is chosen, fish should never be overcooked. The flesh should be just set so that it remains moist and full of flavour.

*Boiling.* This is only recommended for large pieces of fish. The fish should be rubbed with lemon juice to keep it firm and white, then cooked in hot salted water or Court Bouillon (see page 248). Cook the fish in a large shallow pan or fish kettle, if possible in a piece of muslin or foil so that the fish can be lifted out without breaking. Bring the liquid to the boil and then simmer very gently until the fish is just cooked and ready to flake away from the bone. Timing depends on the thickness and shape of the fish, but usually 10–15 minutes per 450 g (1 lb) is enough. Drain the fish well before serving.

*Poaching.* Small pieces of fish or small whole fish may be cooked in this way. If poaching fillets, fold or roll them before cooking. Use milk, fish stock, or a mixture of milk and water in a saucepan or frying pan, and half-cover the fish with liquid. Simmer gently for 10 minutes per 450 g (1 lb). Drain and use the cooking liquid for an accompanying sauce.

*Steaming.* Thin pieces and fillets are best suited to steaming. Place the fish directly in a steamer over a pan of boiling water, and allow 15 minutes to 450 g (1 lb) plus 15 minutes for large fish (fillets will take 20 minutes). Small fillets or cutlets may be cooked on a greased deep plate with 1 tablespoon milk and seasoning over a pan of boiling water, covered with a second plate or lid – this method is particularly attractive for invalid dishes.

*Shallow frying.* Allow just enough fat or oil to prevent the fish sticking, and use a shallow pan. When the fat or oil is just smoking, cook the fish quickly on both sides for a few minutes until golden brown, and finish cooking gently until the flesh loosens from the bone. For shallow frying, the fish may be lightly coated with flour; or with flour, milk and flour again; or with flour, beaten egg and breadcrumbs. The fish should not be prepared until just before frying.

*Butter frying.* A simple and delicious frying method suitable for fillets of flat fish and for small whole fish, if not more than 1 cm (½ in) thick. Dip the fish in seasoned flour, shake off the surplus, and then cook on both sides in hot butter. For 4 fillets, allow 50 g (2 oz) butter and cook for about 5 minutes each side. Place the fish on a serving dish without draining. Add a knob of extra butter to the pan and when hot and frothy, add the juice of half a lemon. Pour over the fish and sprinkle with chopped fresh parsley.

*Deep frying.* The fish should be coated with egg and breadcrumbs (see Shallow frying) or coated with Batter (see page 248). Use a deep pan and wire basket and enough fat to come three-quarters of the way up the pan. Use oil, clarified beef fat or lard, and make sure that the fat is pure and free from moisture. Heat the fat to 180–190°C (350–375°F). Put the fish into the wire basket and place in the hot fat. When the fish is golden, lift out the basket from the fat and drain the fried fish well on absorbent kitchen paper.

*Stir frying.* A new and popular way of cooking fish quickly which uses only a small amount of oil. Use a wok or sauté pan and a tablespoon of oil (peanut oil is particularly good). Heat the pan and add finely chopped seasonal vegetables and small cubes of fish. Toss quickly over the heat and serve as soon as the fish has become opaque.

*Grilling.* Fillets and cutlets may be grilled after being seasoned and sprinkled with lemon juice and brushed well with melted butter or oil. The time taken under a medium grill is from 3–7 minutes on each side, depending on the thickness of the fish. Since fish tends to stick to the wire grill rack, it is best to line the grill pan with foil and to place the fish directly on this (which also makes the pan easier to clean). Whole fish should be scaled first and scored two or three times with a sharp knife on each side. For *barbecuing*, brush the fish well with oil, lemon juice and herbs, and baste it occasionally during cooking, so that the fish remains moist.

*Baking.* An excellent method for cooking whole fish in a greased dish, well-seasoned with salt, pepper and lemon juice. A little milk or water should be poured round the fish, which should be covered with a piece of greased paper. Allow 10–15 minutes per 450 g (1 lb) in a moderate oven, 180°C (350°F) mark 4, depending on the thickness of the fish and whether it is stuffed. As an alternative, the fish may be simply brushed with melted butter and sprinkled with breadcrumbs before baking; this is particularly suitable for cutlets. *Foil-baking* is excellent for cutlets, tail-ends of fish, or small whole fish, such as salmon or trout. Wrap the fish in well-buttered foil with plenty of seasoning, lemon juice and fresh herbs. Place the foil packet on a baking sheet and allow 20 minutes per 450 g (⁛ lb) in a moderate oven, 180°C (350°F) mark 4. The fish is exceptionally moist and full of juices when cooked by this method.

*Microwaving.* Fish cooked in the microwave is full of flavour with an excellent texture and appearance. Add a little lemon juice and seasoning, slit the fish skin in two or three places to prevent bursting, and cover the fish with microwave-proof film. For timing, consult the manufacturer's booklet.

**Covering**

Cook, uncovered, unless otherwise stated. The use of cling film should be avoided in microwave cooking, use microwave-proof film. When a recipe requires you to cover the container, you should either cover with a lid or a plate, leaving a gap to let steam escape.

# WHITE FISH

An interesting collection of recipes for everyday
use and special occasions, from Cornish Cod to
Summer Fish Terrine.

# SAVOURY BREAD AND BUTTER PUDDING

Serves 4

*8 medium-thick bread slices*
*75 g (3 oz) butter*
*150 g (5 oz) Cheddar cheese, grated*
*350 g (12 oz) white fish*
*275 ml (1/2 pint) milk*
*150 ml (1/4 pint) single cream*
*2 eggs*
*salt and pepper*
*few drops of Tabasco sauce*

Heat the oven to 180°C (350°F) mark 4. Remove the crusts from the bread. Spread the bread generously with butter and sprinkle with grated cheese. Cut each slice in half. Remove the bones and skin from the fish and cut the flesh into small pieces. Arrange a layer of bread in an oven-proof dish. Add half the fish and spread it over the bread, then add another layer of bread. Top with the remaining fish and the remaining bread with the cheese uppermost.

Beat together the milk, cream and eggs and season well with salt, pepper and Tabasco sauce. Pour over the bread. Leave to stand for 1 hour. Bake for 45 minutes.

Serve hot with vegetables or a salad.

# FISH CRUMBLE

Serves 4

*450 g (1 lb) white fish, cooked*
*75 g (3 oz) butter*
*1 small onion, finely chopped*
*4 tomatoes, skinned*
*1 garlic clove, crushed*
*1 tbsp fresh parsley, chopped*
*1 tbsp lemon juice*
*150 ml (1/4 pint) water*
*1 tbsp cornflour*
*salt and pepper*
*75 g (3 oz) plain flour*

Heat the oven to 220°C (425°F) mark 7. Flake the fish into a bowl. Melt 25 g (1 oz) of the butter and cook the onion until soft and golden. Discard the seeds from the tomatoes and chop the flesh roughly. Add the tomatoes to the onion with the garlic, parsley, lemon juice and water and simmer for 5 minutes. Mix the cornflour with a little water and stir into the sauce. Simmer for 3 minutes and season well with salt and pepper. Stir in the flaked fish and put the mixture into a greased oven-proof dish. Rub the remaining butter into the flour and sprinkle over the fish. Bake for 20 minutes and serve hot.

A few button mushrooms may be added to the sauce, or some peeled prawns, chopped green pepper or cooked peas, or a mixture of these added ingredients.

# FRENCH FISH CASSEROLE

Serves 4

450 g (1 lb) leeks
50 g (2 oz) butter
1 green pepper, sliced
225 g (8 oz) tomatoes, quartered
salt and pepper
675 g (1½ lb) white fish fillets
1 tbsp lemon juice
1 tbsp fresh parsley, chopped

Heat the oven to 180°C (350°F) mark 4. Clean the leeks well and chop into 2.5 cm (1 in) chunks. Melt 40 g (1½ oz) of the butter and cook the leeks and pepper until soft and golden. Stir in the tomatoes and season well with salt and pepper. Spoon into a greased oven-proof dish. Cut the fish into 4 portions and place on top of the mixture. Sprinkle with lemon juice and parsley and dot with the remaining butter. Cover and bake for 25 minutes. Remove the cover and continue baking for 5 minutes.

Serve at once with boiled potatoes.

# FRUITED FISH CURRY

Serves 4

675 g (1½ lb) white fish
1 medium onion, finely chopped
40 g (1½ oz) butter
1 tbsp curry paste
2 tbsp fruit chutney
1 tbsp sultanas
1 eating apple
40 g (1½ oz) plain flour
275 g (10 oz) long grain rice
1 egg, hard-boiled
100 g (4 oz) prawns, shelled
   (optional)

Skin the fish, remove the bones and cut into serving portions. Cover with water and simmer for 10 minutes. Drain the fish and keep warm, and reserve the cooking liquid for stock. Fry the onion in the butter until soft and golden. Stir in the curry paste and cook for 1 minute. Add the chutney and sultanas. Do not peel the apple, but core and cut the flesh into dice. Stir into the pan and add the flour. Cook until the flour is golden, mixing all the time.

Measure the fish stock and make up to 425 ml (¾ pint) of liquid with water, add to the pan. Bring to the boil and then simmer and stir until the sauce is smooth. Put the fish pieces into the pan and reheat. While the sauce is cooking, boil the rice in salted water for 12–15 minutes and drain well. Arrange the rice in a border on a hot dish and spoon in the fish. Garnish with chopped egg, and prawns if liked.

# WINTER FISH CASSEROLE

Serves 4

675 g (1½ lb) white fish
50 g (2 oz) streaky bacon
40 g (1½ oz) butter
225 g (8 oz) potatoes
225 g (8 oz) carrots
100 g (4 oz) turnips
1 medium onion
1 bay leaf
salt and pepper
275 ml (½ pint) dry cider
25 g (1 oz) plain flour
150 ml (¼ pint) milk

Heat the oven to 190°C (375°F) mark 5. Skin the fish and cut into cubes. Chop the bacon roughly. Melt the butter and stir in the fish and bacon. Cook over a low heat until the fish is golden brown on all sides. Peel the vegetables. Cut the potatoes into cubes and dice the carrots and turnips. Slice the onion thinly. Add the vegetables to the pan and stir well. Put the mixture into a casserole and place the bay leaf on top. Season well with salt and pepper. Pour in the cider and cover and bake for 30 minutes.

Mix the flour with a little of the milk to make a smooth paste and then add the remaining milk. Stir into the casserole, return to oven and continue baking for 10 minutes.

Serve hot with potatoes or rice if liked, or with plenty of crusty bread.

# SUMMER FISH SALAD

Serves 4

450 g (1 lb) white fish fillets
2 hard-boiled eggs, chopped
4 anchovy fillets, finely chopped
2 gherkins, finely chopped
2 tsp capers
2 tbsp olive oil
2 tsp lemon juice
1 tbsp chopped fresh chives
pepper
150 ml (¼ pint) mayonnaise

Poach the fish until just tender. Cool and break into flakes. Mix with the eggs, anchovies, gherkins and capers. Stir together the oil and lemon juice with the chives and plenty of pepper. Pour over the fish and toss lightly. Press lightly into a shallow serving dish and spoon over the mayonnaise. Chill and serve with a green salad and thin brown bread and butter.

# SPANISH FISH SALAD

Serves 4

450 g (1 lb) white fish or smoked
   haddock fillets
225 g (8 oz) long-grain rice
salt and pepper
4 tbsp olive oil
1½ tbsp white wine vinegar
1 garlic clove, crushed
½ tsp French mustard
2 large tomatoes, skinned
4 spring onions
7.5 cm (3 in) cucumber, peeled
1 green pepper, finely chopped
1 red pepper, finely chopped

Poach the fish until tender. Cool and break
into flakes. Meanwhile boil the rice in salted
water until tender. Drain well, rinse in cold
water, drain and leave in a bowl until cool
but not cold.

Mix together the oil, vinegar, garlic,
mustard, salt and pepper. Discard the pips
from tomatoes and chop the flesh roughly.
Chop the spring onions finely. Discard the
seeds from cucumber and dice the flesh
finely. Mix the fish, peppers, tomatoes,
onions and cucumber into the rice and add
the dressing. Toss lightly so that the fish
does not break into very small pieces. Chill
before serving. Peeled prawns or shrimps
may be added before serving.

# FISH CREAMS

Serves 4–6

225 g (8 oz) white fish
25 g (1 oz) melted butter
225 g (8 oz) peeled prawns
150 ml (¼ pint) white sauce
1 egg white
salt and pepper
pinch of ground mace
pinch of cayenne pepper
150 ml (¼ pint) double cream

Heat the oven to 180°C (350°F) mark 4.
Poach the fish until just tender. Drain well
and remove the skin. Put into a food
processor or liquidiser with the butter and
150 g (6 oz) of the prawns. Blend until
smooth. Add the white sauce and egg white
and blend until very smooth. Season well
with salt and pepper, mace and cayenne
pepper.

Whip the cream to soft peaks and fold
into the fish mixture. Place the remaining
prawns in four to six individual oven-proof
dishes. Top with the fish mixture. Place the
dishes in a baking tin with hot water to
come halfway up the dishes. Cover with
greased greaseproof paper. Bake for 30
minutes.

# GRANNY'S FISH SUPPER

Serves 4

675 g (1½ lb) white fish fillets
4 medium onions, thinly sliced
oil or fat for frying
4 medium potatoes, boiled
salt and pepper
25 g (1 oz) Cheddar cheese, grated
1 tbsp fresh parsley, chopped

The fish may be cod, haddock, coley or any other white fish. Poach the fish, cool slightly and remove the skin and any bones. Break into flakes. Fry the onions in a little hot oil or fat until soft and golden, and drain well. Slice the potatoes thinly. Grease an oven-proof dish and put in a layer of potatoes, then onion and fish, seasoning lightly. Continue in layers, finishing with a layer of potatoes. Sprinkle with cheese. Either bake at 180°C (350°F) mark 4 for 25 minutes *or* put under a hot grill to brown if the ingredients are freshly cooked and still hot. Sprinkle with parsley and serve.

This is a useful supper dish as it may be assembled early in the day and refrigerated until needed.

# PAELLA

Serves 8–10

*675 g (1½ lb) long grain rice*
*1 chicken, cut into 8–10 pieces*
*450 g (1 lb) lean pork, diced*
*3 tbsp oil*
*1 large onion, finely chopped*
*3 ripe tomatoes*
*225 g (8 oz) peas*
*3 red peppers, chopped*
*350 g (12 oz) white fish (cod,*
  *haddock, hake)*
*16 mussels in shells*
*225 g (8 oz) prawns in shells*
*1 tsp salt*
*½ tsp pepper*
*pinch of saffron*

A large deep frying pan is best for the preparation of this dish. Ingredients may be varied – runner beans are often substituted for peas. Pieces of eel, crab or lobster may be added to the fish.

Rinse the rice in cold water and drain well. Put the chicken pieces and pork into a pan with the hot oil and cook until brown, add the onion and over a low heat, stirring well, cook until the onion is soft and golden. Peel and deseed the tomatoes. Chop the flesh roughly and add to the pan. Stir and cook for 3 minutes and then add the rice. Cook and stir over a low heat for 10 minutes. Add the peas and peppers; cook for 5 minutes. Add the pieces of fish, and mussels in their shells. Peel half the prawns and add to the pan. Season with salt and pepper and simmer for 10 minutes.

Add the saffron and stir in 1.8 litres (3 pints) boiling water. Bring to the boil and then simmer until the rice is cooked and all the water has been absorbed, stirring occasionally. Stir in the prawns in their shells. To give the paella a rich golden colour, put the pan into a low oven, 170°C (325°F) mark 3, for 5 minutes. Remove from the oven and leave to stand for 2 minutes so that the mixture blends and settles before serving.

# WHITE FISH SUPPER BAKE

Serves 4

450 g (1 lb) white fish
1 medium onion, chopped
2 eggs, beaten
275 ml (½ pint) milk
75 g (3 oz) butter, softened
75 g (3 oz) fresh white or brown
    breadcrumbs
1 tbsp lemon juice
salt and pepper
50 g (2 oz) Cheddar cheese, grated

Heat the oven to 190°C (375°F) mark 5.
Poach the fish until just tender and cool.
Flake the fish into a bowl. Add the onion,
beaten eggs, milk, butter, breadcrumbs,
lemon juice and salt and pepper. Put into a
greased oven-proof dish and sprinkle with
cheese. Bake for 40 minutes.

Serve hot with a mushroom or tomato
sauce and crusty bread.

# HUNGARIAN FISH CASSEROLE

Serves 4–6

6 cod cutlets
40 g (1½ oz) butter
2 medium onions, thinly sliced
1 tbsp paprika
25 g (1 oz) plain flour
275 ml (½ pint) milk
225 g (8 oz) canned tomatoes
salt and pepper
150 ml (¼ pint) soured cream

Heat the oven to 180°C (350°F) mark 4.
Place the fish in an oven-proof dish in a
single layer. Melt the butter in a pan and
add the onions. Cook over a low heat for
5 minutes, stirring well, until the onions are
soft and golden. Stir in the paprika and
cook for 1 minute. Stir in the flour and cook
for 1 minute. Gradually add the milk and
the tomatoes with their juice. Break up the
tomatoes with a fork. Bring to the boil and
then simmer for 20 minutes.

Season well with salt and pepper and
pour over the fish. Cover and cook for
45 minutes. Remove the lid and spoon the
soured cream on top of the fish. Serve at
once with rice or noodles and a green salad.

# SUMMER FISH TERRINE

Serves 6–8

100 g (4 oz) courgettes
100 g (4 oz) French beans
100 g (4 oz) carrots
900 g (2 lb) cod or haddock
50 g (2 oz) fresh white breadcrumbs
4 tbsp double cream
2 tbsp French mustard
2 tbsp lemon juice
2 tbsp dry vermouth
salt and pepper

Heat the oven to 180°C (350°F) mark 4. Wipe the courgettes but to not peel them. Trim the ends and cut into sticks the same size as the beans. Peel the carrots and cut to the same size as the beans. Blanch each vegetable in boiling water for 5 minutes. Drain and dry well and keep to one side. Skin the fish and mince (or use a food processor) with the breadcrumbs, cream, mustard, lemon juice and vermouth. Season well with salt and pepper.

Butter a 1-litre (2-pint) terrine or loaf tin. Spread one-quarter of the fish mixture over the base. Arrange the beans lengthwise on top. Spread on a second quarter of fish mixture and top with the carrots arranged lengthwise. Put on the third quarter of the fish mixture, the courgettes lengthwise and the final layer of fish. Cover with a buttered piece of greaseproof paper and foil or a lid. Place the container in a roasting tin containing 2.5 cm (1 in) water. Bake for 50 minutes. Leave to stand for 30 minutes. Drain off any liquid and unmould on a serving dish. Slice carefully and serve warm or cold as a first course, or with salad.

# COD IN TOMATO SAUCE

Serves 4

4 cod steaks
1 large onion, finely chopped
100 g (4 oz) streaky bacon rashers,
    chopped
½ green pepper
1 tbsp oil
450 g (1 lb) canned tomatoes
½ tsp fresh mixed herbs
salt and pepper

Grill or fry the cod steaks until golden on both sides. While the fish is cooking, fry the onion, bacon and pepper in oil for 5 minutes over a low heat, stirring well. Add the tomatoes and their juice with the herbs, salt and pepper. Bring to the boil and simmer for 10 minutes. Place the cod steaks on a warm serving dish and pour over the sauce. Serve at once with boiled potatoes or crusty bread.

The sauce is very quickly made and may be served with any white fish or with seafood such as scallops or scampi which can be prepared while the sauce is cooking.

# PORTUGUESE COD

Serves 4

4 cod steaks
salt and pepper
275 ml (½ pint) water
juice of 2 lemons
1 medium onion, chopped
1 garlic clove, crushed
4 tomatoes, peeled and chopped
25 g (1 oz) butter
1 tbsp fresh parsley, chopped
pinch of thyme
100 g (4 oz) button mushrooms

Heat the oven to 180°C (350°F) mark 4. Arrange the cod steaks in a greased oven-proof dish and sprinkle with salt and pepper. Cover with a piece of foil and bake for 10 minutes. While the fish is cooking, put the water, lemon juice, onion, garlic, tomatoes and butter into a pan and simmer together for 10 minutes. Add the parsley, thyme and small whole mushrooms.

Remove the foil from the fish and pour over the sauce. Continue baking for 15 minutes.

Serve with potatoes or rice and a green salad.

# CORNISH COD

Serves 4

675 g (1½ lb) cod fillets
salt and pepper
milk
plain flour
75 g (3 oz) butter
24 mussels, cooked
100 g (4 oz) prawns or shrimps,
    peeled
2 tsp lemon juice
1 tbsp fresh parsley, chopped
lemon wedges to garnish

Divide the fish into 4 fillets and season with salt and pepper. Dip in the milk and then flour. Melt 50 g (2 oz) of the butter and fry the fish on both sides until golden. Place on a warm serving dish and keep hot. In a clean pan, melt the remaining butter and toss the mussels and prawns or shrimps over a low heat. Add the lemon juice and pour the mixture over the fish. Sprinkle with parsley and serve at once with lemon wedges to garnish.

The mussel and prawn or shrimp garnish may be used for other white fish, including plaice or sole. For a less rich dish, the fish may be grilled if preferred.

# FISH PUDDING

Serves 4

450 g (1 lb) cod fillets
1 small onion
575 ml (1 pint) white sauce
    (see page 87)
50 g (2 oz) fresh white breadcrumbs
2 eggs
salt and pepper

Skin the fish and cut the flesh into pieces. Mince the fish and onion, or blend together in a food processor. Mix with the white sauce, breadcrumbs and beaten eggs. Season well with salt and pepper. Spoon into a well-greased 750-ml (1½-pint) pudding basin. Cover with greaseproof paper and foil and steam for 1 hour. Turn out and serve with parsley sauce (see page 85). Garnish with a few prawns or some button mushrooms tossed in a little butter.

If preferred, the mixture may be placed in a pie dish and baked at 180°C (350°F) mark 4 for 1 hour, when it will puff up and be golden-brown on the surface.

# FISHERMAN'S CHOWDER

Serves 6-8

*900 g (2 lb) mixed smoked and
  white fish*
*50 g (2 oz) butter*
*1 large onion, thinly sliced*
*100 g (4 oz) bacon, chopped*
*4 celery sticks, chopped*
*1 red or green pepper, chopped*
*1 large potato, diced*
*575 ml (1 pint) water*
*1 tbsp cornflour*
*575 ml (1 pint) creamy milk*
*salt and pepper*

Use a mixture of smoked haddock or cod fillets with some coley, cod, haddock or whiting. Skin the fish and cut into cubes. Melt the butter in a large pan and add the onion, bacon, celery, pepper and potato. Stir over a low heat for 5 minutes. Add the water and simmer for 5 minutes. Add the fish cubes and continue simmering for a further 5 minutes. Blend the cornflour with a little of the milk. Stir in the remaining milk and add to the pan. Season well with salt and pepper and stir over a low heat until the liquid has thickened slightly.

Serve hot with crusty white or wholemeal bread.

# GRAPEFRUIT GRILLED FISH

Serves 4

*butter*
*4 haddock or cod steaks*
*few drops of Tabasco sauce*
*salt and pepper*
*paprika*
*1 grapefruit*

Line a grill pan with foil and grease the foil lightly with a little butter. Put fish in pan and sprinkle with Tabasco sauce, salt, pepper and paprika. Grill for 4 minutes on each side. Meanwhile peel the grapefruit and cut off all the white pith. Remove the grapefruit segments with a sharp knife so that they are unskinned. Arrange the segments on top of the fish and continue grilling for 4 minutes.

Serve with vegetables or a salad.

# HADDOCK WITH GRAPE SAUCE

Serves 4

*675 g (1½ lb) haddock fillets*
*25 g (1 oz) butter*
*25 g (1 oz) plain flour*
*3 tbsp double cream*
*100 g (4 oz) white grapes, peeled*
*salt and white pepper*

Skin the fish and cut into 4 even-sized portions. Poach in water until tender but unbroken, reserve the liquid. Lift carefully on to a serving dish and keep warm. Melt the butter and work in the flour, and stir over a low heat for 1 minute. Add 275 ml (½ pint) of the cooking liquid and stir over a low heat until smooth and creamy. Stir in 2 tablespoons cream and take off the heat. Add peeled and halved grapes, and season to taste. Pour over the fish. Drizzle the remaining cream on top and put under a hot grill to glaze.

# BAKED STUFFED HADDOCK

Serves 6

*900 g (2 lb) whole haddock*
*2 tbsp oatmeal*
*2 tbsp dripping, melted*
*1 small onion, finely chopped*
*2 tsp fresh parsley, chopped*
*2 tsp fresh thyme*
*salt and pepper*
*25 g (1 oz) butter, melted*
*25 g (1 oz) fresh white or brown*
    *breadcrumbs*

Heat the oven to 190°C (375°F) mark 5. Clean the fish and leave whole. Mix together the oatmeal, dripping, onion, herbs and plenty of seasoning. Stuff the fish and close the opening with cocktail sticks. Put the fish into a well-greased oven-proof dish and brush the surface of the fish with a little of the butter. Bake for 30 minutes, basting once or twice. Sprinkle the surface of the fish with the breadcrumbs and sprinkle on the remaining butter. Cover with greaseproof paper and bake at 200°C (400°F) mark 6 for 20 minutes. Remove the cocktail sticks before serving.

# MEXICAN FISH SALAD

Serves 4

450 g (1 lb) halibut or haddock
  fillets
4 limes
1 crisp lettuce
4 tomatoes, skinned
1 green pepper, finely chopped
4 tbsp olive oil
1 tbsp wine vinegar
2 tbsp fresh parsley, chopped
2 tbsp fresh marjoram, chopped
salt and pepper

Skin the fish and remove any bones. Cut into small cubes and put into a shallow dish. Grate the rind from 1 lime and squeeze out all the juice from all the limes. Sprinkle the rind and juice over the fish, cover and leave in the refrigerator for at least 3 hours. Arrange the lettuce leaves in a serving bowl. Discard the seeds from the tomatoes and chop the flesh roughly. Mix the tomato and pepper pieces and arrange in the bowl. Mix the oil, vinegar, parsley, marjoram, salt and pepper together and sprinkle over the tomatoes. Arrange the fish on top.

The fresh lime juice has the effect of cooking the fish, which retains a beautifully fresh flavour. Bottled lime juice cordial should *not* be used for the dish.

# BRITTANY HALIBUT

Serves 4

*675 g (1½ lb) halibut fillets*
*50 g (2 oz) butter*
*1 medium onion, finely chopped*
*25 g (1 oz) plain flour*
*150 ml (¼ pint) dry cider or dry*
  *white wine*
*2 garlic cloves, crushed*
*2 tbsp fresh parsley, chopped*
*2 tbsp lemon juice*
*salt and pepper*
*pinch of cayenne pepper*
*flour*
*oil for frying*

Divide the fish into 4 pieces. Melt the butter and cook the onion over a low heat until soft and golden. Stir in the flour and cook for 1 minute. Stir in the cider or wine, with the garlic and parsley. Simmer for 5 minutes. Add the lemon juice and season well with salt, pepper and cayenne pepper.

While the sauce is cooking, flour the fish lightly and cook in a little hot oil for 3 minutes each side until just golden. Put the fish in a single layer in a shallow oven-proof dish and cover with the sauce. Place under a hot grill for 2–3 minutes until golden and bubbling, and serve at once with boiled potatoes. Cod or haddock may be used instead of halibut.

# HALIBUT AND HORSERADISH

Serves 4

*675 g (1½ lb) halibut steaks, boned*
*150 ml (¼ pint) white sauce*
*150 ml (¼ pint) single cream*
*3 egg yolks*
*1 tbsp horseradish cream*
*1 tbsp wine vinegar*
*salt and pepper*
*1 hard-boiled egg, finely chopped*

Heat the oven to 180°C (350°F) mark 4. Place the halibut steaks in a greased oven-proof dish. Add 3 tablespoons of water, cover and bake for 20 minutes. Drain off the liquid and place the fish on a serving dish to keep warm. Warm the white sauce and remove from the heat. Beat in the cream and egg yolks and heat just enough to warm through, but do not boil. Stir in the horseradish cream, vinegar and seasoning. Coat the fish with the sauce and sprinkle with chopped egg.

Serve at once with boiled or sauté potatoes and peas.

# NORFOLK FISH PIE

Serves 6

450 g (1 lb) halibut, haddock or cod
225 g (8 oz) lobster or scampi
4 scallops
butter
100 g (4 oz) shrimps, peeled
100 g (4 oz) button mushrooms
4 eggs
275 ml (½ pint) white sauce
salt and pepper
450 g (1 lb) mashed potatoes

Heat the oven to 180°C (350°F) mark 4. Poach the white fish and flake the flesh into large pieces. Mix with the lobster or scampi. Remove the corals from the scallops and cut the white part into two circles. Cook for 2 minutes in a little butter and mix the white parts and corals with the white fish. Stir in the shrimps. Wipe the mushrooms but do not peel and cook in the butter for 2 minutes. Stir into the fish. Beat the eggs into the white sauce and add all the fish mixture. Season well and put into a pie dish. Cover with the mashed potatoes and mark lightly with a fork. Bake for 30 minutes.

This is a rich and delicious fish pie, but the ingredients may be varied according to season and budget. Some smoked haddock may be included, mussels may be added and prawns may be used, but the important thing is to get a variety of texture, colour and flavour. The fish may be fresh, canned or frozen, so it is always possible to get an interesting mixture, and while the result is a little expensive, the pie is good enough for a really special meal with guests.

# TROUT WITH ALMONDS

Serves 2

*2 rainbow trout*
*25 g (1 oz) plain flour*
*salt and pepper*
*100 g (4 oz) butter*
*50 g (2 oz) flaked almonds*
*1 tsp lemon juice*

Clean and gut the trout but leave the heads and tails intact. Season the flour well with salt and pepper and lightly coat the trout with the flour. Melt half the butter and fry the trout over a low heat for 5 minutes each side. Lift the fish on to a warm serving dish. Add the remaining butter to the pan and toss the almonds over a medium heat until golden. Add lemon juice to the pan and pour the almonds and pan juices over the trout.

Serve immediately with plainly boiled potatoes and vegetables, or a salad.

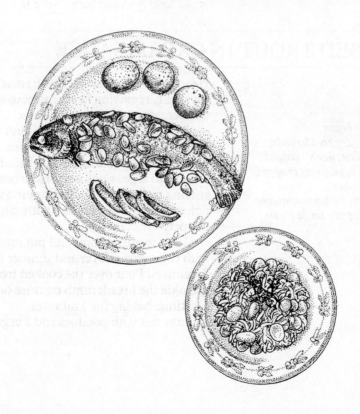

# TROUT WITH BACON STUFFING

Serves 4

4 trout
40 g (1½ oz) butter
4 streaky bacon rashers, finely
    chopped
1 small onion, finely chopped
100 g (4 oz) mushrooms, finely
    chopped
50 g (2 oz) fresh brown breadcrumbs
2 tbsp fresh parsley, chopped
2 tsp lemon rind, grated
salt and pepper
1 egg

Heat the oven to 190°C (375°F) mark 5.
Clean and gut the fish. Melt the butter and
cook the bacon, onion and mushrooms over
a low heat until soft and golden. Remove
from the heat and mix with the
breadcrumbs, parsley, lemon rind, salt,
pepper and egg. Stuff the fish and secure
with cocktail sticks. Arrange in a
well-buttered oven-proof dish in a single
layer. Bake for 25 minutes.

Serve with boiled or sauté potatoes and a
vegetable.

# HERBED TROUT IN CREAM SAUCE

Serves 4

4 trout
50 g (2 oz) butter
50 g (2 oz) dry breadcrumbs
1 small onion, finely chopped
2 tsp fresh sage, finely chopped
salt and pepper
225 g (8 oz) button mushrooms
150 ml (¼ pint) single cream

Heat the oven to 180°C (350°F) mark 4. Gut
the trout, removing heads, although this is
not necessary. Place in a buttered
oven-proof dish and cover with buttered
greaseproof paper. Bake for 20 minutes.
Melt the butter and stir in the breadcrumbs,
onion and sage. Cook over a low heat,
stirring well, until the breadcrumbs are
lightly golden. Season well with salt and
pepper.

Slice the mushrooms and put into a pan
with the cream. Cover and simmer for
3 minutes. Pour over the cooked trout and
sprinkle the breadcrumb mixture on top.
Continue baking for 5 minutes.

Serve hot with potatoes and a vegetable.

# CRISP BROWN TROUT

Serves 4–6

6 brown trout
2 medium onions, chopped
1 tbsp oil
1 garlic clove, crushed
salt and pepper
25 g (1 oz) fresh white or brown
    breadcrumbs
50 g (2 oz) butter, melted
2 streaky bacon rashers
1 tbsp fresh parsley, chopped

Heat the oven to 180°C (350°F) mark 4.
Clean and fillet the fish. Fry the onions
gently in the oil until soft and golden. Stir in
the garlic and season well. Place the trout in
an oiled oven-proof dish. Cover with the
onion mixture. Mix the breadcrumbs with
butter and season with salt and pepper.
Sprinkle on top of the onions. Bake for 25
minutes. While the fish are cooking, grill
the bacon crisply and crumble into small
pieces. Sprinkle the bacon and parsley on
the fish and serve with boiled potatoes.

# SUMMER PLAICE WITH COURGETTES

Serves 4

450 g (1 lb) courgettes
50 g (2 oz) butter
1 tbsp fresh parsley, chopped
1 tsp rosemary
salt and pepper
8 plaice fillets
25 g (1 oz) fresh breadcrumbs
25 g (1 oz) butter, melted
1 tbsp Parmesan cheese, grated

Heat the oven to 190°C (375°F) mark 5.
Wipe the courgettes and slice them thinly
without peeling. Melt the butter and fry the
courgettes with the parsley and rosemary
for 3 minutes. Remove from the heat,
season well and place in the bottom of a
shallow oven-proof dish. Fold the plaice
fillets in half, skin side inwards and arrange
on top of the courgettes. Sprinkle with
breadcrumbs, drizzle with butter and
sprinkle with Parmesan cheese. Bake for
20 minutes.
    Serve at once with new potatoes and a
salad.

# PLAICE IN LEMON BUTTER

Serves 4

8 *small plaice fillets*
25 g (1 oz) *plain flour*
*salt and pepper*
75 g (3 oz) *butter*
1 *tbsp oil*
1 *tbsp lemon juice*
1 *tbsp fresh parsley, chopped*
*lemon wedges to garnish*

Dry the fish on kitchen paper. Season the flour with salt and pepper and coat the fish lightly on both sides. Put 50 g (2 oz) of the butter into a frying pan with the oil, and heat until the butter has melted. Fry the fish for 4 minutes on each side until cooked through and golden. Lift on to a warm serving dish.

Add the remaining butter, lemon juice and parsley to the pan and heat until golden brown. Pour over the fish, garnish with lemon wedges and serve at once.

# BURNHAM PLAICE

Serves 2

2 *small whole plaice*
25 g (1 oz) *brown breadcrumbs*
1 *celery stick, finely chopped*
4 *tbsp tomato juice*
3 *tbsp lemon juice*
100 g (4 oz) *peeled prawns*

Garnish
*parsley sprigs*
*lemon wedges*

Heat the oven to 200°C (400°F) mark 6. Clean and trim the fish but leave them whole. Place the fish on a flat surface with the white skin uppermost. Use a sharp knife to make a long slit down the backbone, and with the point of the knife, ease the flesh away from the backbone along both sides to make a pocket.

Mix the breadcrumbs with the celery, tomato juice, lemon juice and half the prawns. Pack the mixture into the pockets in the fish, allowing it to spill loosely. Place the fish in a shallow oven-proof dish. Cover with greased greaseproof paper and bake for 20 minutes. Lift the fish on to individual plates and garnish with remaining prawns, parsley and lemon wedges.

# PLAICE ROLLS IN LEMON SAUCE

Serves 4

8 plaice fillets
100 g (4 oz) shrimps or prawns
15 g (½ oz) butter
15 g (½ oz) plain flour
275 ml (½ pint) milk
juice of 1 lemon
salt and pepper

Heat the oven to 180°C (350°F) mark 4.
Place the fish on a flat surface and divide the
shrimps or prawns between the fillets. Roll
the plaice round them and stand the fish
upright and close together in a greased
oven-proof dish. Melt the butter and work
in the flour. Stir in the milk over a low heat
and cook gently until the sauce thickens.
Remove from the heat and stir in the lemon
juice. Season well and pour over the fish.
Bake for 25 minutes.
    Serve with potatoes and vegetables.

# HAKE BAKE

Serves 4

50 g (2 oz) butter
1 garlic clove, crushed
2 medium onions, sliced
175 g (6 oz) mushrooms, sliced
1 tsp fresh mixed herbs
4 hake cutlets or steaks (or cod)
salt and pepper
25 g (1 oz) fresh brown or white
    breadcrumbs

Heat the oven to 190°C (375°F) mark 5.
Melt the butter and reserve half of it. Use
the rest to cook the garlic, onions,
mushrooms and herbs over a low heat for
5 minutes, stirring well. Place in an oven-
proof dish. Season the fish on both sides
with salt and pepper and place it on top of
the vegetables. Sprinkle with breadcrumbs
and the remaining butter. Bake for
30 minutes.

# HAKE WITH CAPER SAUCE

Serves 4

4 hake cutlets
1 small onion, finely chopped
225 g (8 oz) canned tomatoes
salt and pepper
25 g (1 oz) butter
4 tsp capers

Garnish
parsley sprigs
lemon wedges

Heat the oven to 190° (375°F) mark 5.
Place the fish in a greased, shallow
oven-proof dish. Mix the onion with the
chopped tomatoes and their juice. Season
well and pour over the fish. Cut the butter
into flakes and dot over the fish. Cover and
bake for 25 minutes. Remove the fish and
place on a serving dish. Sieve the tomato
mixture from the dish. Reheat and stir in
the capers. Pour over the fish and garnish
with parsley and lemon wedges.

# SOLE WITH PRAWN AND MUSHROOM SAUCE

Serves 4

4 large fillets lemon sole
1 small onion, thinly sliced
1 bay leaf
8 peppercorns
150 ml (¼ pint) dry white wine
150 ml (¼ pint) water
squeeze of lemon juice
25 g (1 oz) butter
25 g (1 oz) plain flour
salt
50 g (2 oz) mushrooms, sliced
100 g (4 oz) prawns, shelled
8 tbsp double cream

Heat the oven to 180°C (350°F) mark 4.
Fold the fillets in three and put in a buttered
oven-proof dish in a single layer. Add the
onion slices, bay leaf and peppercorns. Pour
over the wine and water and add a squeeze
of lemon juice. Cover and bake for 15
minutes. Strain off and reserve the liquid
and keep the fish warm.
  Melt the butter and work in the flour.
Cook for 1 minute over a low heat.
Gradually blend in the cooking liquid and
stir over a low heat until the sauce has
thickened. Season lightly with salt. While
the sauce is cooking, simmer the
mushrooms in 1 tablespoon water with a
squeeze of lemon juice until just cooked.
Drain the mushrooms and add to the sauce
with the prawns. Stir in the cream and
adjust seasoning to taste. Pour over the fish
and serve at once.

# PIKE QUENELLES

Serves 4

*450 g (1 lb) pike*
*salt and pepper*
*pinch of ground nutmeg*
*2 tbsp fresh parsley, chopped*
*2 egg whites*
*150 ml (¼ pint) double cream*
*275 ml (½ pint) fish stock*
*275 ml (½ pint) dry white wine*

Remove the skin and bones from the fish and mince the flesh finely (or make into a purée in a liquidiser or food processor). Mash the flesh with salt, pepper, nutmeg and parsley, and put through a sieve. Beat in the egg whites until completely blended and chill for 1½ hours. Gradually work in the cream to make a light but firm mixture.

Grease a shallow pan. Using two tablespoons dipped in hot water, shape the fish mixture into egg-shapes and place in the pan, leaving space between them as they swell during cooking. Bring the stock and wine to the boil in a separate pan and pour over the fish shapes. Poach gently until the shapes puff up and feel firm. Lift from the pan, draining well and place on a warm serving dish.

Serve at once with Hollandaise Sauce .

# STUFFED JOHN DORY

Serves 4

*900 g (2 lb) John Dory*
*1 small onion, finely chopped*
*50 g (2 oz) butter*
*50 g (2 oz) fresh white breadcrumbs*
*150 g (5 oz) Cheddar cheese, grated*
*1 egg*
*salt and pepper*
*1 tbsp grated Parmesan cheese*

Heat the oven to 190°C (375°F) mark 5. Prepare the fish as fillets. Put the onion and butter into a pan and cook gently for 5 minutes until the onion is soft and golden. Add the onion and butter to the breadcrumbs and Cheddar cheese and then add the beaten egg. Season well.

Place half the fillets in a greased oven-proof dish and top with half the breadcrumb mixture. Cover with remaining fillets and then the remaining breadcrumb mixture. Sprinkle with Parmesan cheese. Bake for 35 minutes.

Serve with vegetables or salad.

# MONKFISH KEBABS

Serves 4

*100 g (4 oz) button onions, peeled*
*100 g (4 oz) courgettes*
*450 g (1 lb) monkfish, skinned*
*225 g (8 oz) streaky bacon*
*225 g (8 oz) mussels, cooked*
*100 g (4 oz) button mushrooms*
*8 bay leaves*
*salt and pepper*
*50 g (2 oz) butter, melted*

Use four long kebab skewers, not short meat skewers. Blanch the onions in boiling salted water for 2 minutes. Wipe the courgettes but do not peel them, and cut into 4 cm (1½ in) thick slices. Blanch the courgettes for 2 minutes. Drain the onions and courgettes very thoroughly.

Cut the monkfish into cubes. Derind the bacon and stretch the rashers with the back of a knife. Cut each rasher in half and wrap a piece round each mussel. Wipe the mushrooms but do not peel.

Thread a bay leaf on each skewer and then add the various ingredients, alternating vegetables and fish, and placing a bay leaf half-way. Season well with salt and pepper, and brush with the melted butter. Preheat the grill to a medium heat, and grill for 6 minutes. Turn the skewers, brush with butter, and continue grilling for 6–8 minutes.

Serve with rice or warm pitta bread and fresh tomato sauce.

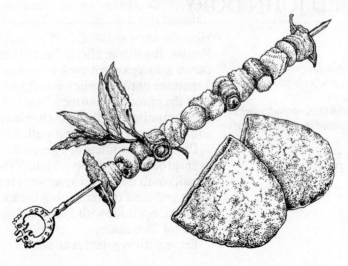

# BAKED RED MULLET

Serves 4

*4 red mullet*
*150 ml (¼ pint) dry sherry*
*2 tsp tomato ketchup*
*2 tsp anchovy essence*
*50 g (2 oz) button mushrooms,*
  *chopped*
*1 small onion, finely chopped*
*grated rind of 1 lemon*
*2 tsp fresh parsley, chopped*
*salt and pepper*
*2 tbsp brown breadcrumbs*
*50 g (2 oz) butter*

Heat the oven to 180°C (350°F) mark 4. Clean the mullet, removing the heads and tails. Score the fish with two diagonal cuts on each side and place in a shallow oven-proof dish. Mix together the sherry, ketchup, anchovy essence, mushrooms, onion, lemon rind, parsley, salt and pepper. Pour over the fish. Cover with the breadcrumbs and with flakes of butter. Bake for 25 minutes.

Serve with vegetables or a green salad.

# SKATE IN BLACK BUTTER

Serves 4

*900 g (2 lb) skate wing pieces*
*850 ml (1½ pints) water*
*5 tbsp white wine vinegar*
*salt*
*6 parsley stalks*
*blade of mace*
*100 g (4 oz) butter*
*2 tbsp capers*
*2 tbsp fresh parsley, chopped*
*pepper*

Put the skate into a large shallow pan and cover with the water. Add 1 tbsp of the vinegar, 1 tsp salt, the parsley stalks and mace. Bring to the boil and then simmer gently for 12 minutes until the fish is tender. Drain the fish very thoroughly, and take off the skin. Place the fish on a warm serving dish.

Put the remaining vinegar into a small thick pan and boil hard until reduced to half. Cut the butter into small pieces and add to the pan. Heat until brown but not burned. Stir in the capers and parsley, and season with salt and pepper. Pour over the fish and serve at once.

# JELLIED EELS

**Serves 4**

*900 g (2 lb) eels*
*850 ml (1½ pints) water*
*4 tbsp vinegar*
*2 tsp salt*
*1 tsp crushed peppercorns*
*1 medium carrot, sliced*
*1 medium onion, sliced*
*6 sprigs parsley*
*2 tbsp fresh parsley, chopped*

The eels can be skinned, but if the skin is very tough, it may be left on and removed after cooking. Cut the fish into 2.5 cm (1 in) slices. Put the water, vinegar, salt, peppercorns, carrot, onion and parsley sprigs into a pan. Bring to the boil and then simmer for 30 minutes. Strain the liquid into a clean pan.

Add the pieces of eel and simmer for 15 minutes. Lift the eel from the pan and remove and discard bones. Put the pieces of eel into a bowl. Boil the liquid hard until it is reduced by one third. Stir in the chopped parsley and pour over the eel. Cool and then chill until the liquid forms a soft jelly.

Serve with brown bread and butter.

# GRILLED WHITING WITH ORANGE BUTTER

Serves 4

*4 small whiting*
*25 g (1 oz) plain flour*
*salt and pepper*
*50 g (2 oz) butter*
*1 orange*
*4 streaky bacon rashers*

Remove the heads and tails from the whiting. Wash and dry the fish and toss in the flour seasoned with salt and pepper. Score the skin diagonally two or three times on each side of the fish. Line a grill pan with foil and place the fish in the pan. Spread with half the butter. Grill under a medium heat for 7 minutes on each side.

While the fish are cooking, grate the orange rind and mix with the remaining butter. Remove the white pith from the orange and cut out the segments so that they have no skin. Derind the bacon and stretch the rashers with the back of a knife. Cut each rasher in half and roll up. Grill the bacon rashers with the fish. When the fish is nearly cooked, spread over the orange butter and arrange the orange segments in the pan. When the orange pieces are hot, lift the fish on to a warm serving dish and garnish with orange segments and bacon rolls. Spoon over the pan juices and serve with mashed potatoes or rice and a green salad.

# OILY FISH

These fish are very nutritious and particularly
rich in vitamins A and D as well as mineral salts.

# SOUSED HERRINGS

Serves 4–6

6 herrings
salt and pepper
150 ml (¼ pint) wine or cider
  vinegar
150 ml (¼ pint) water
1 tbsp mixed pickling spice
4 bay leaves
2 small onions, thinly sliced

Heat the oven to 150°C (300°F) mark 2. Clean and fillet the herrings. Season each fillet well with salt and pepper and roll up each fillet, skin inwards, from the tail end. Place close together in a single layer in an oven-proof dish. Mix the vinegar and water and pour over the fish. Sprinkle on the pickling spice and arrange the bay leaves and onion rings on top. Cover with a lid or foil and bake for 1½ hours. Leave to cool in the liquid, then drain the herrings and place on a serving dish garnished with onion rings.

Serve with salad.

# CROFTER'S CASSEROLE

Serves 4

4 large herrings
salt and pepper
1 large onion, thinly sliced
4 large potatoes, thinly sliced
50 g (2 oz) butter, melted

Heat the oven to 200°C (400°F) mark 6. Clean and fillet the herrings and open them out flat. Arrange in a greased, shallow oven-proof dish and sprinkle with plenty of salt and pepper. Arrange the onions on top and then the potatoes. Season well and brush with butter. Cover with a lid or foil and bake for 50 minutes. Remove the lid or foil and continue baking for 15 minutes.

Serve with vegetables or a salad.

# CRISPY HERRING FRIES

Serves 4–6

*4 large herring*
*25 g (1 oz) plain flour*
*2 eggs*
*salt and pepper*
*100 g (4 oz) porridge oats*
*½ tsp mustard powder*
*oil for deep frying*

Garnish
*lemon or orange wedges*
*parsley sprigs*

Fillet the herrings to yield 8 pieces of fish. Cut into 5 cm (2 in) strips and coat with flour. Beat the eggs in a shallow bowl and season well with salt and pepper. Dip in the pieces of herring and then coat them in the oats mixed with mustard.

Heat the oil to 180°C (350°F). Fry the herring pieces in batches for about 5 minutes until crisp and golden. Serve very hot, garnished with lemon or orange wedges and parsley sprigs.

# SHETLAND TURNOVERS

Serves 4

*350 g (12 oz) shortcrust pastry*
*3 medium herrings*
*100 g (4 oz) streaky bacon rashers*
*1 large potato, grated*
*grated rind of ½ lemon*
*salt and pepper*
*milk for glazing*

Heat the oven to 220°C (425°F) mark 7. Roll out the pastry and cut to make four 15 cm (6 in) squares. Clean and fillet the herrings and grill them flat, skin-side down for about 8 minutes until cooked through. Remove the skin and flake the fish coarsely. Grill the bacon for 2 minutes. Chop into small pieces and mix with the fish. Add the potato, lemon rind and plenty of salt and pepper.

Place the filling in the centre of the pastry squares. Fold over and seal the edges firmly with a fork. Place on a baking sheet and brush well with milk. Bake for 10 minutes then reduce the heat to 190°C (375°F) mark 5 and continue baking for 25 minutes. Serve hot or cold.

# SWEET AND SHARP HERRINGS

Serves 4

4 medium herrings
150 ml (¼ pint) malt vinegar
150 ml (¼ pint) water
1 tbsp tomato ketchup
1 tsp fresh parsley, chopped
3 bay leaves
6 peppercorns
50 g (2 oz) demerara sugar
1 tsp mustard powder

Heat the oven to 180°C (350°F) mark 4. Clean and fillet the herrings. Arrange in a single layer in an oven-proof dish. Mix the vinegar, water, tomato ketchup, parsley, bay leaves and peppercorns. Pour over the fish and cover with a lid or foil. Bake for 1 hour. Remove from the oven and uncover. Mix together the sugar and mustard and sprinkle over the fish. Do not cover but return to the oven for 15 minutes. Leave the herrings to cool in the liquid. When cold, drain the fish and serve with salad.

# APPLE HERRINGS

Serves 4

4 herrings
salt and pepper
1 medium onion, thinly sliced
1 bay leaf
8 black peppercorns
4 cloves
blade of mace
150 ml (¼ pint) white wine vinegar
150 ml (¼ pint) apple juice

Sauce
450 g (1 lb) cooking apples
2 tbsp lemon juice
2 tbsp light soft brown sugar
pinch of ground ginger
pinch of ground nutmeg

Heat the oven to 180°C (350°F) mark 4. Clean the herrings and divide each fish into two fillets. Season with salt and pepper and roll up the fish from the tail end, with the skin outwards. Place in a single layer in a shallow oven-proof dish. Arrange the onion slices on top of the fish with the bay leaf, peppercorns, cloves and mace. Mix the vinegar and apple juice and pour over the fish. Cover and bake for 45 minutes.

While the fish are cooking, prepare the sauce. Peel, core and slice the apple and put into a pan with the remaining ingredients. Cover and simmer over heat until the apples are soft. Sir the sauce. Drain the fish and top with the sauce. The dish may

# SPICED SALT HERRINGS

Serves 4

2 salt herrings
1 small onion, thinly sliced
1 small lemon, thinly sliced
1 bay leaf
pinch of pepper
pinch of ground nutmeg
5 tbsp dry cider
3 tbsp salad oil

Clean and bone the herrings and leave to soak in cold water for 12 hours. Skin the fish and cut the fillets into narrow strips. Arrange the strips in a shallow serving dish with the onion and lemon slices on top. Break the bay leaf into pieces and sprinkle over the top. Sprinkle with pepper and nutmeg. Mix the cider and oil and pour over the herrings. Cover and leave in a cool place for 3 hours.

Serve with salad or with bread and butter or with small new potatoes.

# ROLLMOP HERRING SALAD

Serves 4

8 rollmop herrings
450 g (1 lb) potatoes
150 ml (¼ pint) mayonnaise
1 tsp French mustard
2 red eating apples
lettuce or Chinese leaves
parsley sprigs for garnish

Chop the rollmop herrings into small pieces. Chop the onions with which they are pickled and mix with the herrings. Boil the potatoes until cooked, drain very well and leave until lukewarm. Mix the mayonnaise and mustard. Dice the potatoes and stir into the mayonnaise. Leave until just cold. Do not peel the apples, but core and dice them. Mix together the potato salad with the herring and onion pieces and apples. Arrange on a bed of lettuce or Chinese leaves and garnish with parsley sprigs. Serve freshly made.

# HERRINGS WITH CREAM SAUCE

Serves 4

4 medium herrings
25 g (1 oz) butter, melted
salt and pepper
150 ml (¼ pint) double cream
2 tsp made mustard
2 tsp lemon juice
1 small onion, grated
lemon wedges to garnish

Clean the herrings and remove heads and tails. Brush all over with the butter and sprinkle well with salt and pepper. Grill under a medium heat for about 7 minutes on each side until cooked through and slightly crisp.

Whip the cream to soft peaks and fold in the mustard, lemon juice and onion. Place the herrings on a warm serving dish with a garnish of lemon wedges. Serve the sauce separately.

# HERRINGS WITH MUSTARD BUTTER

Serves 4

4 medium herrings
75 g (3 oz) butter
1 tsp mustard powder
salt and pepper
4 tomatoes

Heat the oven to 190°C (375°F) mark 5. Clean and fillet the herrings and open them out flat. Cream the butter with the mustard powder, salt and pepper and spread on the flesh of each fish. Fold in half and wrap each fish in a piece of greased foil. Place on a baking sheet and bake for 15 minutes. Cut the tomatoes in half and place on the baking sheet. Season well and dot with a little butter. Continue baking for 10 minutes.

Serve at once with brown bread and butter.

# MARGARETTA HERRINGS

Serves 4

*4 large herrings*
*50 g (2 oz) butter*
*salt and pepper*
*4 tbsp single cream*
*3 tsp tomato purée*
*3 tsp made mustard*

Heat the oven to 180°C (350°F) mark 4. Fillet the herrings to yield 8 pieces of fish. Divide the butter into 8 pieces and put a piece on the surface of each fillet. Roll up the fish, skin side outwards, and pack into an oven-proof dish, in a single layer. Sprinkle with salt and pepper. Mix together the cream, tomato purée and mustard and pour over the fish. Bake for 30 minutes.

Serve at once with plain boiled potatoes and peas, or a green salad.

# HERRING ROE SAVOURIES

Serves 4

*4 very large tomatoes*
*225 g (8 oz) mixed hard and soft roes*
*25 g (1 oz) butter*
*salt and pepper*
*few drops of Worcestershire sauce*
*25 g (1 oz) grated Parmesan cheese*
*4 small slices buttered toast*

Heat the oven to 180°C (350°F) mark 4. Cut a thick slice from the top of each tomato. Scoop out the insides, leaving a thick 'wall' for each tomato. Discard the seeds but reserve the pulp and liquid. Fry the roes in the butter until just firm. Mix with the tomato pulp and liquid and season well with salt, pepper and Worcestershire sauce. Pile into the tomato cases and sprinkle with cheese. Put into a dish and bake for 20 minutes. Serve each tomato on a piece of buttered toast.

# CREAMED HERRING ROES

Serves 4

450 g (1 lb) soft herring roes
25 g (1 oz) plain flour
salt and pepper
50 g (2 oz) butter
275 ml (½ pint) single cream
2 tsp lemon juice
4 slices wholemeal toast
1 tbsp fresh parsley, chopped

Rinse the roes under cold running water. Drain well and pat dry with kitchen paper. Season the flour well with salt and pepper and dust the flour lightly over the roes. Melt the butter and fry the roes for 5 minutes over a low heat, turning them often. Stir in the cream and lemon juice and bring just to the boil. Pour over the toast and sprinkle with parsley.

# SOFT ROE PATE

Serves 4–6

225 g (8 oz) soft roes
salt and pepper
150 g (5 oz) butter
1 tbsp lemon juice
1 tbsp fresh parsley, chopped

Season the roes with salt and pepper. Melt 25 g (1 oz) of the butter and fry the roes lightly until cooked through which will take about 10 minutes. Mash with a wooden spoon. Soften the remaining butter and work into the roes and mix well until smooth and evenly coloured. Mix with lemon juice and parsley and spoon into a serving dish.

Serve with hot toast or thin brown bread and butter.

# SALMON STEAKS IN CREAM SAUCE

Serves 4

4 × 2.5 cm (1 in) thick salmon
    steaks
2 tbsp fresh parsley, chopped
2 tsp lemon rind, grated
salt and pepper
1 bay leaf
275 ml (½ pint) single cream

Heat the oven to 190°C (375°F) mark 5. Grease a shallow oven-proof dish and put in the salmon steaks in a single layer. Sprinkle with parsley, lemon rind, salt and pepper. Put the bay leaf on top and pour over the cream. Bake for 25 minutes, basting occasionally during cooking.

Serve at once with new potatoes and peas.

# GREENWICH WHITEBAIT

Serves 4

*450 g (1 lb) whitebait*
*salt and pepper*
*pinch of curry powder or cayenne*
  *pepper*
*40 g (1½ oz) plain flour*
*oil for deep frying*

Garnish
*parsley sprigs*
*lemon wedges*

Make sure that the whitebait are completely dry by patting them with kitchen paper. Mix the salt, pepper, curry or cayenne with the flour and coat the fish lightly. Heat the oil to 180°C (350°F). Put about one-third of the whitebait into frying basket and place in the oil. Shake them as they cook for 3 minutes until just coloured. Drain and place on a warm serving dish. Repeat the process with the other fish.

Return all the fish to the frying basket. Let the oil reheat to the correct temperature and return the fish to the pan for about 1½ minutes, shaking the basket as they become golden and crisp. Drain quickly on kitchen paper and serve very hot with parsley sprigs and lemon wedges to garnish, and an accompaniment of thin brown bread and butter.

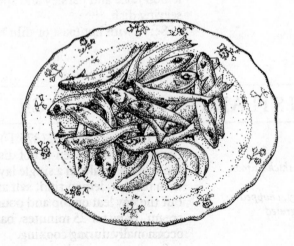

# MACKEREL WITH GREEN PEPPER SAUCE

Serves 4

4 mackerel
75 g (3 oz) butter
1 lemon
salt and pepper
225 g (8 oz) tomatoes, skinned and
    chopped
1 garlic clove, crushed
2 green peppers, chopped

Garnish
lemon wedges

Heat the oven to 190°C (375°F) mark 5.
Clean the mackerel and place on a piece of
foil greased with 50 g (2 oz) of the butter.
Add the grated rind and juice of the lemon
and season well with salt and pepper. Fold
over the foil to form a sealed packet. Bake
for 45 minutes.

While the mackerel are cooking, prepare
the sauce. Melt the remaining butter and
add the tomatoes, garlic and peppers.
Simmer over a low heat until the peppers
are soft. Place the mackerel on a serving
dish and spoon over the sauce. Serve with
lemon wedges.

# STUFFED BAKED MACKEREL

Serves 4

4 mackerel
salt and pepper
lemon juice
225 g (8 oz) mushrooms, finely
    chopped
2 medium onions, finely chopped
1 tbsp fresh parsley, chopped
4 sprigs fennel

Heat the oven to 180°C (350°F) mark 4.
Fillet the fish, keeping each mackerel in one
piece. Sprinkle inside with salt, pepper and
lemon juice. Take a large piece of foil and
place on a baking sheet. Mix the
mushrooms, onions and parsley and season
well with salt and pepper. Fill each fish with
this mixture and arrange on the foil which
has been well-buttered. Put a sprig of fennel
on each fish. Fold over the foil to make a flat
parcel.

Bake for 30 minutes. Open the foil
carefully. Remove and discard the fennel.
Slash the top of each fish diagonally three
times at equal intervals. Do not cover again
but return to the oven for 10 minutes. Lift
the fish carefully on to a serving dish and
spoon over any cooking juices.

Serve at once with boiled potatoes and a
vegetable.

# MACKEREL KEBABS

Serves 4

*4 small mackerel*
*8 lean bacon rashers*
*20 button mushrooms*
*8 bay leaves*
*salt and pepper*
*1 tbsp lemon juice*
*½ teaspoon fresh mixed herbs*
*6 tbsp oil*

Prepare the mackerel to yield eight fillets. Cut each fillet into six pieces. Derind the bacon and spread out each rasher thinly with a broad-bladed knife. Divide each rasher into three pieces, and roll up each piece of bacon.

Take four long kebab skewers and thread on the mackerel, alternating with bacon rolls, mushrooms and bay leaves. Season well with salt and pepper and sprinkle with lemon juice and herbs. Place on a dish and sprinkle with oil. Cover and chill in the refrigerator for 2 hours. Grill under a medium heat for 15 minutes, turning the skewers frequently.

Serve with Mustard Sauce (see page 85), brown bread and a green salad.

# ESSEX PICKLED MACKEREL

Serves 4–6

*6 small mackerel*
*25 g (1 oz) butter*
*4 bay leaves*
*4 cloves*
*1 tsp peppercorns*
*575 ml (1 pint) vinegar*
*1 tbsp thyme*
*1 tbsp fresh parsley, chopped*
*1 tbsp fresh fennel, chopped*
*salt and pepper*

Heat the oven to 180°C (350°F) mark 4. Fillet the fish, wash and dry them. Arrange in a single layer in a greased oven-proof dish and dot with pieces of butter. Bake for 20 minutes. Put the bay leaves, cloves, peppercorns and vinegar into a pan and bring to the boil. Simmer for 10 minutes. Leave until cold and strain over fish. Leave in a cold place for 6 hours. Lift out the fish and drain well. Arrange on a serving dish and sprinkle with the herbs and plenty of salt and pepper.

# BAKED MACKEREL IN CIDER SAUCE

Serves 4

4 mackerel
salt and pepper
1/2 lemon
1 medium onion, thinly sliced
sprig of thyme
sprig of rosemary
2 bay leaves
425 ml (3/4 pint) dry cider
150 ml (1/4 pint) water
2 tsp arrowroot

Heat the oven to 180°C (350°F) mark 4. Slit each fish along the belly and remove the guts. Use kitchen scissors to cut off the heads and fins. Wash the fish well, drain, and season well inside each fish with salt and pepper. Arrange the fish head to tail in a single layer in an oven-proof dish. Peel the rind thinly from the lemon and arrange on top of the fish with the sliced onions and herbs. Pour over the cider and water, and cover with foil. Bake for 30 minutes.

Arrange the fish and onions on a warm serving dish and keep hot. Strain the cooking liquid until it measures 425 ml (3/4 pint). Mix the arrowroot with a little cold water and stir into the cooking liquid. Bring to the boil, stirring all the time. Simmer gently, stirring often, until the sauce is clear. Pour over the fish and serve at once with jacket or boiled potatoes, and a vegetable or green salad.

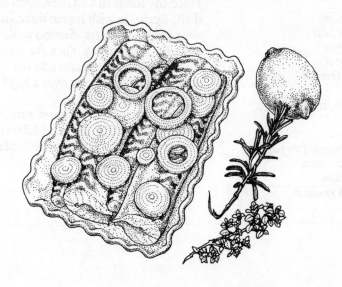

# MEDITERRANEAN MACKEREL

Serves 4

4 medium mackerel
8 tbsp oil
5 tbsp dry white wine
few drops of Tabasco sauce
salt and pepper
50 g (2 oz) black olives
2 oranges
4 bay leaves

Clean and gut the mackerel and remove the heads. Make two or three diagonal slashes across both sides of each fish. Line a grill pan with foil and place the fish in the pan. Mix the oil, wine, Tabasco sauce and plenty of salt and pepper and pour over the fish. Leave to stand for 2 hours, turning the fish occasionally. Preheat the grill and grill the fish for 8 minutes on each side. Lift the fish on to a serving dish and pour over the pan juices. Leave until cold.

Peel the oranges and cut them across into thin rings. Garnish the fish with olives, orange rings and bay leaves, and serve with brown bread and butter and a green salad.

# MACKEREL WITH MUSTARD CREAM

Serves 4

8 mackerel fillets
2 tbsp lemon juice
25 g (1 oz) butter
salt and pepper
6 tomatoes, skinned
2 tbsp oil
1 garlic clove, crushed

Sauce
4 tbsp mayonnaise (see page 88)
4 tbsp double cream
juice of 1 lemon
2 tsp French mustard

Heat the oven to 200°C (400°F) mark 6. Place the fillets in a shallow oven-proof dish. Sprinkle with lemon juice and top with flakes of butter. Season well, cover and bake for 20 minutes. Slice the tomatoes thickly. Heat the oil and add the tomato slices and garlic. Cook over a high heat for 2 minutes.

Place the tomato slices on a hot serving dish. Arrange the mackerel fillets on top. Mix together the sauce ingredients and spoon over the top.

# BAKED SPRATS

Serves 4

900 g (2 lb) sprats
salt and pepper
pinch of ground nutmeg
1 medium onion, sliced
4 bay leaves
275 ml (½ pint) white wine vinegar
25 g (1 oz) butter
sprig of fennel
1 tsp fresh parsley, chopped
½ tsp fresh thyme

Heat the oven to 180°C (350°F) mark 4. Remove the heads and tails from sprats. Wash and pat dry with kitchen paper. Arrange the fish head to tail in a shallow oven-proof dish. Season with salt, pepper and nutmeg. Break the onion slices into rings and arrange on top of the fish with the bay leaves. Pour over the vinegar and a little water if necessary to cover. Dot with flakes of butter and put on the fennel sprig.

Cover with foil and bake for 1 hour. Cool and then chill in the refrigerator. Just before serving, drain the sprats and arrange on a serving dish. Sprinkle with parsley and thyme and serve with Tartare Sauce or Green Mayonnaise .

# DEVILLED SPRATS

Serves 4

450 g (1 lb) sprats
50 g (2 oz) plain flour
2 tsp mustard powder
1 tsp cayenne pepper
salt and pepper
oil for deep frying

Gut the fish through the gills, leaving the heads and bodies intact. Dry the fish with kitchen paper. Season the flour with the mustard, cayenne pepper, salt and pepper. Coat the fish evenly. Fry in hot deep oil for 3–4 minutes until crisp and golden.

Serve with brown bread and butter and lemon wedges.

# SEAFOOD (SHELLFISH)

Seafood is extremely versatile, highly nutritious
and simple to prepare.

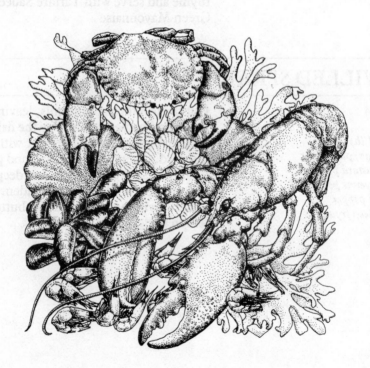

# QUICK PRAWN PIZZA

Serves 4–6

225 g (8 oz) self-raising flour
salt and pepper
pinch of cayenne pepper
50 g (2 oz) block margarine
100 g (4 oz) Cheddar cheese, grated
6 tbsp milk
4 large tomatoes
225 g (8 oz) peeled prawns
50 g (2 oz) black olives, halved
50 g (2 oz) gruyère cheese
3 tbsp oil

Heat the oven to 200°C (400°F) mark 6. Sieve the flour, salt, pepper and cayenne pepper into a bowl. Rub in the margarine until the mixture is like fine breadcrumbs. Stir in the grated cheese and mix to a dough with milk. Roll the dough out to a 23 cm (9 in) circle. Place on a lightly oiled baking sheet.

Slice the tomatoes and arrange on top of the dough. Cover with 150 g (5 oz) of the prawns and the halved olives. Cut the cheese into very thin slices and arrange on top. Sprinkle with oil, and season with salt and pepper. Bake for 30 minutes. Garnish with the remaining prawns. Serve freshly baked.

# SWEET AND SOUR PRAWNS

Serves 3–4

225 g (8 oz) prawns, shelled
1 tbsp dry sherry
salt and pepper
2 tbsp oil
1 large onion, thinly sliced
1/2 green pepper, chopped
1/2 red pepper, chopped
5 tbsp chicken stock
4 rings canned pineapple
1 tbsp cornflour
2 tsp soya sauce
5 tbsp wine vinegar
50 g (2 oz) sugar

Put the prawns into a bowl and add the sherry, salt and pepper. Heat the oil and soften the onion and peppers over a low heat for 5 minutes. Add the stock. Cut the pineapple into small pieces and stir into the pan. Cover and cook gently for 5 minutes. Mix together the cornflour, soya sauce, vinegar and sugar. Stir into the pan and stir over a low heat until the sauce thickens. Stir in the prawns, cover and turn off the heat. Leave to stand for 2 minutes and serve with boiled rice.

# SAILORS' MUSSELS

Serves 4

*60–70 mussels in shells*
*1 small onion, finely chopped*
*1 garlic clove, crushed*
*275 ml (½ pint) dry cider or dry*
*  white wine*
*150 ml (¼ pint) water*
*pepper*
*25 g (1 oz) butter*
*15 g (½ oz) plain flour*
*1 tbsp fresh parsley, chopped*

Put the mussels in cold water and discard any that float. Scrub the mussels very thoroughly, removing any 'beards' by tugging with a sharp knife. Discard any mussels that are broken and any which remain open. Place in a large pan with the onion, garlic, cider or wine, water and pepper. Cover and cook very gently until the shells open, about 5–7 minutes. Always check mussels after cooking and this time discard any whose shells have not opened. Drain the mussels, retaining the liquid. Remove the top shells from mussels and discard. Divide the mussels in half shells between 4 individual bowls.

Put the cooking liquid into a clean pan and bring to the boil. Soften the butter and mix well with the flour. Add tiny pieces of this mixture to the hot liquid and simmer until the liquid has thickened slightly. Season with salt and pepper to taste and stir in parsley. Pour over the mussels and serve at once.

# MEDITERRANEAN SCAMPI

Serves 4

*450 g (1 lb) scampi*
*3 tbsp olive oil*
*1 small onion, finely chopped*
*1 garlic clove, crushed*
*4 tomatoes*
*1 tbsp fresh parsley, chopped*
*2 tsp lemon juice*
*salt and pepper*

If the scampi is frozen, thaw and then drain well. Heat the oil in a thick pan and fry the onion and garlic until the onion is soft and golden. Skin the tomatoes and discard the pips. Chop the flesh roughly and add to the pan with the scampi. Cook over a low heat, stirring well, for 6 minutes until the scampi are tender. Remove from heat and stir in the parsley, lemon juice, salt and pepper.

Serve hot with buttered rice or with crusty bread.

# SCAMPI NEWBURG

Serves 4

24 shelled scampi
50 g (2 oz) butter
1 small onion, finely chopped
1 garlic clove, crushed
1 tbsp concentrated tomato purée
salt and pepper
275 ml (½ pint) single cream
2 egg yolks
3 tbsp brandy

The scampi may be frozen but should be thawed and well drained before use. Melt the butter and stir in the onion and garlic. Cook gently over a low heat for 5 minutes. Add the scampi and stir over a low heat for 2 minutes. Stir in the tomato purée and season well with salt and pepper.

Mix the cream, egg yolks and brandy. Stir into the scampi and heat through but do not boil.

Serve with boiled rice.

# CURRIED SHRIMPS

Serves 4

1 large onion, finely chopped
25 g (1 oz) butter
1 tbsp curry powder
1 cooking apple, peeled and chopped
275 ml (½ pint) chicken stock
1 tbsp concentrated tomato purée
2 tbsp fruit chutney, finely chopped
350 g (12 oz) peeled shrimps
1 tbsp lemon juice

Cook the onion in the butter for 5 minutes until soft and golden. Stir in the curry powder and continue cooking for 3 minutes. Add the apple and stir over a low heat for 3 minutes. Add the stock, tomato purée and chutney, stir well and bring to the boil. Cover and simmer for 20 minutes. Stir in the shrimps and lemon juice and heat thoroughly.

Serve with boiled rice or as the filling for scooped-out baked jacket potatoes.

# POTTED SHRIMPS

Serves 4

175 g (6 oz) butter
225 g (8 oz) shrimps, peeled
ground black pepper
ground nutmeg
squeeze of lemon juice

Melt 100 g (4 oz) of the butter over a low heat. Add the shrimps and a good seasoning of pepper and nutmeg, preferably freshly ground. Add the lemon juice. Toss over a low heat until the shrimps are coated in butter. Spoon into 4 individual ramekins. Leave until cold.

Melt the remaining butter and strain over

the shrimps, being careful not to let the milky residue from the butter go through the strainer. Leave until cold and set.

The shrimps will keep in a refrigerator for up to 7 days. They are best served just warm with plenty of hot toast, so that the butter is soft but not melted. If heated through, the shrimps form a useful emergency sauce for white fish, or they are very good with scrambled eggs.

# SCALLOPS IN CHEESE SAUCE

Serves 4

8 scallops
425 ml (¾ pint) milk
25 g (1 oz) butter
25 g (1 oz) plain flour
50 g (2 oz) Cheddar cheese, grated
pinch of mustard powder
salt and pepper
50 g (2 oz) prawns, shelled
25 g (1 oz) fresh breadcrumbs
25 g (1 oz) butter, melted
25 g (1 oz) Parmesan cheese, grated

Heat the oven to 180°C (350°F) mark 4. Put the scallops into a shallow pan and cover with the milk. Simmer over a low heat for 5 minutes. Drain the scallops, reserving the milk, and slice each one in two horizontally, to make 16 pieces and the 8 'corals'. Arrange in a shallow oven-proof dish. Melt the butter and work in the flour. Cook over a low heat for 1 minute and gradually add the warm milk. Stir over low heat until the sauce thickens. Remove from the heat and stir in the Cheddar cheese, and season with mustard, salt and pepper. Sprinkle the prawns over the scallops and pour on the cheese sauce.

Sprinkle the breadcrumbs on top of the dish. Drizzle on the melted butter and sprinkle with the Parmesan cheese. Bake for 15 minutes.

Serve at once with rice or potatoes and a green salad.

# SCALLOPS IN WINE SAUCE

Serves 4

8 scallops
275 ml (½ pint) dry white wine
1 small onion, finely chopped
sprig of parsley
sprig of thyme
1 bay leaf
75 g (3 oz) butter
2 tbsp lemon juice
100 g (4 oz) button mushrooms
25 g (1 oz) plain flour
salt and pepper
25 g (1 oz) Cheddar cheese, grated
25 g (1 oz) fresh white or brown
   breadcrumbs
1 tbsp Parmesan cheese, grated

If possible, keep four deep scallop shells for the presentation of this dish, but otherwise use individual oven-proof dishes. Put the scallops into a pan with the wine, onion and herbs. Simmer for 5 minutes and drain the scallops, reserving the liquid. Chop the scallops into three white pieces and the coral. Melt 50 g (2 oz) of the butter and add the lemon juice. Add the mushrooms and cook over a low heat for 5 minutes. Add the remaining butter to the pan and stir in the flour. Cook for 1 minute and then strain in the cooking liquid from the scallops. Simmer for 3 minutes. Take off the heat, season and stir in the Cheddar cheese. Add the scallops. Spoon into scallop shells or individual dishes. Mix the breadcrumbs and Parmesan cheese and sprinkle on top. Put under a hot grill to brown the breadcrumbs.

# COCKLE PIE

Serves 4

575 ml (1 pint) cooked cockles
225 g (8 oz) shortcrust pastry
   (see page 93)
6 spring onions or 1 small onion,
   finely chopped
100 g (4 oz) streaky bacon rashers,
   finely chopped
pepper

Freshly-cooked cockles will produce their own liquor, but if they have been bought from a fishmonger or frozen, chicken stock may be used in finishing the pie.

Heat the oven to 200°C (400°F) mark 6. Line a 20-cm (8-in) flan ring with pastry. Bake blind for 15 minutes. Put a layer of cockles in the base and sprinkle with onion and bacon. Season with pepper and repeat the layers and top with a few cockles. Sprinkle on 150 ml (¼ pint) cockle liquor or chicken stock. Make a lattice from any remaining pastry and place over the filling. Turn the oven down to 180°C (350°F) mark 4 and bake for 30 minutes. Serve hot or cold.

# SMOKED FISH

# SMOKED MACKEREL PASTIES

Serves 4

*350 g (12 oz) shortcrust pastry*
*275 g (10 oz) smoked mackerel*
*225 g (8 oz) potatoes, diced*
*1 medium onion, diced*
*2 tomatoes*
*4 tbsp tomato ketchup*
*1 tsp lemon juice*
*salt and pepper*
*milk for glazing*

Heat the oven to 200°C (400°F) mark 6. Roll out the pastry and cut into four 15 cm (6 in) circles. Skin the fish and remove any bones. Cut into small pieces, and mix with the potatoes and onion. Skin the tomatoes and discard the pips. Chop the flesh roughly and mix with the fish and with the tomato ketchup, lemon juice and plenty of salt and pepper. Divide the mixture between the pastry circles, placing it in the centre of each one. Dampen the edges with water and seal the pastry in the centre to give a pasty shape.

Place on a lightly greased baking sheet and brush well with milk. Prick each pasty two or three times with a fork. Bake for 10 minutes, then reduce the heat to 150°C (300°F) mark 2 and bake for 25 minutes.

Serve hot or cold, with vegetables or a salad.

# PEPPERED SMOKED MACKEREL SALAD

Serves 4

*2 peppered smoked mackerel*
*450 g (1 lb) potatoes*
*1 eating apple, peeled and diced*
*1 green pepper, chopped*
*5 tbsp oil*
*2 tbsp lemon juice*
*1 tbsp fresh chives, chopped*
*salt and pepper*
*pinch of turmeric*

Remove the skin and any bones from the mackerel and break the fish into large flakes. Boil the potatoes, cool and dice. Mix together the fish, potatoes, apple and green pepper. Mix the oil, lemon juice, chives, salt, pepper and turmeric and pour over the fish. Toss lightly and serve on a bed of lettuce or other salad greens.

Plain smoked mackerel may be used for this recipe, but the variety which is coated in cracked black peppercorns is particularly delicious. The fish is also available with a thick coating of herbs.

# SMOKED HADDOCK SALAD

Serves 4

450 g (1 lb) haricot or red kidney
  beans, cooked
450 g (1 lb) smoked haddock
milk and water
150 ml (¼ pint) natural yoghurt
2 tbsp lemon juice
1 tbsp fresh parsley, chopped
2 tsp curry powder
salt and pepper
crisp lettuce or Chinese leaves
1 hard-boiled egg, sliced

For speed of preparation, canned beans may be used if well drained. Poach the fish in a mixture of milk and water for 10 minutes and drain well. Cool the fish and remove the skin and bones. Flake the fish and mix with the beans. Mix the yoghurt, lemon juice, parsley, curry powder and seasoning together. Pour over the fish and mix well. Shred the lettuce or Chinese leaves and arrange in a bowl or on a flat platter. Spoon on the fish mixture and garnish with sliced egg.

# BRANDADE OF SMOKED HADDOCK

Serves 6–8

675 g (1½ lb) smoked haddock
275 ml (½ pint) milk
275 ml (½ pint) olive oil
2 garlic cloves, crushed
150 ml (¼ pint) single cream
salt and pepper
pinch of ground nutmeg
1–2 tsp lemon juice
fried bread triangles

Poach the fish in the milk until just tender. Drain well and discard the skin and bones. Flake the fish finely into a bowl over a pan of hot water. Heat the oil and garlic together in another pan until hot but not boiling. Put the cream into a small pan and also heat gently to lukewarm.

Pour a little oil in to the fish, beating with a wooden spoon. Add a little cream and beat well. Alternate oil and cream, beating well, but do not overbeat the mixture or it will separate. When all the oil and cream has been absorbed, season to taste with salt, pepper, nutmeg and lemon juice. Put the fish mixture into a warm serving bowl and surround with fried bread triangles.

# KEDGEREE

Serves 4

175 g (6 oz) long grain rice
450 g (1 lb) smoked haddock or cod
   fillet
2 eggs, hard-boiled
2 tsp curry powder
2 tsp lemon juice
salt and pepper
100 g (4 oz) butter
1 tbsp fresh parsley, chopped

Cook the rice in boiling salted water for
12–15 minutes until just tender. Drain very
well and keep warm. Meanwhile poach the
fish in water until cooked but unbroken.
Drain well and remove the skin and any
bones. Break into large flakes and mix with
the rice. Chop the whites of the eggs
roughly and mix into the rice with the curry
powder, lemon juice, salt and pepper. Flake
the butter and stir into the rice. Pile on a hot
serving dish and sprinkle with the chopped
egg yolks and parsley.

# ARNOLD BENNETT OMELETTE

Serves 2

175 g (6 oz) smoked haddock fillet
4 large eggs
50 g (2 oz) gruyère cheese, grated
salt and pepper
25 g (1 oz) butter
275 ml (½ pint) cheese sauce
25 g (1 oz) Parmesan cheese, grated

Poach the haddock until tender. Drain well,
cool and remove the skin and any bones.
Flake the fish. Beat the eggs until light and
frothy. Add the cheese, haddock and
seasoning to the eggs. Melt the butter in an
18-cm (7-in) omelette pan and pour in the
egg mixture. Cook gently, lifting the egg
and moving it with a fork until the omelette
is almost set. Spoon on the warm cheese
sauce and sprinkle on the Parmesan cheese.
Do not fold the omelette but put under a
hot grill to brown quickly. Serve
immediately.

# FISHERMAN'S PIE

Serves 4

*450 g (1 lb) smoked haddock or cod
  fillet*
*275 ml (½ pint) dry cider*
*150 ml (¼ pint) milk*
*40 g (1½ oz) butter*
*40 g (1½ oz) plain flour*
*3 hard-boiled eggs, chopped*
*100 g (4 oz) peas, cooked*
*salt and pepper*
*350 g (12 oz) puff pastry*
*egg for glazing*

Heat the oven to 220°C (425°F) mark 7. Poach the fish in the cider and milk until just cooked. Drain the fish, reserving the cooking liquid. Remove the skin and bones, and break the fish into chunks. Melt the butter and stir in the flour. Cook for 1 minute over a low heat and gradually add the strained cooking liquid. Bring to the boil, stirring well, and then simmer until smooth and creamy. Remove from the heat and stir in the fish, chopped eggs and peas. Season well with salt and pepper. Turn into a pie dish.

Roll out the pastry and cover the pie dish, using any trimmings to make decorative leaves. Brush well with beaten egg to glaze. Bake for 30 minutes.

Serve with mashed potatoes and vegetables.

# QUICK KIPPER PIZZA

Serves 4–6

225 g (8 oz) self-raising flour
1/2 tsp salt
40 g (1 1/2 oz) butter
150 ml (1/4 pint) milk

Topping
100 g (4 oz) Cheddar cheese, grated
1 tsp mustard powder
1/2 tsp fresh mixed herbs
225 g (8 oz) tomatoes
8 kipper fillets
8 black olives, stoned
paprika

Heat the oven to 200°C (400°F) mark 6. Sieve the flour and salt, and rub in the butter until the mixture is like fine breadcrumbs. Work in the milk to make a firm soft dough. Roll out lightly to make a 30 cm (12 in) circle. Place on a greased baking sheet.

Mix the cheese, mustard and herbs in a basin and sprinkle over the dough. Skin the tomatoes and slice them thinly. Arrange on top of the cheese. Arrange the kipper fillets on top in a wheel pattern. Place the olives between the fillets. Sprinkle with paprika. Bake for 30 minutes. Serve hot.

# KIPPER SALAD

Serves 4–6

8 kipper fillets
6 tbsp olive or nut oil
3 tbsp white wine vinegar
2 tsp French mustard
2 tsp dill seed (or dill weed)
pepper
lettuce or Chinese leaves

Skin the raw kipper fillets by inserting a sharp pointed knife under the skin and stripping back the skin carefully. Cut the fillets into 1 cm (1/2 in) thin strips. Place in a bowl. Mix the oil, vinegar, mustard, dill seed and pepper and pour over the kippers. Cover and leave in a cool place for 12–24 hours, stirring the mixture occasionally. Arrange the lettuce or Chinese leaves on a serving dish and spoon on the kipper pieces and dressing.

# CANNED FISH

A collection of quick and easy recipes which
can be made straight from the store cupboard.

# SALMON BAKE

Serves 4

*225 g (8 oz) can pink or red salmon*
*1 × 4 cm (1½ in) thick slices of*
*    white bread*
*150 ml (¼ pint) milk*
*1 egg*
*25 g (1 oz) butter, melted*
*½ tsp lemon juice*
*salt and pepper*

Heat the oven to 180°C (350°F) mark 4. Drain the salmon and discard the liquid. Remove the bones and skin and mash the salmon with a fork. Remove the crusts from the bread and soak the bread in milk for 20 minutes. Beat the bread and milk with a fork and work in the salmon, egg, butter, lemon juice and seasoning (the fish is usually rather salty, so be careful not to over salt). Mix well and put into a 500-ml (1-pint) oven-proof dish which has been well greased. Bake for 1 hour.

Serve hot with new potatoes or mashed potatoes and vegetables, or cold with salad. Leftovers make an excellent sandwich filling.

# SALMON MOUSSE

Serves 4–6

*225 g (8 oz) can red or pink salmon*
*½ lemon*
*salt and pepper*
*3 drops Tabasco sauce*
*150 ml (¼ pint) natural yoghurt*
*150 ml (¼ pint) mayonnaise*
*4 tsp gelatine*

Garnish
*lemon slices*
*parsley, chopped*

Drain the salmon and remove the skin and bones. Mash with a fork. Add the grated rind and juice of the lemon, the salt, pepper, Tabasco sauce, yoghurt and mayonnaise and mix thoroughly until evenly coloured. Put 1 tablespoon water into a cup and sprinkle on the gelatine. Put into a pan containing a little hot water and heat gently until the gelatine has dissolved and is syrupy. Stir into the salmon mixture. Cool and just before the mousse sets, spoon into a serving dish or into 4–6 individual dishes. Chill for 2 hours. Garnish with lemon slices and parsley just before serving.

# ANCHOIADE

Serves 4

*100 g (4 oz) can anchovy fillets*
*2 garlic cloves, crushed*
*3 tbsp olive oil*
*1 tbsp lemon juice*
*pepper*
*4 × 5 cm (2 in) thick slices French
   bread*
*1 tbsp fine breadcrumbs*
*1 tbsp fresh parsley, chopped*

Heat the oven to 190°C (375°F) mark 5.
Chop the anchovy fillets and put into a bowl
with the oil from the can. Mash with a
spoon and work in the garlic, olive oil,
lemon juice and pepper. Spread on the
slices of French bread and put on to a
lightly oiled baking sheet. Sprinkle with
breadcrumbs and parsley. Bake for 15
minutes.

# SUMMER SEAFOOD SALAD

Serves 4

*1 crisp lettuce*
*225 g (8 oz) button mushrooms*
*3 tbsp lemon juice*
*450 g (1 lb) tomatoes, skinned*
*3 eggs, hard-boiled*
*225 g (8 oz) canned tuna in brine*
*225 g (8 oz) prawns, peeled*
*4 tbsp olive oil*
*2 tbsp wine vinegar*
*salt and pepper*

Shred the lettuce and place in a large
serving bowl. Do not peel the mushrooms
but wipe and then trim the stems and slice
the mushrooms thinly. Put them into a
separate bowl and sprinkle with lemon
juice. Leave to stand while preparing the
rest of the salad.

Quarter the tomatoes. Quarter the eggs
lengthwise. Place on the lettuce. Drain the
tuna and break into chunks. Add to a
bowl with the prawns. Stir in the
mushrooms. Mix together the oil, vinegar,
salt and pepper. Pour over the salad and
toss lightly so that the eggs do not break.

Serve with a bowl of lemon-flavoured
mayonnaise.

# CURRIED TUNA PUFF

Serves 4–6

*350 g (12 oz) puff pastry*
*1 small onion, finely chopped*
*1 eating apple, peeled and finely*
  *chopped*
*15 g (½ oz) butter*
*2 tsp curry powder*
*2 tsp plain flour*
*150 ml (¼ pint) stock or water*
*1 tbsp mango chutney*
*salt*
*50 g (2 oz) long grain rice*
*225 g (8 oz) canned tuna fish,*
  *drained*
*egg for glazing*

Heat the oven to 220°C (425°F) mark 7. Divide the pastry in half. Roll out into two rounds, one measuring 23 cm (9 in) and the other slightly larger. Place the smaller round on a baking tray.

To make the filling, cook the onion and apple in the butter over a low heat until soft and golden. Stir in the curry powder and flour and cook for 1 minute. Blend in the stock or water and chutney and simmer for 5 minutes, stirring well. Season to taste with salt. Meanwhile cook the rice in boiling salted water for 12 minutes until tender. Drain well and add to the curry mixture. Flake the fish, add to the mixture, and leave until cold.

Place the curry mixture in the centre of the pastry round, spreading it to within 1 cm (½ in) of the edge. Brush the edge of the pastry circle with beaten egg. Put the other piece of pastry on top and seal the edges well. Roll out any trimmings and cut out leaves to decorate the top of the pastry. Brush leaves with beaten egg and cut two slits in the top of the pastry. Bake for 30 minutes.

Serve hot with vegetables or a salad.

# SALAD NICOISE

Serves 4

1 crisp lettuce
4 tomatoes, skinned
2 eggs, hard-boiled
100 g (4 oz) cucumber
100 g (4 oz) French beans, cooked
1 green or red pepper, chopped
225 g (8 oz) canned tuna in oil or
   brine
50 g (2 oz) anchovy fillets
50 g (2 oz) black olives
6 tbsp olive oil
3 tbsp wine vinegar
salt and pepper

Break the lettuce leaves into pieces and line
a large salad bowl. Quarter the tomatoes
and eggs and place in the bowl. Do not peel
the cucumber but dice and add to the bowl.
Cut the beans into chunks and add to the
bowl with the chopped pepper. Drain the
tuna very well and break into chunks. Add
to the bowl and garnish with anchovy fillets
and olives. Mix the oil and vinegar and
season well, and pour over the salad. Serve
at once, with a bowl of mayonnaise if liked.

This is a favourite French dish and it
makes a substantial and delicious meal
accompanied by chunks of crusty bread and
butter. If liked, some tiny new potatoes may
be added to the salad. If the large
full-flavoured outdoor tomatoes are used,
they should be cut into eight or twelve
sections.

# SAUCES, STUFFINGS AND PASTRIES

This chapter gives several savoury sauces and
butters to serve with fish as well as stuffings
and pastry recipes.

# INSTANT PARSLEY SAUCE

Serves 4

275 ml (½ pint) soured cream
½ lemon
2 tsp tomato purée
3 tbsp fresh parsley, chopped
salt and pepper

Put the soured cream into a bowl. Add the grated rind and juice of the lemon. Stir in the tomato purée and parsley. Beat well to combine ingredients and season with salt and pepper.

Serve with white fish or smoked fish.

# MUSTARD SAUCE

Serves 4

1 medium onion, finely chopped
2 sprigs parsley
275 ml (½ pint) dry white wine
25 g (1 oz) butter
25 g (1 oz) plain flour
1 tsp French mustard
salt and pepper

Put the onion and parsley into a pan with the wine. Simmer for 5 minutes and leave to stand while preparing the rest of the ingredients. In a small pan, melt the butter and stir in the flour. Cook over a low heat for 1 minute, stirring well. Remove from the heat and stir in the strained wine. Return to the heat and cook over low heat, stirring well for 5 minutes. Stir in the mustard, salt and pepper.

Serve with oily fish.

# GOOSEBERRY SAUCE

Serves 4

225 g (8 oz) gooseberries, fresh or
   frozen
4 tbsp water
2 tsp sugar
25 g (1 oz) butter
squeeze of lemon juice

Put the gooseberries into a pan with the water and simmer gently until the fruit has broken and is soft. Put through a sieve into a clean pan. Stir in the sugar, butter and lemon juice. Heat gently and serve hot.

Serve with oily fish.

# TOMATO SAUCE

Serves 4

1 small onion, finely chopped
1 small carrot, finely chopped
15 g (½ oz) butter
1 tbsp oil
1 garlic clove, crushed
1 tsp fresh parsley, chopped
pinch of marjoram or basil
225 g (8 oz) fresh ripe tomatoes,
    skinned
salt and pepper

Fry the onion and carrot in the butter and oil for 5 minutes over a low heat. Add the garlic and cook for 1 minute. Stir in the herbs and chopped tomatoes. Simmer over a low heat for 10 minutes. Sieve and reheat, adjusting seasoning to taste. If preferred, canned tomatoes may be used, but the sauce will be thinner, and it is better to strain the juice and keep it in reserve to adjust the consistency as required.

Serve with white or oily fish.

# HOLLANDAISE SAUCE (QUICK METHOD)

Serves 4

3 egg yolks
1 tbsp lemon juice
1 tbsp warm water
salt and white pepper
100 g (4 oz) unsalted butter

Mix the egg yolks, lemon juice and water in a blender or food processor. Season lightly with salt and pepper. Melt the butter without browning and pour into the machine while it is running. Adjust the seasoning when the sauce is thick, and serve warm.

*Variations*
*Aurora Sauce* Fold 3 tablespoons mayonnaise and 150 ml (¼ pint) whipped cream into the sauce. Serve warm with cold fish.
*Mousseline Sauce* Fold 150 ml (¼ pint) whipped cream into the sauce. Serve warm with cold fish.
*Orange Hollandaise* Stir 1 teaspoon grated orange rind and 1 tablespoon orange juice into the sauce and serve warm with cold fish.

# WHITE SAUCE

Serves 4

*25 g (1 oz) butter*
*25 g (1 oz) plain flour*
*275 ml (½ pint) milk*
*salt and white pepper*

Melt the butter over a low heat. Stir in the flour and cook for 1 minute. Remove from the heat and stir in the milk. Cook over a low heat for 5 minutes, stirring gently until smooth and creamy. Season to taste and add flavouring ingredients as preferred.

*Variations*
*Cheese Sauce* Remove the sauce from the heat and stir in 75 g (3 oz) grated cheese just before serving.
*Egg Sauce* Add 2 finely-chopped hard-boiled eggs to the sauce.
*Parsley Sauce* Add 2 tablespoons chopped fresh parsley to the sauce.
*Hot Mustard Sauce* Add 2 teaspoons mustard powder to the sauce.
*Shrimp Sauce* Stir 75 g (3 oz) peeled shrimps into the sauce and season with a few drops of Tabasco sauce.
*Hot Tartare Sauce* Add 1 teaspoon chopped fresh parsley, 1 teaspoon finely chopped onion, 3 finely chopped pickled gherkins and 12 chopped capers to the sauce.
*Mushroom Sauce* Cook 50 g (2 oz) chopped mushrooms in 25 g (1 oz) butter until just tender and stir into the cooked sauce.

# CIDER SAUCE

Serves 4

275 ml (½ pint) dry cider
40 g (1½ oz) butter
40 g (1½ oz) plain flour
425 ml (¾ pint) fish or chicken stock
salt and pepper

Put the cider into a small pan and cook quickly until reduced by half. Melt the butter in another pan; add the flour and stir over a low heat for 1 minute. Gradually work in the stock and stir over a low heat until thick and smooth. Add the cider and season well. Stir over a low heat for 3 minutes and serve hot.

# MAYONNAISE (QUICK METHOD)

Serves 4–6

1 egg and 1 egg yolk
½ tsp mustard powder
salt and white pepper
275 ml (½ pint) olive or salad oil
1 tbsp wine vinegar or lemon juice

Place the egg, egg yolk, mustard, salt and pepper in a blender or food processor. With the machine running, pour half the oil through the feeder tube and process until well mixed. Gradually add the remaining oil drop by drop and process until the mixture is thick. Stir in vinegar or lemon juice.

*Variations*
*Curry mayonnaise* Add 1 tablespoon tomato purée, 1 tablespoon curry paste, 1 teaspoon lemon juice and 2 tablespoons double cream to the mayonnaise and process just enough to blend. Serve with crab or prawns.
*Green mayonnaise* Add 1 chopped garlic clove, with 1 tablespoon chopped parsley, 1 tablespoon chopped chives and 1 tablespoon chopped basil to the mayonnaise and process until well blended. Serve with white fish.
*Tartare sauce* Fold in 1 teaspoon chopped fresh parsley, 1 teaspoon finely chopped onion, 3 finely chopped pickled gherkins and 12 chopped capers. Serve with grilled or fried white fish.

# CUCUMBER SALAD

Serves 4–6

*1 large cucumber*
*salt and pepper*
*5 tsp white wine vinegar*
*150 ml (¼ pint) double cream*

Peel the cucumber and dice finely. Sprinkle with a little salt and put into a sieve. Leave to drain for 30 minutes. Put in a bowl and season with pepper. Sprinkle on the vinegar. Whip the cream to soft peaks and fold into the cucumber. Serve with fried or grilled fish.

# FLAVOURED BUTTERS

Serves 4–6

*100 g (4 oz) unsalted butter*
*flavouring*
*seasoning*

The butter should be at room temperature and may be prepared by hand or in a blender or food processor. When the butter has been creamed, flavouring and seasoning may be added. The butter should be formed into a cylinder, wrapped in foil and chilled before slicing into pats.

*Variations*
*Anchovy butter* Add 2 teaspoons anchovy essence while creaming the butter, and season with salt and pepper to taste.
*Parsley butter* Add 2 tablespoons finely chopped parsley, a squeeze of lemon juice and seasoning to taste.
*Watercress butter* Add ½ bunch watercress to machine while blending so that the watercress is finely chopped. Season with salt, pepper and 1 tablespoon lemon juice.

# MUSHROOM STUFFING

Serves 4

100 g (4 oz) fresh white or brown
    breadcrumbs
2 tbsp butter, melted
50 g (2 oz) mushrooms, finely
    chopped
1 tbsp fresh parsley, chopped
squeeze of lemon juice
salt and pepper

Put the breadcrumbs into a bowl and add the butter. Add the mushrooms, parsley, lemon juice and seasoning and mix.

Enough for 1 large fish or 4 smaller ones.

# LEMON PARSLEY STUFFING

Serves 4

100 g (4 oz) fresh white breadcrumbs
2 tbsp melted butter
2 tbsp fresh parsley, chopped
1 lemon
salt and pepper
milk

Put the breadcrumbs into a bowl. Add the butter and parsley with the grated rind and juice of the lemon. Season well with salt and pepper. Add a little milk just to bind the ingredients but to leave them slightly crumbly.

Enough for 1 large fish or 4 smaller ones.

# TOMATO STUFFING

Serves 4

100 g (4 oz) fresh white or brown
    breadcrumbs
2 tbsp butter, melted
3 large tomatoes, skinned
1/2 red pepper, finely chopped
1 garlic clove, crushed
salt and pepper

Put the breadcrumbs into a bowl and add the butter. Chop the tomatoes roughly and discard the pips. Add to the breadcrumbs with the pepper and garlic, and season well with salt and pepper.

Enough for 1 large fish or 4 smaller ones.

# COATING BATTER

100 g (4 oz) plain flour
2 tbsp oil or melted butter
2 eggs, separated
pinch of salt
150 ml (¼ pint) warm water

Sift the flour into a bowl. Add the oil or butter with the egg yolks, salt and water. Beat well and leave to stand for 1 hour. Whisk the egg whites to stiff peaks and fold into the batter just before using.

To use the batter, dip the fish in a little plain flour to coat it lightly. Coat fish with batter and allow surplus batter to drain off. Fry at once in hot oil or fat.

# COURT BOUILLON

1.2 litres (2 pints) water (or water
    and white wine)
75 g (3 oz) onions
1 medium carrot
1 garlic clove
1 celery stalk
1 parsley sprig
1 thyme sprig
½ bay leaf
1 clove
2 tsp salt
4 peppercorns

Put all the ingredients into a pan, cover and simmer for 30 minutes. Strain, cover and refrigerate for up to 3 days.

Use for poaching or boiling fish.

*Variation*
**Fish Stock**  Use only water with flavourings and add fish trimmings and bones from raw fish. Cover and simmer for 30 minutes. Strain and use for cooking fish.

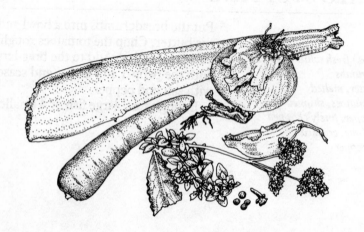

# PUFF PASTRY

Makes 450 g (1 lb) pastry

*225 g (8 oz) plain flour*
*½ tsp salt*
*225 g (8 oz) hard margarine or*
  *butter*
*1 tsp lemon juice*
*150 ml (¼ pint) cold water*

Sieve together the flour and salt. Divide the margarine into four equal pieces. Rub one piece into the flour and mix to a pliable dough with the lemon juice and water. Turn on to a lightly floured board and knead until smooth. Cover and leave to rest for 15 minutes in a cool place.

With two knives, form the remaining fat into a square slab. Roll the dough into a rectangle and put the piece of fat at the top end leaving a margin around sides and top. Fold the rest of the dough over, placing the upper edges of dough together, and brush off the surplus flour.

Turn the pastry round so that the folded edge is on the left-hand side. Press the open edges together with a rolling pin, and press across the dough 5 times with a rolling pin to flatten. Roll into a rectangle, keeping the edges straight.

Fold the pastry in three by folding the bottom third upwards and top third downwards and over to cover it. Turn so that folded edge is on the left. Seal the edges and roll out as before. Fold, turn and seal the edges as before. Place the pastry on a floured plate in a polythene bag, and leave to rest in a cold place for 20 minutes.

Roll out four more times, always turning and sealing the dough as before. Rest the dough for 20 minutes between each rolling. Roll out to the required size and thickness for baking.

# SHORTCRUST PASTRY

Makes 350 g (12 oz) pastry

*225 g (8 oz) plain flour*
*½ tsp salt*
*50 g (2 oz) hard margarine*
*50 g (2 oz) lard*
*2–3 tbsp cold water*

Sieve together the flour and salt. Rub in the margarine and lard until the mixture is like fine breadcrumbs. Add the water and mix to a stiff dough. Knead lightly until smooth. Roll out to required shape and thickness.

# INDEX